THE UNDERWORLD OF THE EAST

THE UNDERWORLD
OF THE EAST

BEING EIGHTEEN YEARS' ACTUAL EXPERIENCES
OF THE UNDERWORLDS, DRUG HAUNTS
AND JUNGLES OF INDIA, CHINA
AND THE MALAY ARCHIPELAGO

By

James S. Lee

GREEN
MAGIC

Published in 2000 by Green Magic

First published in 1935 by Sampson, Low, Marston & Co., London

This edition published in 2000 by Green Magic
BCM Inspire, London WC1N 3XX

Introduction copyright Mike Jay 2000

A catalogue record for this book is available from
The British Library

Typeset by Academic and Technical, Bristol
Printed and bound by Anthony Rowe, Chippenham, Wilts

Jacket design by Chris Render

ISBN 0 95 366311 6

Contents

Introduction

To the suspicious reader, James Lee's *Underworld of the East: Being Eighteen Years' Actual Experiences of the Underworlds, Drug Haunts and Jungles of India, China and the Malay Archipelago* might at first sight appear to be an elaborate hoax. Far more than almost any other example of the turn-of-the-century travel genre, it presents our jaded modern palates with the sort of Orient of the Mind which we imagine far more often than we get: a twilight world of ports, red-light districts, drug dens and secret chambers of vice from Aden to Kyoto, as strange as opium dreams yet as real as bamboo and stale tobacco, and our guide not some prurient *flaneur* protesting his shock and disbelief at every step but a mining foreman from Yorkshire who, during the course of the book, is largely preoccupied with smoking, swallowing and injecting as many drugs as possible.

This impression of a hoax is continually bolstered by the way in which James Lee seems to go out of his way to make his memoirs especially entertaining and relevant to the modern reader. He tells us how – in 1901 – he started the first motorcycle gang in Calcutta; how he demonstrated sterile needle techniques to cocaine-addicted prostitutes; how he took so many drugs before a night on the town in London that he hallucinated a turbanned Hindu gentleman in the ticket queue at Piccadilly Circus underground station. Even more suspiciously, he defuses the near-universal problem which the modern reader has with colonial memoirs by being resolutely sympathetic and unprejudiced towards the local people – even marrying an Indian girl who he subsequently treats with nothing but love and respect.

But perhaps most suspicious of all is the way in which Lee presents us with an account which significantly rewrites the social history of drugs in the period leading up to their pro- hibition. Into an episode which has been previously explained in terms of the misery of an increasingly opiate-addicted population encouraged by the spread of Oriental habits into the slums of Europe and America, Lee injects a powerful and unique account of working class drug use which is well- informed, vigorously healthy, entirely unproblematic and, far from being a self-inflicted torture, is simply a logical response to the narrowness, paternalism and sheer boredom of turn-of-the-century Britain. (In this context the suspicious mind might even recall that William Burroughs' autobiographi- cal first novel, *Junky*, was published under the pseudonym of Lee.)

Finally, as if all the above were not too good to be true, he tells of his discovery of two mysterious drugs in the jungles of Sumatra which – if their existence and effects are to be believed – would offer not only spectacular new highs to the drug connoisseur but nothing less than a fortune to the pharma- ceutical industry.

But a second glance confirms that *Underworld of the East*, even if it seems too good to be true, is none the less exactly what it claims to be. It's written with an artlessness which would be almost impossible to imitate: short sentences, eccen- trically punctuated, and clearly the work not of a professional writer but merely an extremely interesting person. The author's occupation as a mining engineer is reflected in the way in which his mind turns on mechanical and technical problems, which are addressed with a vigour and period detail which it would be highly demanding if not downright impossible to fake. And, apart from anything else, there's the original edition of the book, a 1930s cloth-bound volume typical of travel mem- oirs of the period: anyone unwilling to accept this last item on faith can locate the yellowing, age-spotted copy in the British Library.

Of all the points of interest in *Underworld*, the most striking is Lee's use of drugs and his detailed descriptions of their effects, benefits and potential pitfalls. This is partly because drugs –

his self-proclaimed "hobby" – are central to the way he himself
sets out his stall (Chapter I is simply entitled *About Drugs*), and
partly because his account plugs a yawning gap in the record of
exactly how and why drugs were being used in a "recreational" (or, at least, not strictly medical) context at the time
when the campaign for their prohibition was building up an
irresistible head of steam.

Since Thomas de Quincey's *Confessions of an English Opium
Eater* in 1821, the increasing consumption of opiates, cocaine
and cannabis preparations had been reflected in a steady interest in drug literature. Some of this was self-conscious aestheti-
cism largely imitative of de Quincey himself (the American Fitz
Hugh Ludlow's *The Hasheesh Eater*, for example); some of it
was more sceptical and analytical in tone (such as Charles
Baudelaire's *Les Paradies Artificiels*); most of it, then as
now, consisted of simplistic morality tales where the reader
was indulged in voyeuristic, sensuous thrills only to be
"saved", along with the protagonist, in a sanctimonious final
paragraph.

Towards the end of the century, however, the mood took an
abrupt turn. Opium overdoses and suicides, though relatively
uncommon, became increasingly regular tabloid-fodder, and
doctors and pharmacists began to lobby enthusiastically for
drug use to be brought under professional control. Simulta-
neously, as the populations of Chinatowns in cities like San
Francisco and London began to increase, anxieties about
drugs, the Yellow Peril and (despite little or no evidence)
dope-for-sex white slave rings all combined to add substances
such as opium and cocaine to the increasingly strident calls by
the Temperance Leagues for the prohibition of alcohol. This
change in tone is strikingly marked in the literature of the
period: Dickens' unfinished novel *Edwin Drood* opens with
the protagonist John Jasper in an opium den, having a vision
of an English cathedral town transformed into a seething
Oriental horror-show, in the company of a woman who has
*"opium-smoked herself into a strange likeness of the China-
man."* Similar descriptions of the degradations of the "opium
den" increasingly find their way into the detective fictions of
Conan Doyle, who only a few years before had been happy to

portray Sherlock Holmes' indulgence in cocaine and morphine as a bohemian eccentricity.

During this period a new pejorative vocabulary – "opium den," "dope fiend" – was coined by a combination of Temperance Leaguers and anti-Chinese xenophobes, and with it a new metaphor for drug use – "plague" or "contagion" – which was all too often taken literally. Cases of dependency on opium and morphine began to be clinically described in the 1870s as "morbid cravings," and within a few years the medical profession was refining and squabbling over the "disease model of addiction," adding terms of their own – "neurasthenia," "constitutional diathesis," "degeneration" – to describe its dangers ever more fully. The "disease model" essentially claimed that addiction to opiates, like alcoholism, was a medical condition which, without proper medical intervention, would destroy the user: "addiction" gradually became synonymous with "use," and opiates with any foreign substance (cocaine or cannabis), until all non-medical drug use came to be regarded as an "addiction" requiring medical supervision. Medical science offered, by today's standards, an odd range of treatments, which included substituting morphine with the substantially more addictive heroin.

There was little dispute among doctors, politicians or church leaders that drug addiction was a "plague" – even though opiate use began to fall after the first medical warnings in the 1870s and continued dropping throughout the subsequent decades. Nor was there any doubt among whom this plague was spreading: the working classes. Drug use by artists and aristocrats, aesthetes and "brain-workers," was regarded as a symptom of their special needs and stresses; the same behaviour by the working classes was a vice which became increasingly synonymous with criminality, miscegenation, hereditary feebleness, dementia and insurrectionary politics. And as for the source of this plague, of that too there was no doubt: the East.

This is the world from which *Underworld of the East* emerges, and it is this which makes Lee's story so particularly enlightening. The debate outlined above was carried, naturally enough, without opposition: who could have the slightest interest in standing up for the cause of the "drug addict"? What purpose could it serve to establish exactly who took drugs, and why, and what sufferings (or, Heaven forbid! — delights) they found in them? And, when these drug addicts were being introduced to the habit by Orientals, who could take seriously the idea that such cross-pollination might take place in an atmosphere not of vicious and squalid contagion but of friendship, mutual respect and cultural *rapprochement*?

By taking up the gauntlet of explaining his use of drugs, Lee's account stands, by default, as the epitaph of the Unknown Soldier in the War on Drugs, a posthumous witness statement for the defence in a case which was never heard. Although he was no doubt an exceptional character, there is every likelihood that he speaks for the vast majority of working class drug users at the turn of the century. The number of drug users who are today classed as "problematic" or addicted is usually estimated at about three percent of the total, and there is no reason to believe that the figure would have differed greatly in a Victorian and Edwardian England which was awash with freely available mood-control drugs: cocaine in Coca-Cola, cannabis in Collis Browne's patent remedies, heroin pushed over the chemist's counter as a cough medicine. Of course, even now, it is the problematic three percent who receive ninety-seven percent of the oxygen of publicity; within the turn-of-the-century debate the case for the informed, self-determining "recreational" user is effectively carried by Lee alone.

The initial question to which Lee supplies a clear answer is motive: why did he take drugs? He did so for the same reason that he sought work placements abroad: not out of unhappiness, "nervous instability" or "pathological weakness," but simply because he found the daily round of life in Britain stultifyingly boring. "*I was getting fed up with life in England,*" he tells us. "*There was too much sameness about it: a place where there is little real freedom, and one had to do just as the next fellow did. To wear the same kind of clothes, with a collar and tie, and talk about football and horse-racing or be considered no sport . . . these were just some of the things that I found irksome.*"

Lee headed for the colonies with none of the gloomy sense of self-sacrifice and exile which many expats took with them, but with a sense of freedom and an appetite for mind-expanding experiences. From the beginning he demonstrates great curiosity about the local people he meets, and sees no point in following colonial form *"by affecting to consider them as inferiors."* It is this which leads directly to his use of drugs: his open-mindedness and discretion mean that he is naturally invited into many private worlds – drug sessions, the underworld of gambling dens, salons and bordellos – which are typically concealed from European eyes. It is these which, increasingly, become the focus of his interest in his Eastern travels, and he begins to select destinations (such as China) where he will have the opportunity to broaden his experience of them: they become the concrete symbols of his urge to penetrate ever more deeply into the alien cultures in which he finds himself.

As this penetration continues, Lee becomes progressively more ambivalent about the "civilisation" he has left behind and the "savagery" in which he finds himself. Despite his use of then-standard terms like "nigger" and "coolie," he remains free of the prejudices which these terms tended to convey. *"These people work for no-one,"* he observes. *"They live in the same state of civilisation that their forefathers did…the greater part of our population are wage-slaves, at the beck and call of their masters…of what benefit is our civilisation to ninety percent of the people, if it brings them barely enough of the coarsest food and the cheapest shoddy clothing?"*

This spontaneous outbreak of socialism would probably have been sufficient grounds at the time to accuse Lee of enslavement to the vices of the Orient; the further knowledge that he was using drugs on a regular basis would have sealed the judgement that he was a pathological and degenerate addict. But Lee, throughout his account, is emphatically not addicted to drugs: he stops using them every few months, often for long periods, to preserve the freshness of their effect; he spends long periods in Britain without using them at all. And it is not the irresistible craving for drugs which brings him back to the

East time and again, so much as the intolerable boredom of the alternative.

Since Lee begins his narrative in a state of drug-naïvety, we are able to follow the process whereby he acquires a body of knowledge which was at the time, as far as we know, otherwise unrecorded. This process is instructive in understanding the relationship between the three sources of information which are traditionally available to the drug user: orthodox medical science, local customs and traditions, and personal self-experimentation.

Lee's baptism into drug use was, like the majority of cases in the Victorian world, initially performed by the medical profession. Finding himself in India, and suffering like most Westerners from touches of malaria, he visits a doctor (who he refers to as "Dr. Babu") who gives him a miraculous and immediate panacea for all his symptoms: an intravenous injection of morphine. This is, as Lee will later discover, merely a high-tech, medicalised version of the traditional cure for malaria and all tropical chills, fevers and diarrhoeas – opium.

Morphine does more than cure Lee's symptoms: it leaves him "*simply purring with content.*" He quickly learns from Dr. Babu the technique of injecting himself: the first and almost the last time his drug "hobby" requires specific medical knowledge. Dr. Babu stresses the importance of sterile needles to avoid sepsis, a lesson which Lee passes on to many other drug users during the course of the book. "*Under his instructions,*" says Lee of the Indian doctor, "*I now started to use drugs scientifically.*"

Lee continues to use morphine on a regular basis without suffering any problems more serious than the perennial curse of the junkie: chronic constipation. "*I was becoming so costive,*" he informs us, "*that no opening medicine had much effect.*" (This is, of course, one of the chief medical values of opium in the tropics where dysentery and diarrhoea, especially in children, can often be fatal.) Returning to Babu with this problem, the obliging doctor solves it at a stroke – with an injection of cocaine. Lee finds this stimulant a perfect complement to the narcotic he has been enjoying, and begins to develop – and record with scrupulous detail – a regime which maintains both his health and his original enjoyment of the drugs: a regime which expands to include opium, hashish and various other substances.

Lee's drug use maintains a medical dimension, as indeed traditional use of drugs like opium and hashish always has done in the regions where they are grown. *"Had I a headache on some rare occasion?,"* he explains. *"I removed it at once with a mixture of morphia and cocaine. A little fever which was natural in this climate and affected every European, I could remove in a few minutes, just as I could remove any kind of pain."* He also comes to appreciate the broader spectrum of traditional uses to which opium is put: lost in the Sumatran jungle, for example, he finds it an essential restorative. *"But for Ali's opium,"* he observes, *"we might never have got back, because such a position calls for the best of the mind and body; calmness, keen perception, staying power, and this opium will supply when wanted."* And, increasingly, he begins to experiment with larger recreational doses – or *"regular binges,"* as he refers to them – during which he learns to encourage the active imagination in developing mental scenarios of the past, of the far future, of previous elements of his own life and of worlds previously unimagined. He is particularly enthusiastic about mixing his drugs: he notes, for example, that when large doses of hashish are *"combined with a certain proportion of cocaine, it is possible almost to experience anything one wishes, quite realistically."*

This gives us a valuable perspective on the claim which was then in the process of being enforced by law: that the use of drugs can be understood by the medical profession alone and, by the same token, is too dangerous for the layman to explore unaided. Lee demonstrates that the knowledge required to use drugs is both less than medical and more. Dr. Babu's ground rules were essential to get him started – though they amounted to little more than basic first aid skills – but the construction of a regime of personal use, though drawing on medical knowledge, was Lee's own work. Compared to the contemporary medico-psychiatric formulations of "chronic intoxications" and "morbid cravings," most of which read today like parodies of *Reefer Madness*-style propaganda, Lee's own accounts of dosage, tolerance, dependence, detoxification and withdrawal remain startlingly clear and accurate. He was not magically immune to the pains of withdrawal, but was constantly perfecting his techniques for its management. After one of his reduction programmes (on his return to England) he tells us: "*I admit that at the end I had a little craving, but it was nothing really ... still, I decided that the system was not perfect, and I meant to continue experimenting ...*"

His transcendence of medical knowledge is nicely illustrated by his return to England, where he finds himself sharing a cabin with a young medical student. The medical student discovers that Lee is using drugs "*and gave me a terrible lecture on the consequences of the habit. I asked him if he had ever taken any himself, and he confessed that he had not, and that he was going on what he had heard.*" We can imagine the conversation left the medical man's pride somewhat dented and, as Lee drily adds, "*Shortly afterwards I missed my syringe*" – an illustration in microcosm of the all-too-common relationship between prohibition and ignorance.

The attitude which marks Lee's use of drugs is, in a word, responsibility. It never seems to occur to him for an instant that the onus is on anyone but himself to ensure that his "hobby" is safe, or that it would be anyone's fault but his own if it went wrong. Medical opinion is not something to follow blindly nor to dismiss out of hand, but something to use along with the other available sources of information. His philosophy is plainly stated in the preface: "*The life of a drug-taker can be a happy one; far surpassing any other, or it can be one of suffering and misery; it depends on the user's knowledge.*"

This philosophy marks a divergence not merely from orthodox medical opinion but from the tradition of drug literature up to this point – a tradition of which Lee shows no signs of being aware. Central to Thomas de Quincey's telling of his tale is that the pleasures and pains of opium cannot be separated, and that the continued use of drugs leads only to abysses of despair. Baudelaire, influenced no doubt by what Gustave Flaubert called a "*leavening of Catholicism,*" insisted that the use of drugs was inevitably a *"forbidden game"* which plays into the hands of man's *"natural depravity."* These tropes were almost invariably followed by subsequent writers on the subject: even the great modern chronicler of the drug experience, William Burroughs, regarded addiction as a *"disease of exposure,"* a living hell which is the inevitable consequence of playing the game to its limits. But Lee has no truck with any such fatalism: even after a serious motorcycle accident which left him hospitalised, he observes that *"drugs were a godsend to me . . . the three months or so that I was laid up were happy ones."*

In the end, he does give up using drugs, but only as a result of the change in the law. *"When the Dangerous Drugs Act came into force,"* he tells us, *"I gave up using all drugs, because the danger and risk of obtaining them was too great. The paltry quantities, about which the authorities make such a fuss, were of no use to me, and I was able to give them up without any trouble or suffering."* There is a clear tone of contempt for the hypocrisy and humbug of this new legislation – and, more than that, an insistence that it is not merely cowardly but profoundly mistaken: *"All these narcotic drugs, which are commonly known as Dangerous Drugs, are really the gift of God to mankind. Instead of doing him harm, they should really be the means of preserving his health, and making his life a state of continual happiness."*

This alternative view is, in a sense, Lee's main project: to describe from personal experience how this "state of continual happiness" can be attained by the correct use of drugs. Naturally, this requires a radically different view of drugs and their effects from that of the prevailing medical and religious dogma – and no aspect of this difference is more radical than that Lee, unlike almost anyone else whose testimony has survived from the period, clearly knows whereof he speaks.

Thus Lee gives us a full account of the "how" of his drug use – the knowledge and techniques which he developed to separate its pleasures entirely from its pains. Beyond, this, the next interesting question is the "why": exactly what it was which he enjoyed about it and learnt from it, and the ways in which it changed his views of the world.

In this, as in his methods of drug use, what is perhaps most striking from a modern perspective is not what is present but what is absent. Just as his "hobby" is notable for its absence of withdrawal pains and bad conscience, so is his view of the world notable for the absence of the almost universal modern concomitant of drugs and the Orient: Eastern spirituality. Lee is a thoroughgoing rationalist: his interest in Eastern religions is at best detached and ethnographic, and he never gives any indication that he regards its metaphysical language as a better descriptor for the mysteries of existence than that of good old-fashioned empirical science. In a period when count-less Westerners were returning with wild tales of fakirs, levita-tions and, particularly, the legendary Indian Rope Trick, Lee's considered judgement is that *"the Indian rope trick is a fable, and never has been done, and never will be done, and the man who says he has seen it is a foolish person."*

Nevertheless, the experience of strong psychoactive drugs is perennially difficult to contain within the accepted language of mechanistic science, and one of Lee's most explicit pleasures in his mind-expanding *"regular binges"* is that of the cosmic viewpoint which they bring, the sense that the normally impreg-nable defences of the ego are somehow breached and an alto-gether vaster perspective becomes temporarily visible through the cracks. Lee devotes much time to these experiences – chapters with titles like *"Strange Waking Dreams"* and *"Strange Thoughts and Visions"* in which he hallucinates vividly and wildly, or constructs scenarios of the far distant future and the ultimate destiny of the earth which bear striking similarities to the cosmic extrapolations of fellow-rationalists like H.G. Wells or Olaf Stapledon. As we approach the death of the sun in the far future, he prophesies, *"the whole of man-kind will be living at the equator, a land of ice and snow, and semi-darkness. They will be dressed in skins and the sun will appear as a purple-coloured ball in the sky."*

Of course, we cannot rationally expect our civilised values to persist through such cosmic changes, and such visions fuel Lee's feelings that the differences between "civilisation" and "savagery" are ephemeral and, ultimately, irrational. He finds it hard to take revealed religion seriously – he describes it as a *"profession which was originally introduced and carried on almost solely with the object of providing a fat living for those who professed to teach that which no man can know."* But, especially during his drug revelations, he is struck with increasing force by the insights which result from imagining a vaster perspective on the cosmos in which man is entirely insignificant. This leads him to a formulation of what would now be described as Gaia theory, one which is quite remarkable for the period and which almost certainly reflects his professional occupation: *"Is the earth a great living organism, with an intelligence of its own, and are we the parasites which live on its surface and occasionally burrow into its skin?"*

During the course of the book he develops such insights into what he refers to as his Evolutionary Law, which describes the tendency of everything from atoms to human societies to galaxies to merge and integrate: a law which always keeps one foot on the ground of science while frequently poking its head into the clouds of metaphysics. The Evolutionary Law even generates a rational system of religion and ethics: *"All religions must in time, according to the Evolutionary Law, join together and form one ... and there will be only one sin: 'the doing of an injury or injustice to another', and the magnitude of the sin will be the injury intended, not that inflicted."* This is a measure of how far Lee's drug use was both cause and effect of a radical perception of the world, diametrically opposed to the one where, for example, an individual's decision to use drugs was regarded not only as a sin but also as a crime and a disease. For him the castigation of drug use as "savage" by "civilised" societies is in fact, from a wider perspective, an indication of just how far our concept of civilisation still has to evolve. It is also notable that, despite the closeness of his formulation to the Eastern concept of *karma*, he shows little or no conscious interest in the parallel.

Finally, no commentary on *Underworld* would be complete without an assessment of Lee's claims to have discovered two extraordinary drugs which, if genuine, remain entirely unknown to science and potentially revolutionary in their implications. Again, we might here suspect a hoax: he is economical with the provenance of these mysterious substances, referring only to their preparations as *"Drug No. 1"* and *"Drug No. 2,"* and telling us that he concocted them himself from plant samples which were brought to him by natives in the Sumatran jungle and exchanged for opium.

But, as with the rest of the book, it seems unlikely that Lee is having us on. First, to do so would be entirely out of keeping with the artlessness and honesty with which he tells the rest of his story. Second, the accuracy of his descriptions of the drugs which we know gives broader credibility to his details of the effects of Drugs No. 1 and 2. Third, it is entirely possible that the jungles of Sumatra contain many psychoactive plants of whose existence we are entirely ignorant. The ethnobotany of plant drugs is a relatively recent academic discipline, and has been focused almost entirely on the New World − partly because the discipline is predominantly American, and partly because Central and South America provide the broadest and most accessible range of traditional cultures which are still focused around the use of psychoactive plants: the mushrooms, cacti and *ayahuasca* brews of Mexico, the Amazon and the Andes. It is only now becoming clear, for example, that the highlands of New Guinea offer a broad spectrum of sacred plant use which includes species previously unknown to science, and by contrast even with New Guinea Sumatra remains virgin territory to the ethnobotanist. It is also entirely possible that any traditional Sumatran use of Drugs No. 1 and 2 may have died out since Lee's visit.

Drug No. 1, from Lee's description, is a psychedelic, but one which despite his variety of previous experiences made him *"intoxicated in an entirely new manner."* Having tested small doses of it for toxicity on some captive rats − his standard and classically scientific procedure − he takes measured doses steadily through one afternoon, breaking for a curry and then continuing, adding injections of cocaine and *"looking forward to some new experiences in the Spirit World."* The effects he describes are unusual in the extreme: whereas most psychedelic drugs produce what are clinically described as "illusions" − perceptions which are enhanced or distorted − Drug No. 1 leads to a series of "true hallucinations," whereby Lee spends several hours in the company of entities and objects which were plainly not there but which nevertheless appeared entirely real: beautiful men and women, crowds of lepers and eventually hovering luminous globes. While there are known plant drugs which produce these effects – the tropane alkaloids in belladonna and datura, for example – Lee's description suggests that Drug No. 1 is an unusually dissociative psychedelic, and one possibly unrelated to any other plant substances we know.

But if Drug No. 1 is unusual, the effects of Drug No. 2 are astonishing in the extreme. Taking it first while high on cocaine, Lee is astonished to find that its effect is to return him, physically and mentally, to a state of normal health, even to the point of contracting his dilated pupils. Later, he finds that it has the same effect on opiates (although a larger dose is required); and, when taken in the absence of other drugs, it simply produces "*a feeling of great vitality, the absolute perfection of mental and bodily health.*" He concludes that its essential *modus operandi* is to restore the system, from whatever state it is in, to the peak of its condition. After his initial experiments he makes up a supply of this drug which he takes with him on his subsequent travels and continues to use frequently to bring him down from the effects of other drugs, to aid his reduction programmes after extensive opiate use, and simply as a general tonic. After a while, he simply refers to it as "*the Elixir of Life.*"

Here is a drug which in most contexts would be dismissed as pure fantasy, but which in Lee's account, even allowing for a little pride in his chemical detective-work and some consequent exaggeration, remains a tantalising discovery. In a sense, it also forms a perfect counterpoint to the book he has already given us. His story is a unique contribution to the social history of drugs, a Rosetta Stone which allows us to decode anew the official version of the "menace" and "Oriental contagion" of late Victorian drug abuse which our current drug laws persist in their attempts to control and eradicate. If Drug No. 2 were to be rediscovered, and were to match Lee's claims for it, he would certainly have contributed to our future as much as he has to our past. The final words of *Underworld* stand, like the testimony of Lee himself, as an invitation, a promise and a challenge: *"Years ago I destroyed my syringes, apparatus and drugs, but somewhere in the island of Sumatra there exists the plant from which I made the drug I called 'The Elixir of Life'."*

CHAPTER 1

About Drugs

Before commencing with my story in its proper order, I will say a few words about the drug habit generally.

During the thirty years in which I was a constant user of drugs of many kinds, various people, including some doctors, and chemists, have asked me how it was that I was able to continue in the habit for so long a time, and use such large quantities of drugs, and still remain in good health.

This true story of my experiences will explain the reason, and also may show the drug habit in an entirely new aspect.

It is now many years since I gave up using all drugs, but during the thirty years with which this story deals, I have used morphia, cocaine, hashish, opium, and a good many other drugs, both singly and in combination.

The doses which I became able to take, after so many years of the habit, may seem almost impossible, yet it is a fact that I have increased my dose gradually, until I could inject eighty grains of pure cocaine a day; sufficient to kill many persons, if divided amongst them.

At other times when I favoured morphia, I have injected as much as ten grains per day, although the medical dose is a quarter of a grain.

My arms, shoulders and chest are a faint blue colour, which, if magnified, reveals the marks of thousands of tiny punctures; hypodermic syringe marks.

Many years I have searched the jungles of the Far East for new drugs; testing strange plants, bulbs, and roots, making extracts, and then testing them first on animals, and in some cases on myself, and I will describe later some of the strange effects produced; particularly in the case of one drug, which I will call "The Elixir of Life."

If some of the things I describe are horrible, they are nevertheless true. What strange sights may a man not see during seven years in a country like China, if he goes to look for them below the surface? It is a country of camouflage and hidden ways. Innocent looking junks, quietly floating down the rivers and canals, may be really sumptuously furnished gambling dens and drug haunts, where orgies of many kinds are carried on. No European, unless he is introduced by a trusted Chinese, will ever have entry to these places.

The life of a drug taker can be a happy one, far surpassing that of any other, or it can be one of suffering and misery; it depends on the user's knowledge.

1

The most interesting period will only be reached after many years, and then only if perfect health has been retained; using several kinds of drugs (for one drug alone spells disaster), and increasing the doses in a carefully thought out system; a system which was first made known to me by the Indian doctor who initiated me into the drug habit.

Waking visions will then begin to appear when under the influence of very large doses, and it is these visions which are so interesting.

I have sat up through the night taking drugs until the room has been peopled with spirits. They may be horrible, grotesque, or beautiful, according to the nature of the drugs producing them. Strange scenes have been enacted before my eyes; scenes which were very real and lifelike, and which I will describe later.

When the Dangerous Drug Act came into force I gave up using all drugs, because the danger and risk of obtaining them was too great. The paltry quantities, about which the authorities make such a fuss, were of no use to me, and I was able to give them up without any trouble or suffering, owing to my experiments and discoveries.

This story will be as a message of hope to all drug addicts. The cure is easy, but not by the method generally adopted, that of gradually reducing the dose; a method which will only cause intense suffering, and sometimes even death.

CHAPTER 2

I Go Out to India

Far up on the north-east frontier of India is a little mining settlement. Here is the last outpost of civilisation. Situated on the borders of Assam and the wild hill country of the savage Nagas and Singphoos, it lays in the valley at the foot of the towering jungle-clad hills, from which the coal is being mined.

Picture to yourself a large open space which has been, at much labour, cleared of jungle, extending about a mile in every direction.

A single line railway track runs into it, and finishes at the foot of the hills, alongside a small bungalow, which does duty as a railway station and telegraph office.

Scattered about the irregular-shaped clearing are several European bungalows; single story wooden structures, with grass-thatched roofs, and a wide verandah all round, or at back and front only, the whole floor being several feet above the ground and built on poles. Further along, there is a little wooden post office, and several native shops built of bamboo framework and plastered inside and out with a mixture of clay and cow dung, which sets hard and smooth like cement.

On an open space slightly above the level of the rest, there are long lines of native huts or barracks, arranged in streets, and housing the hundreds of coolies of both sexes who work in the mines.

Far up on top of a high hill, stands a watch tower and camp, in charge of a corporal and small company of Gurkhas. They are acting as sentinels and guards to keep watch on the further valley and hills beyond, over which may appear, at any time, death in the shape of the savage "Nagas."

Here I found myself in the year 1894. I was just twenty-two years of age, and I had come out as mechanical engineer to the mines.

I had been an assistant-instructor at one of the chief technical colleges in London, but I had always wanted to see something of the world. I regarded this simply as a starting off place, and now I had arrived at the scene of my labours for the next three or four years.

My bungalow was a small three-roomed affair built like most of the others, and standing on the top of a small hill in its own little compound, containing a few banana trees, and other fruits and plants; a two-roomed bamboo and mud structure at the rear, which acted as cookhouse, and accommodation for the servants.

The bungalow was furnished with many odd pieces of furniture bought from time to time from previous residents in the district who were leaving the country, and I had arranged to take the whole lot over at a valuation, the previous owner having died of fever.

Even the old Mohammedan cook and the "paniwallah," or water carrier, had worked for the dead man who was now a permanent resident in the little plot of fenced ground in the jungle which did duty as a cemetery; a place in which were already one or two crosses with brass tablets attached. Wild animals roamed over their graves at night time, but they were buried deep.

In memory I see that little compound now. Abdul, a bare-legged old man with a bushy beard, now probably dead and cremated, his ashes scattered by the winds. I see him sitting at the cookhouse door buttering my morning toast with a chicken feather dipped in a tin of liquid known as butter, or, later in the day, squatting at his little home-made brick stove, cooking my curry and rice. The "paniwallah," a coal black native, stretched out almost naked, asleep under the shade of a tree. Mulki, the sweetest little brown-skinned girl in the world, long since dead and buried in Stratford Cemetery, near London; I see her sitting in the corner of the verandah, showing to some of her girl friends the "sarais" and bangles the sahib had given her.

Those were happy days, too, before I had learned to use drugs. I was young and full of optimism; life was before me. In the early morning Abdul would come into the room with tea and bananas, and I would get up and go on to the verandah, where I would look out on to the valley below. It would be generally shrouded in thick white mist, showing just the tree tops of the jungle; a mist which would clear away as the sun rose higher. The jungle would be full of sound; chiefly the call and chattering of monkeys in many tones of voice, celebrating the coming of another day, and the loud croaking of frogs. A thin wisp of smoke could be seen on the top of the highest hill, where the Gurkhas were cooking their morning meal.

High up the hillside and near the top where the ground began to flatten out, lay the entrance to the "Upper Level Mine."

Picture a couple of hundred yards of flat surface where the hill had been cut back and levelled. The mine entrance; a tunnel leading into the side of the hill. A small engine-house in which worked the hauling engine. A large vertical boiler near the latter and a steam-driven fan, built into the side of the hill for ventilating the mine.

The jungle-clad hills towered above on one side, and sloped down to the valley below on the other.

As I entered the mine tunnel carrying my safety lamp, I walked along, keeping my eyes on the rope pulleys between the rails, to see that they were working freely. The rope, polished bright by constant friction, passed over the pulleys with what seemed to be, by the dim light of my lamp, an incredible speed.

The roof, floor and walls of the tunnel were of shining coal, and as I moved along, the light from my lamp seemed to be some kind of shield which surrounded me, always cleaving into the pitch blackness ahead as I advanced, and keeping at bay the darkness which followed me closely, as though it was some living thing, which, but for the lamp, would pounce upon and engulf me.

A faint rumbling sound began to be heard ahead; the rails vibrated, and presently a small glimmer of light appeared in the distance. It was a long way off, but it got brighter and brighter, and I pressed myself in against the coal wall of the tunnel, as a long line of full coal tubs rushed past, with a coolie squatting on the buffers of the last tub. The light became smaller and faded away.

I turned off down one of the many side passages, along which a full tub of coal was coming slowly towards me, being pushed by a woman.

The air became thicker and coal dust could be seen dancing in the beam cast by the lamp. Faint sounds of tapping could be heard ahead. Scrambling up a shoot cut in the coal, I found myself in a large chamber, the floor of which was covered with loose coal some feet in depth. Several women were working here; some of them filling baskets with coal, while others were carrying them away on their heads, and tipping them into a coal tub standing at the top of the shoot.

The chamber was hot, and the women had loosed their "serais" and tied them round their middle, and from the waist upwards and the knees downwards they were bare. Their skins were moist with perspiration, and glistened in the lamp-light like polished brown marble.

I always felt uncomfortable among a crowd of coolie women; they eyed me with such curiosity, and made personal remarks, a few words of which I was beginning to understand. When the remarks are lewd and obscene, the Hindustani language can be very expressive. There were more women in the mine than men, because they were better workers and cheaper. Many of them were young girls of about sixteen or less. Morality was very low amongst them, and sometimes I was almost afraid to go along some of the far parts of the workings; I was little more than a boy and I had heard tales of lone men being carried off into disused portions of the mine, by three or four women, some of whom were under the influence of "bhang" or "ganja."

"Oh, Sukie. Here is the young sahib come to see you," called out one of them, to a pretty little girl, who answered with a shrill laugh.

One bold young thing, with glittering eyes and a grin showing ivory white teeth, advanced towards me with a mincing gait similar to that sometimes adopted by comedians on the music-hall stage, and, without bothering to cover her breasts, she stood before me, a beautiful image of symmetry, and then she started to wriggle her body in the manner of the Nautch dancers, evoking a scream of laughter from the rest.

Another girl, whose mouth and lips were blood red with chewing betel nut, or "pahn," as it is called, came up and offered me a chew.

None of these women were in my department, and I had no authority over them, so they were much freer than they would have been in the presence of one of the mine foremen.

I walked out into the passage again, and then crawled up a steep incline, which was so narrow that I had to proceed on all fours; and then I came to another chamber. Here there were some men cutting into the coal face with pickaxes, at the ground level; after a certain distance had been cut in, a shot would be fired and the coal above the cut would fall. The air inside of the chamber was getting very thick and almost unbreathable. There was no means of getting any ventilation into it from the gallery outside, except by means of a hand-worked rotary fan which I intended to fix outside, with a pipe leading into the chamber.

I could hear a continuous kind of groaning noise, and I looked up at the roof of the chamber. I knew that there was a pressure of hundreds of tons from above tending to close up the place. The earth was trying to heal its wound.

Is the earth a great living organism, with an intelligence of its own, and are we the parasites that live on its surface and sometimes bore into its skin?

Any wound on the earth's surface will heal up in time; a time perhaps no greater in comparison to its span of life than the time taken for our wounds to heal. Tunnels, excavations and scars, if left to nature, will fill up.

Man bores into the earth's skin for coal, and then nature makes an effort to heal the wound. Water will form in the tunnel, softening the surrounding sides, so that they may cave in and fill up, if left alone. But man pumps the water out, and puts in props to support the roof.

Nature will then form explosive gas in the excavation, but man draws it away by means of fans. As time goes on, spontaneous combustion occurs, and there is an explosion. The wound is cleansed and cauterised by the flame; the props are blown out, and the roof sinks. The wound is healed.

The earth was probably born in the same way as we were. Some thousand million years ago a star was approaching towards the sun. For perhaps a thousand years they were travelling towards each other, during which time the gravitation pull of each was increasing. At the nearest point of approach the pull was so great that millions of tons of molten matter were torn out of each. These two portions joined together, and by natural laws, took the shape of a globe, just as a soap bubble or a drop of water does. The globe became a planet, revolving round its parent the sun. It journeys through space taking in its nutriment from the ether. Its internal heat is no greater, in proportion to its bulk, than ours is to us.

What are volcanoes if not similar to boils which burst on the human body, and discharge hot matter? Have we no vegetation growing on our bodies in the shape of hair just as the earth has trees and jungle, and are we not sometimes subject to rumblings and twitchings which correspond to earthquakes and explosions of natural gas?

The wind is the earth's breath, and the rain its tears. We humans, who burrow into the earth's surface for coal and minerals, are we not like the parasites which sometimes bite into the human skin and suck our blood?

When the earth was young, its skin was smooth and free from wrinkles, while with age came the folds and undulations; the rising mountain ranges, and deep depressions; the wrinkles and furrows of advancing age.

Yes, the earth is getting old. The vegetation is not so luxurious as formerly, in the time when the mammoth roamed the enormous forests, even in the North Polar regions. These latter are now bare, for the earth is getting bald on the top. No longer is the earth upright, but leans over as it moves along its path. It is getting slower in its movements, and it is not travelling so far, because it is drawing nearer to the sun. Its internal fires are cooling down and the time will come when it will be cold and dead like the moon.

Lumley, the mine foreman, came into the chamber with a safety lamp, which he pushed up as high above his head as he could reach, and I saw that there was gas in the roof. He listened to the sounds of the groaning and cracking above, and looked worried.

I walked out into the passage, along which a line of women were moving, each with a basket of coal on her head. The passage was dark, and some of them were in a playful mood, and I felt almost like blushing before I got clear.

Proceeding deeper into the workings, I came to a place where I had to ascend a steep incline by means of an empty coal tub which was pulled up by a full one descending on the adjacent track.

Passage-ways would lead sometimes to blank chambers, and I was in one of these, inspecting a hand-worked rotary fan arrangement, which was being fixed up. The chamber was full of explosive gas, and no naked light was allowed anywhere near.

I tested the air with my safety lamp.

Down near my feet the air was all right, but as soon as I held the lamp up to the level of my shoulders, I could see by the minute and continuous tiny explosions inside the gauze of the lamp, that the air was highly explosive, and even knee high there was a little gas. Just then I saw a glow of light, and there, standing at the entrance of the chamber, was a coolie – one of the poorest and most ignorant coal-black type – and he had in his hand a naked lamp.

These lamps were used in most parts of the mine except where there was gas. They were about the size of a large ink bottle, and had a long thick wire with a hooked end, attached to the lamp, for carrying by the finger, so that the lamp was nearly touching the ground when one walked along.

My heart nearly stopped beating.

Would the poor, ignorant blighter raise the lamp as high as his knee before I could get to him? If he did, I and many others would be burnt alive.

I dare not speak to him for fear he would not understand me, and then, to get a better view of my face, he would raise the lamp.

With as unconcerned a face as I could assume, for fear of startling him, I turned and commenced to leave the chamber.

What a relief. It was like a condemned man receiving a reprieve when my hand seized the handle of his lamp.

This is a dangerous occupation. Even in England, with intelligent white miners, coal mining is not one of the safest of callings, but here, working with ignorant coolies, in very thick seams, it is distinctly risky.

I had three different mines to visit and look after the machinery.

This one, however, was the only one which had a hauling engine for hauling the full coal tubs along the main tunnel.

Along this tunnel, fixed to the coal sides, was a stout wire. It passed through eye staples spaced at intervals on the wall, and in the event of any train of tubs which was being hauled out getting off the track, the man riding on the last tub pulled the wire and rang a gong in the engine-house, and the haulage stopped.

We decided to put up an electric bell in the engine-house in place of this antique arrangement.

Having fixed up the bell and batteries in the engine-house, I ran from there two wires, spaced close together, one above the other, and supported on insulators fixed in the wall; running the whole length of the main tunnel.

All that it was necessary to do now, to stop the haulage, was to press the two wires together, and the bell would ring in the engine-house.

"Would the coolies ever learn to use it?" "Never." They would seize a wire as before and pull hard, when down would come the wires, insulators and brackets. These would get entangled in the moving train, which had not stopped because the bell had not rung, and the whole of the half mile of wire, insulators and fastenings, would be hauled out by the engine.

It seemed to me to be like a great monster which could undo a whole week's work of mine in a few minutes.

I refixed it two or three times and then scrapped it, and went back to the old system.

Some of the women were very beautiful; they came from all parts of India. There were the tall, fair-skinned girls from Northern India with splendid features; the gentle and shy Hindu girls who cast down their eyes when one approached; the dark skinned little Bengali girls with fine eyes, cheeky and full of life, and the coal black negroid type from the central provinces; girls with statuesque figures, and smiling happy faces. I was beginning to feel lonely in my bungalow by myself, and I decided to keep my eyes open. I had not met Mulki yet.

CHAPTER 3

The Coming of the Tiger

I was in grand form; I found life very interesting, for there was plenty of variety here.

I have seen a man eater, a tiger. Not only that, but I have smelt its foul breath in my face, and have almost felt its claws when reaching for me, within a few inches of my body. Yet I am still alive, but the memory of it will live with me for ever. Those hours of fear were torture far more acute than any pain; a mental torture which I never before realised was possible to be produced by fear. Yes, believe me, fear can be more agonising than bodily pain.

In imagination I see the reader smile, but then probably you have never experienced real fear; very few people have; for remember, there are degrees of fear, and I think that I have experienced the greatest of them all.

I was sleeping in my bed when I was awakened in the early hours of the morning by a coolie standing under my window, calling, "Sahib! Sahib!"

As soon as I awakened, I got up and went to the open window; a window which contained no glass; only a wooden-louvred shutter.

"Sahib, harkul bund hai," said the coolie, meaning "The fan has stopped."

This was a very serious matter. I knew that there were more than a hundred men and women working underground on the night shift, and soon the air underground would be unbreathable, and work would have to stop. The fan must be got going at once. I got up and dressed quickly, meanwhile sending the coolie for one of my fitters, who had a hut just below my compound.

Luckai, the fitter, an old man something like an Egyptian mummy in appearance, came up to my compound, carrying a hurricane lamp and a large pipe wrench, while the coolie fireman followed carrying some tools.

It was no joke, really, for we had to walk about half a mile through the jungle, before we got to the fan, which was situated in an isolated spot, right in the heart of the jungle, and high up the hill side.

I was always scared on this trip at night time, and I had made it a few times under similar conditions; the fan had a habit of stopping sometimes at night. It might be the feed pump of the boiler which had gone wrong, or perhaps the coolie had allowed the water to get out of sight in the gauge glass, then he would get scared, draw the fire, and come down for a fitter.

9

I was scared because the jungle was known to be infested by tigers and leopards, and many natives had been killed at one time or another in the district.

As we walked along the winding path up the side of the hill, with thick jungle on either side, the old man was fairly trembling, and muttering to himself: "Khun roj Bargh kyh-ager," which means literally, "Some day tiger eat."

The coolie was the only one of us who appeared not to be afraid, but then perhaps he had no imagination; he was a poor specimen of humanity; naked with the exception of a loin cloth, and coal black, with spindle legs and big feet; and his face and arms were covered with syphilitic sores.

I could certainly have taken my rifle with me, but it would not have been much protection at night time.

A tiger could spring out on us before I could use it, or a leopard could jump down on us out of a tree as we passed underneath; besides, I knew that I would come in for a good deal of chaff from the other Europeans. I carried a hunting knife only.

Although I reckoned that the chances of us meeting a tiger were about 100 to 1 against, this did not seem to help much.

Arrived at the spot (not the mine entrance already described), I proceeded to investigate.

The place was a levelled and cleared portion of the hill side towering above us. Here there was a horizontal engine and a large vertical boiler, standing on a massive concrete foundation, and driving, by means of a leather belt, the fan, which was built in the hill side. In front of me the jungle sloped away steeply down to the valley below.

The boiler fire was out, and the steam had fallen to a few pounds pressure, and steam and water were leaking into the furnace.

I knew that there was a tube leaking, probably the uptake tube. It was a very old boiler and all I could do was to make a temporary repair.

Leaving Lukai and the coolie to blow off the water and take off the manhole cover, I proceeded down the hill by a different route to the mine entrance, to see the foreman miner, and tell him to withdraw the coolies; the repair would take the rest of the night to make.

By the time I got back, I found that they had got the water blown off, and the manhole opened, leaving an opening into the boiler several feet above the ground.

They had a ladder placed against the boiler, and Lukai was on the domed roof, taking off the chimney, while the coolie was down below raking out the ashes, and taking out the firebars, so that I could stand upright when inside the furnace. The interior was still hot, so we started to partly fill the boiler with cold water as high as the furnace crown on which we would have to stand when inside the steam space.

Although we had thrown buckets of cold water all round inside the furnace door, the interior was also fairly hot and stifling when I crept inside with a small lamp.

Meanwhile Lukai got into the boiler through the manhole overhead, and between us we located the leak. As I expected, it was a small leak through the uptake tube. It had worn thin just there. Really it was dangerous, but as it would take a week to get another boiler up, and we could not stop the mine working, I had to patch it up as quickly as I could.

I next got in the manhole beside Lukai, and while he held the lamp, I punched a round chisel or drift through the leak until I had made a round hole large enough for a $\frac{1}{2}$-inch bolt to pass through.

This done, we got outside and found two pieces of plate of about 2 inches square, with a hole through the centre of each, for the bolt to pass through. These plates or washers were slightly curved, so as to fit the tube.

Wrapping the neck of the bolt with spunyarn, and covering it with red and white lead, I threaded on a plate, first passing the second piece of plate up to Lukai who had climbed into the manhole.

Again getting inside the firedoor, I reached up the tube, and pushed the bolt through the hole, until the plate, well-covered with lead and spunyarn, was pressing firmly against the tube.

Lukai now threaded his piece of plate on to the bolt from the other side of the tube; first well leading and wrapping it, and all that now required to be done, was for him to put on the nut and tighten up, so that the leak would be tightly gripped by the plates, inside and outside.

Just then I heard the coolie scream, and saw his legs and feet scampering up the ladder.

He was now on top of the boiler shouting, "Bargh" ("tiger").

The sudden realisation of my position now struck me for the first time. I was trapped like a rat in a trap. I was on the ground level, and there was an open hole into the chamber.

"Could the tiger reach me with its claws, through the open door?" I felt that it could, and I knew then real fear, such as few people ever experience.

Thoughts raced through my brain, quickly following one another. I thought of our relative positions.

The coolie was on top of the boiler, high up out of reach of the tiger, and therefore safe. Lukai was inside the boiler, and the only opening into this part, was the manhole, and this was several feet above the ground. He was fairly safe I thought, because the tiger could not climb up the smooth steel side. My position was the only one which was dangerous. I could now hear it moving about outside, and once or twice I caught a glimpse of its stripes, as it passed the door opening, because the night was not dark, the stars were shining above us.

The creature evidently had not yet discovered my presence, and was concentrating its attention on the coolie above.

It moved in silence, and both Lukai and the coolie were now silent.

Suddenly, with a terrible snarl, it sprung upwards, and I could hear its claws rasping on the steel plate, as it slipped back. Its rage and snarls were now horrible, and all the time I was pressing myself back against the far side of the boiler as hard as I could.

"Could it reach me when it discovered my presence?"

I measured the distance with my eye, and I felt more hopeful.

Suddenly the snarling stopped, and I saw its head at the opening. It had found me.

First it tried to force itself through the door, but it could only get its head through, and its fangs soon were snapping within a couple of feet of my body. Its breath came in horrid, foul gusts, filling the chamber with a sickening odour, and its roars inside the confined space were enough to hurt my ear drums, while its eyes were glaring into mine.

I stood there fascinated with horror.

I now knew that it could not reach me that way, but would it start reaching in with its claws? My imagination now began to visualise its claws reaching me, and speculating as to what part of me it would rip up first. The constriction on my heart had become almost like a physical pain. Just then I heard something strike the boiler plate with a loud clang. Lukai had thrown his hammer. "Of course." How foolish of me. I had forgotten my hunting knife, which was in my belt. I would wait until it put its head in again, and then try and jab the blade through its eye into the brain.

Now it was reaching for me with its paw through the door opening, and its claws came within a few inches of my body, opening and shutting in a horrible manner. It could not reach me, but I knew that if it had the intelligence of a human being, it would reach in sideways, and then all would soon be over.

It was too dangerous to try and slash its paw; besides, it would do little good. I would wait.

Again it had got its head in the opening and I raised my knife, but found that its teeth followed my hand, and it was risky to strike, because it was snapping all the time. Its top lip was lifted, exposing fangs which seemed enormous, and its whiskers were trembling with rage.

Then I struck with all the suddenness I was capable of. I had missed, and the knife only slashed down its nose, because its head had moved.

Quickly the tiger backed out with a roar. Its rage now was so terrible that it even bit at the plate of the door opening. It was behaving outside like a rampaging demon; lashing its tail and sometimes springing up at the coolie, who had now recovered his courage, when he found himself beyond reach. Both he and Lukai were spitting and hissing and hurling abuse at it.

Once on its upward spring it got its paw in the manhole door opening and hung there a minute while the rest of its claws were slipping and rasping on the steel plates of the boiler side. Then Lukai brought his spanner down with all his force on its paw, nearly cutting it through on the sharp edge of the door opening.

Now the creature was almost insane with rage. It had first been hit by Lukai on the back with a hammer, then its nose had been split by my knife, and lastly its paw had been nearly cut off by the last blow.

Presently it put its head in the fire door again, and, following Lukai's example, I struck it a heavy blow on the nose with my large hammer.

Now a tiger's nose is a very tender and sensitive spot, and it is intended to be so, because its whiskers have to guide it through the thick undergrowth in the dark, and it feels the touch of any obstruction first through these, and then through its nose; consequently the pain must have been extremely acute, judging by the noise it made. It then bounded off into the jungle.

However, none of us ventured to leave our refuge before it was broad daylight, and in the meantime, we completed the work.

CHAPTER 4

I Meet Mulki

Abdul met me in the compound, as I was coming from the mine. Although he was a dignified-looking old man with a long beard which was almost white, he was very childish in his manner, in the presence of Europeans. Now he stood before me with a bashful smile on his face, while he scraped his big toe backwards and forwards in the soil. I knew that he had something on his mind; it was generally a favour that he had to ask when he behaved in this odd manner.

"Well, what is it?" I enquired, speaking in the little Hindustani that I had already picked up.

"Saunders Sahib Mem hai," he said with a glance at the cookhouse door.

I had already taken over the poor fellow's bungalow and bought his furniture, but I was not quite prepared to take over his wife. However, I thought I would have a look at her.

Abdul called out "Mem Sahib," and the cookhouse door opened and the girl came out with a loud clanking and jingling noise. She wasn't bad looking except that she was very black, but she had bracelets half way up to her elbows, and on her ankles were several heavy silver anklets which together must have weighed pounds. Through her nostrils there were two small gold buttons about the size of sixpences. She even had rings on her big toes.

She was extremely shy or nervous, and I felt sorry for the poor girl, having to go back and work in the mine, after being a "Mem Sahib," but I got rid of her as nicely as I could.

After that Abdul seemed to take it for granted that I intended to change my state of single blessedness. As I half assented to the idea, I was consequently not surprised that Abdul had so many friends visiting him. They were mostly females, and young and pretty. I found strange young women sitting in my compound, talking to Abdul, nearly every day.

It is surprising how news travels, for some of them, I found, had come by train from quite a distance.

They just sat with their eyes downcast, when I passed, but I knew that they had had a look at me.

I finally selected a tall, good-looking girl of the "Khaisto" caste, with classical features, and very large eyes.

14

At first I thought she was very shy; I should have known better. Her talk was chiefly about love, and sex matters. Soon she was treating all natives as though they were so much dust beneath her feet.

I soon had a first class row going on around me. Going away by train next day to bring her clothes, she marched into the first class carriage, which was reserved for Europeans. She refused to budge for the guard.

The station bungalow was situated quite close to mine, and I could hear a babel of voices, and a great deal of excitement, but I did not pay much attention until the Station Master Babu came himself for me.

At the station I found a large crowd of coolies, who were interested spectators to a battle of words between the Khaisto girl and the whole of the station staff, train crew included.

What a gift of language she had. She told the characters of the station master, and guard, as well as that of their fathers and mothers, and female relations.

I was rather amused than otherwise, until one night, having been away up the line, and arriving home earlier than expected, viz. about 2 a.m. by trolley, I found her entertaining a gentleman friend, so I decided to part with her.

Then one day I met Mulki. I first saw her working outside the mine. She was carrying baskets of coal on her head. Small, slender, and perfectly formed, she had a light skin that was as fine and smooth as silk. An oval face, with sensitive features, and an expression which reminded me of pictures I had seen of the "Madonna." Her eyes were large and beautiful. An altogether lovely face. A good face I thought.

Next day I saw her again and spoke to her.

She did not know her age, but I put it down at sixteen, and she came from somewhere in the Central Provinces. I could tell that she did not belong to the coolie class, for she spoke in a refined voice, the best type of Hindustani. She told me her story, which in after years I found to be true.

Her father was a farmer, owning land and cattle, and it had been decided by her family that she should marry a neighbouring landowner, a man old and ugly, and as her objections were of no account and she was going to be handed over on a certain date, she ran away.

Wandering to the nearest large town, she met a labour recruiter, who pulled a tale about a fine job she could have as a "Nautch Wallah" or dancing girl, to travel all over India.

She was persuaded to place her thumb mark on a printed form, and was then sent off by train with others to Calcutta, and afterwards by river steamer to the mines in Assam.

The sad fact only dawned on her when it was too late, that she had contracted to work in the mines for four years as a contract labourer, at the rate of six rupees per month (eight shillings), and keep herself.

She was very pleased to get away from the hard, labouring work of the mine, and we got on so well together that she was with me many years, travelling to many parts of the world with me.

Poor girl, she died suddenly in London, while we were staying at a small private hotel in Bow Lane, Cheapside, in 1915, from an overdose of some drug, I think morphia.

After the coroner's inquest she was buried in Stratford Cemetery.

I will have a good deal more to tell about her in this story, as she is bound up with much of it.

CHAPTER 5

I Learn to Inject Morphia

Beautiful places in the tropics, I have heard, are often unhealthy, and this I found was one of them, and it was not long before I got a touch of malaria.

Malaria causes an absolutely rotten feeling, with headache and all the rest of it, so one day when I had an attack rather worse than usual, I sent over to the hospital for the Indian doctor or "Babu," who was in charge there.

He was a fat and jolly Hindu of about forty years of age. After feeling my pulse and taking my temperature, he said, speaking through his nose like most Babus do, "Yes, sir. You have a little fever, but I will soon cure you."

Then he called Abdul to bring a glass of water, and taking a little case out of his pocket, he opened it and took out a small glass syringe; the first hypodermic syringe I had ever seen. Withdrawing the glass plunger, he selected a tabloid from a small tube and dropped it in the syringe, replaced the plunger and drew the syringe three-quarters full of water. Placing a hollow needle on the end of the syringe, he first shook it until the tabloid was dissolved, and then injected the contents into my arm. I will never forget that first injection; the beautiful sensation of ease and comfort; the luxurious dreamy feeling of indolence and happiness which immediately ensued. Every distressing symptom of the fever had disappeared, and I only wanted to sit still in my chair. I was simply purring with content. The voice of the Dr. Babu, who was a great talker, was like a gentle murmur, and I saw him through a pleasant haze.

I must have sat there for hours after he had gone, and it was growing dark, and Abdul came in with the lamp, and commenced laying the table for dinner. It was the first meal that I had really enjoyed for some days, and that night I slept well, and awakened fresh next morning.

As the day wore on, I felt not quite so well, rather tired and a little depressed, and I thought that perhaps I required a little more of the medicine the Babu had given me the day before; also I felt that I would like to have another dose, so I went over to the hospital and saw the Babu. He greeted me with a pleasant smile, and made no trouble about giving me another injection.

"What sort of medicine is this, doctor?" I asked him.

"It is morphia," he said, "the most useful medicine in the world."

The word morphia meant little to me then. Of course I had heard about morphia addicts, but I thought that I was quite capable of controlling any impulse I might have of making a habit of it, and I thought a few doses could not make much difference; moreover, the second dose seemed to be even more potent than the first; no doubt he had given me a larger one.

I even persuaded the doctor to give me a syringe and a tube of $\frac{1}{4}$-grain tabloids.

After a time I found myself looking forward to the afternoon when the day's work was over, and I could take a larger dose and lay dreaming rosy dreams; meanwhile I had got in a supply of tabloids from Calcutta.

There were only day dreams it is true, for I had not yet reached the stage where visions appear while asleep, much less that stage which extremely few drug addicts ever reach, the time when absolutely life-like visions appear while awake. This stage can never be reached on morphia alone.

After a few months of regular indulgence in morphia I began to feel that to get the same results I had to increase my dose and also that the effect wore off more quickly.

Also, I found that my digestive system was getting out of order, and I was becoming so costive that no opening medicine had much effect. The latter symptom was causing me considerable inconvenience, and I was getting scared. I was using now about 4 grains a day, injected a grain at a time instead of the $\frac{1}{4}$ dose as at first, yet the effect was not so pleasant.

I decided that the drug habit was getting too great a hold on me, and that the time had come when I must give it up; never expecting any difficulty in doing so.

I had heard that morphia users broke themselves of the habit generally by reducing their dose a little every day, until they had given it all up.

I smile at my ignorance now, but then it seemed quite simple, so I started.

Next day I took my usual supply of morphia for the day: 4 grains, and mixed it in a small vial containing six syringes full of water, viz. 120 minims. I now drew up into the syringe one tenth of the mixture (12 minims) and threw it away replacing it by this quantity of water.

Next day I felt all right, "Hurrah, it is easy."

The second day I threw away 24 minims and added only 18 minims of water, thus reducing the quantity of liquid per injection from 20 minims to 19 minims; the mixture also being not so strong.

Now I did not feel so good. I found my thoughts constantly turning to morphia, and going over again the pleasant sensation I had experienced. This seemed to emphasise my present state. I really felt uncomfortable and rather irritable, and I kept thinking what a pleasure it would be to take a thumping big dose.

Pride and fear made me stick to my intention, and persevere with this so-called system, until I had reduced my consumption of morphia to $\frac{1}{2}$ grain a day. Beyond this I could not possibly go. I was suffering terribly; I could not sleep, nor sit still, and I was on the fidget all the time. I had a horrible toothache, and I was jumpy and nervous. I could not get a wink of sleep at night, for I would be up half a dozen times walking about the room, as I had cramps in my feet and legs, which I could not keep in one position while lying in bed for more than a minute, before they began to ache again.

I felt wretched in the extreme, and I think that the worst symptom of all was the horrible feeling of depression and gloom – so terrible that it defies description. Moreover, I found that every reduction of the dose increased the sufferings, not only in proportion, but probably four-fold, and I had a tolerable idea that what I was suffering then would be only a fraction of what I would suffer when I got down to the quarter of a grain.

I could not stand it any longer, and I injected a whole grain dose.

Can anyone possibly describe the sensation of relief I felt? I think not; no words possibly could do so. It was simply Heavenly, and that is all I can say. I was now thoroughly scared, because I was back on my 1 grain doses, and soon I even began to feel that I would like to increase them.

I decided to see the Dr. Babu, so I went over to the hospital, where I found he was attending to the outpatients.

I went into his room and waited, and began to think.

I had often noticed a peculiar look in his eyes, when I met him. Sometimes I noticed that the pupils were mere pin points, while at other times they were so large as to almost fill his iris. Moreover, I had noticed that sometimes he would be calm and dreamy in his manner, while again he would be full of life and energy. His moods appeared to change in many different ways.

I remembered the peculiar smile on his face when I told him that I was going to gradually reduce my dose of morphia until I had given it up.

He had enquired two or three times how I was getting on, and each time I had told him of my success he had smiled. I wondered why he had not told me how difficult morphia was to give up; so when he came in I tackled him about it.

"Sir," he said, "morphia is a very strange medicine, it is both Heaven, and Hell. It is very difficult to give up, but it can be done."

Morphia should not be used by anyone for longer than a few months, he told me, because by that time it will begin to lose its pleasant effect, and it will also begin to affect the health, because the action of the drug is continually in one direction.

He told me that he used many kinds of drugs, each in turn; changing over from one to another, using them sometimes singly, and at other times in combinations, so that no one drug ever got too great a hold on him. Each time he changed over, the drug he had been using regained all its old potency and charm when commenced again.

I complained about the binding effect of the morphia.

"Yes," he said "that is one of the principal reasons why the long use of morphia alone is so destructive to health. Its deadening effect on the bowels and the digestion. Although purgatives are of little use, and, moreover, are dangerous to a morphia addict, there is one sure remedy."

Then he gave me my first dose of cocaine.

I found the effect extremely pleasant, although I only had a beginner's dose, $\frac{1}{2}$ grain. It was stimulating, and exhilarating, producing a feeling of well being;

of joy and good spirits. Large doses will produce great self-confidence, and absolutely banish every feeling of self-consciousness in the most difficult situations; in fact it will make the user glory in becoming conspicuous.

Cocaine in large doses also has another effect, which I will not describe here, and this effect is considerably increased when certain other drugs are mixed with it. It is a strange fact that although cocaine, in itself, is not an opening medicine when used by any other person, the effect is immediate when taken by a morphia addict whose bowels have become inoperative.

Following the Dr. Babu's instructions, I first mixed up an ounce solution containing 1 grain of morphia to each 20 minims of water, and another of a 5 per cent solution of cocaine.

Starting with 20 minims of the morphia solution, injected three times a day, i.e. 3 grains of morphia a day, I reduced the dose by 1 minim each day, and added 1 minim of the cocaine solution, until in twenty days I was using no morphia at all, only cocaine.

I experienced no inconvenience at all, or craving for morphia, only increased pleasure.

My health improved, and I became so full of life and energy, and good spirits, that everyone noticed the change in me. No one suspected that I had been using morphia, they had put the change in me, from the health and spirits which I had when I first arrived, to the listless and dreamy state I had been in for some time, to malaria.

The increased brilliance of my eyes, due to the cocaine, appeared only to be an excessive state of good health and vitality.

I now experienced even greater pleasure from the indulgence in cocaine, than I had experienced when commencing to use morphia; and the fact that I had been able to give up the latter so easily, filled me with pride, because in the last week or two I had read a good deal about the drug habit. I was studying a book by an Indian writer, which the Babu had lent me.

It is true that I was now using cocaine, instead of morphia, but then cocaine is much easier to give up than morphia. The deprivation does not cause such distressing and terrible symptoms.

I had not yet discovered the perfect cure for all drug habits, this was to come later, but just out of curiosity I tried a beginner's dose of morphia again, and I found that it had regained all the potency and effect that it had when I was first introduced to it.

Cocaine, I found, banished all desire for sleep, and as loss of proper sleep is one of the reasons why the drug quickly ruins the health, I saw the doctor about it.

I had become very friendly with him, and perhaps because I treated him differently from the way most Europeans treated the educated Indian in those days – by affecting to consider them as inferiors – he imparted to me knowledge about many strange drugs, and their effects. He had devoted many years to the study of this subject, and it was due to him that I first got my great idea, with which I will deal in succeeding chapters.

He next initiated me into the art of smoking opium in the Chinese fashion, and I found that a few pipes of this, smoked just before retiring, procured me a refreshing and sound sleep, which is essential to the cocaine addict, but is so seldom obtained.

The opium is smoked in a manner which has been so often described in books that I will not say much about it here. Opium has the appearance of thick black treacle before it is cooked on a skewer, over a small spirit lamp until it becomes of the consistency of cobblers' wax. This is then rolled into a pellet the size of a large pea, and stuck on the pipe bowl with the skewer. When the latter is withdrawn there remains a small hole through the centre of the pellet.

The pipe, which is a hollow bamboo, is then held over the flame and the smoke sucked into the lungs.

The effect is extremely soothing and sleep-producing, more so than any other drug, and it is a mistake to think that it produces dreams. When once the smoker is asleep, it is a sound and dreamless sleep.

It is preceded by a very pleasant, dreamy state, in which the imagination is very active, and everything appears beautiful, so that even an ugly woman would appear charming.

I found that I could vary my dose of cocaine very considerably, and occasionally I would have a regular binge and then bring myself back to normal with the aid of a little morphia injected.

I was again in fine health and spirits, and I was becoming more interested in my surroundings.

No one suspected that I was using drugs, for there was nothing about my manner to indicate my habit, especially as during the day I used only small doses.

The Dr. Babu was a jolly old soul and fond of female society, and frequently when I went over to his bungalow of an evening, I would find him entertaining some of the prettiest girls in the settlement, and sometimes he had "Nautch Wallahs," i.e. professional dancing girls, giving an exhibition. Sometimes, also, there were other entertainments which I will not describe.

In those days I was very young and shy, and many things easily shocked me.

I found cocaine became more and more fascinating as the doses were increased and time went on. The small doses such as are taken by a beginner, will produce only a remarkable increase of mental and bodily vigour, with a feeling of great strength, but without any intoxication, but if the dose is considerably increased, a kind of intoxication which is quite different from that produced by drink will ensue, a kind of intoxication which I will endeavour to describe later on.

CHAPTER 6

Strange Waking Dreams

I was now using fairly large quantities of cocaine, often tempered with morphia, and smoking a little opium every night.

The morphia and cocaine, of course, I injected, and I soon found that the punctures of the needle left red spots, which sometimes would inflame, and even, as in one instance, cause a sore, and it was this latter that caused me to mention it to the Dr. Babu.

He looked at my arm, and then told me a few truths that I did not know before, nor had ever thought of.

Like most Babus, he spoke slowly, in copy book English, with a slight nasal accent, choosing his words carefully.

"Do you know, sir, that every time you obtain a puncture in the flesh by means of the hypodermic needle, you introduce into the internal portion of the body considerable agglomerations of bacteria."

I listened to his lecture, and understood from it, that I should only use an all-glass syringe, which should be boiled frequently and put away in sterilizing solution, while a second one was being used. The needles, of which I required several, should be kept in solution and the points never touched with the fingers before using, and also that the place where the injection was going to be made should be first wiped with cotton wool dipped in spirits of wine.

All this was most important (he informed me) in a case where so many injections are constantly being used, otherwise a minute portion of septic matter would be introduced into the system each time. It was this, he informed me, that was one of the causes for quickly undermining the health of drug injectors. Their system becomes poisoned by septic matter. Many germs are introduced with each injection.

A single drug, used by itself, cannot be continued with for so long as a combination of two or more drugs. The former will quickly ruin the health, because the action is always in one direction.

No wonder the drug habit is considered so deadly, and makes so many mental and physical wrecks.

A person uses cocaine only for several months, or a year say. He uses it continuously without any other drug to correct its action from always being in the same direction. He is in a constant state of exhilaration and stimulation of the nervous system. He hardly ever sleeps because cocaine

22

banishes sleep, neither does he ever feel hungry, because one of the attributes of this drug is to banish hunger.

He soon becomes like a living skeleton, although appearing to be full of life and energy to the last, but it is false energy; just the effort of the cocaine, using up his nervous energy at a greater rate than his system is making it.

Soon a complete collapse must occur.

It is the same with morphia, only the result is brought about in the reverse direction. The morphia user lives in a pleasant, dreamy state, of soothing comfort and reduced heart's action, which in time gradually makes him almost dead to everything in the world but morphia.

A confirmed morphia addict of long standing loses all sex instinct and feeling; although this is not permanent, it returns when the drug is given up, or if cocaine is substituted.

Cocaine, on the other hand, will, in time, if used entirely alone, produce a kind of sex mania.

In after years I have come in contact with thousands of drug addicts in India, China, Japan, the Malay Archipelago and other parts of the world, where I have specially sought them out.

The popularity of the various drugs differs with the country, but opium heads all the others, followed by cocaine, morphia, hashish, ganja, bhang, etc.

Then there are various kind of liquor which are almost like drugs. Spirits of wine, absinthe, sumsu or rice spirit, arack, made from raisins, and aniseed, and many others.

There are also secret drugs known only to a few in China, drugs which are terrible in their after-effects, but which are more alluring than any of those mentioned. I do not give the names of them here.

For the sore place on my arm, the Babu mixed up some cocaine into a paste and applied it, informing me that this drug is the finest healer known, only it is nearly always used in a solution, which is too weak.

Under his instructions, I now started to use drugs scientifically.

I watched my bodily condition carefully, and corrected at once any adverse symptoms.

Had I a headache on some rare occasion? I removed it at once with a mixture of morphia and cocaine.

A little fever which was natural in this climate and affected every European, I could remove in a few minutes, just as I could remove any kind of pain.

Suppose I was feeling too wakeful to sleep, then a few pipes of opium would send me into a sound, dreamless sleep. Any tendency towards worry, or that commonplace feeling of being dissatisfied with things, could be banished in a few minutes.

Drugs alone could do this, if rightly used, but unfortunately, they are hardly ever used so.

All these narcotic drugs, which are commonly known as Dangerous Drugs, are really the gift of God to mankind. Instead of them doing him harm, they should really be the means of preserving his health, and making his life a state of continual happiness.

I was now able to use large quantities of any particular drug for a time without it harming my health in the slightest, in fact I seemed to benefit by it in every way.

If I had been taking heavy doses of cocaine for some time, living in a state of mental exhilaration and stimulation of every bodily faculty, then I knew that I must reverse, and give the nervous system a perfect rest, under the soothing influence of morphia; and obtain long sound sleeps, with the aid of opium. Moreover, these alternative drugs were equally fascinating. It would be difficult to say that one was more so than another, and the contrast in their action made each one seem more attractive than the last.

The appetite must not be neglected. The stomach will digest enormous quantities of food perfectly, under certain forms of stimulation, if only the nervous energy at the moment is sufficient.

Morphia and brandy together will produce a voracious appetite, and it is a fact that I have eaten a meal at midnight, consisting of three-quarters of a pound of cheese with pickles, half a pound of roast pork, a small loaf of bread and butter and three or four cups of coffee and brandy. Afterwards I have slept soundly and felt fresh and well next morning.

Think of the amount of nutriment the system will obtain from such a meal, enjoyed and perfectly digested.

The study of the effects of different drug combinations became for me a fascinating hobby, and when I tried "hashish," I found it to be the strangest drug of all. I will tell the reader something about it later, also about "ganja" and "bhang."

One of the first effects felt after a dose of cocaine, is a marvellous clearness of vision, and a feeling of perfect well being and happiness. Any tired feeling will be instantly banished and replaced by a feeling of great strength and power. The brain will become powerfully stimulated and clear in thought.

Further doses will produce a peculiar kind of intoxication and extreme fertility of the imagination.

If morphia is added, the thoughts will become calmer and even more fertile, and waking dreams will occur; dreams which are marvellously clear.

Thoughts passed through my mind with an amazing sequence, and problems appeared, only to be immediately solved.

I thought of evolution, and I realised that there is one hard and fast principle which never varies. No matter what example we consider, whether it is the evolution of mankind, nations, cities, science, language, religion, machinery, music, war, or even the evolution of the earth itself, the principle or law never varies.

This law may be stated thus:

There is a constant coming together of Atoms or Units, to form one whole, and a gradual concentration of same. A constant increase in density.

From this principle, I was able to visualise the future of this earth and the human race step by step, until I came to the conclusion that, at some future time, the whole of mankind would become one family, having one Government, one language, and even one colour, and that eventually the earth and all the other planets would fall into the sun and make one body.

Let us consider some examples of the working of this Law.

Prehistoric man wandered through the jungles, in isolated units; these units gradually came together and formed tribes. In time several tribes joined together and formed nations; two or more of which, joining, became an empire. As the process goes on, the whole of the peoples of the earth must come under one Government, they will have one language, and one colour.

To become convinced of this, you must convince yourself that the evolutionary process works in this way without exception. There are no exceptions to this rule. What may appear an exception at first sight is not so, when further considered.

Let us consider some more examples.

The human body commences as a few isolated cells, and these increase and concentrate as the body grows, until maturity is reached.

Great cities commence as a few isolated houses, these grow in number, and become more congested. Outlying villages are gradually absorbed, and the whole extends in every direction, many towns being joined together, to form a great city – London for instance.

Speech commenced as a few simple sounds, meaning food, pain, pleasure, fear, etc.

Music also commenced as an isolated note or two which caught the savage ear.

Science and Arts grew in the same way, increasing, and multiplying their parts and becoming more concentrated, one branch becoming dependent on another.

The great steamship of the present day, containing hundreds of thousands of parts, is evolved from the dug-out, a single unit.

Compare the crude art of the Ancient Egyptians with a modern picture, and you will see in the former a few isolated figures of birds, animals, and humans, seemingly having no connection, one with another, while in the latter you will see a picture, containing many parts all knitted together so as to form one whole.

The great armies of the present day, in which many nations join together in war, each sending their millions of units to form a single whole, have evolved from the isolated savage warrior of prehistoric times.

Consider the means of production and distribution.

Prehistoric man produced and carried for himself alone. Next we have the small traders and carriers acting for a few, then the big manufacturers and railways, producing and carrying for thousands. Later these combined and formed great trusts and amalgamations, reaching out and embracing other countries.

Eventually according to the law, the whole of the means of production and distribution for the world will come under one organisation.

The same with Governments. Prehistoric man was his own government. Gradually these isolated units came together under one who made himself chief. In time this chief, along with others, came together under one overlord or Baron. The various Barons met for the purpose of War, and appointed one to rule over them, as King.

Again several Kings came under one who was styled an Emperor.

The peoples of the world are coming closer together and eventually they will all be under one authority.

Regarding the colour of races; even now the red man is dying out, as is also the black man of Australia and New Zealand and the Pacific islands. The black man will die out along with the red.

Either the white man or the yellow man will predominate or it may be that as travel facilities increase and the two races come nearer to each other, they will intermarry and produce only one colour.

Even the earth is following this evolutionary law.

Scientists are agreed that it has evolved from atoms of nebulous matter floating in space. It is still increasing in size and density, because millions of tons of meteoric and nebulous matter are constantly falling to it out of space; increasing its mass, and it is cooling and contracting; thus increasing its density.

Its atoms are multiplying, and coming closer together. There comes a time when the evolutionary process has reached its zenith, and then it reverses, and dissolution commences.

The units now, instead of increasing and concentrating, decrease, and become more separated.

The human body after maturity, commences to decline, and at death its atoms are separated into dust.

Great cities disintegrate, pass away, and are lost, like Babylon, Nineveh and others.

War will pass away when its evolutionary process has reached the zenith.

The human race itself will pass away; it will first commence to dwindle; to finally disappear at some future time when this earth, like the moon, is no longer able to support life. When its internal heat has gone, all the water now on the surface will sink into the interior, and there will be no heat to turn it into steam and throw it back to the surface. At present no water can penetrate beyond a certain depth without being returned to the surface.

The air will also condense into liquid air, owing to the great cold, and it also will sink in along with the water, and the earth will be airless and waterless, like the moon.

The human race will then have passed away.

The earth is one of the atoms, or units, which will take part in the sun's evolution.

The earth's velocity will gradually decrease, and therefore its centrifugal force. It will be drawn nearer and nearer to the sun, until at last, when it is motionless and dead, it will fall in and increase the sun's bulk.

The rest of the planets will all, either have taken, or will take the same course.

"Can we go further?"

It is known to astronomers that our sun is moving in the direction of the Constellation of Hercules, and is travelling round a gigantic circle; a path which takes it 18,200,000 years to cover in one revolution. It, along with thousands of other suns, is moving round this unknown centre, which may be a gigantic sun, and if so, by the laws of attraction, this central sun must be greater in bulk than the combined mass of all these thousands of suns.

"Will they, in turn, fall in on the centre and form one body?"

The earth's revolution on its axis will gradually slow down, until eventually there will be only one revolution, and then it will always turn one, and the same face to the sun, just as the moon does to the earth. There will then be only one season.

"Will the sexes at some future time be combined into one sex?"

Some medical scientists say that there are already signs of this.

The laws of Nature are truly wonderful. There is a most perfect system, which governs every natural law in the universe. "Can it have all come about by chance, order out of chaos, or has it been designed?"

CHAPTER 7

The Return of the Tiger

It was Sunday morning, and the scene was one of peace as I stood looking out over the compound. It was bathed in sunlight except where shaded by the banana trees and tall ferns. Abdul was squatting at the cookhouse door, plucking a chicken for my tiffin, and the paniwallah as usual was asleep.

Mulki was sitting in the corner of the verandah, playing with the parrot and monkey. She was as happy as the day is long, and since she had left the mine she had become more beautiful than ever.

Sounds of several "Tom-Toms" being beaten floated over from the coolie lines, and from down below, at the foot of the little hill on which my bungalow stood, I could hear the voice of Lukai, scolding his young wife.

Although he was a skinny old man with a hawk-like nose and bald head, he seemed to be full of life and energy. He had a fresh wife about every month. The present one was about thirteen or fourteen years old; he liked them young.

For a native he was wealthy, with his sixty rupees a month; ten times a coolie's pay. He was something of a miser, and there was much speculation as to where he had his money buried.

At night, the wives lived in the hut; a little one-roomed bamboo and mud affair, that he had built himself, but during the day they worked in the mine, because he would not pay the money required to cancel the girls' contract. Perhaps the girls came with some idea of finding the buried hoard. He never gave his wives any silk "sarais," or silver bangles, and they used to come up into my compound in their white cotton, and regard with much envy Mulki's laundered Assam silk "sarais" of many yards' length, with flowered edges; garments that gave Mulki much happiness; that she would finger and look at several times a day.

Lukai was in an abject state of fear. His hut was the nearest of all to the jungle, and word had come in that the tiger had made a kill near the Singphoo village. It could easily put its paw through the thin bamboo walls, but luckily a tiger does not often have sufficient intelligence for this.

I went over to the bungalow of Simpson, one of the mine foremen. He was a well educated and studious young fellow, and he was sitting on the verandah with a book.

"I have just heard that the tiger has killed a cow near the Singphoo village, and I am thinking of going out there this evening, and I want you to come along," I said. "We will sit up, and wait; it is almost sure to return to the carcase for another feed."

Simpson was eager for the adventure; he had never been after a tiger before.

"I've only got a Winchester repeater," he said; "the bullets are small, but it fires seventeen shots."

"That will be all right; I will take my Cape gun; it fires a big bullet; big enough for an elephant almost."

Mulki heard of our intended adventure, and she was very anxious about my safety.

"What thing, Sahib? Me not wanting Sahib going. By and bye tiger eating. Not going, Sahib."

She was learning a little English, but as yet pidgin English; the pidgin English of India; a language quite different from that of China, which in turn is nothing like the attempt made by the natives on the West Coast of Africa. Each one is entirely different, while the pidgin English as spoken in Malay Archipelago and the South Seas, stands in a class by itself. It is a perfect scream.

In this book you will see some examples of pidgin English as it is really spoken in the various countries. They differ almost as much as Dutch differs from German.

After tiffin we set off, taking a coolie with us to carry a basket containing food, and a hurricane lamp.

We had a few miles to go along the railway track and I sent for my two trolley wallahs and the trolley.

We sat on the seat in front, and the coolie squatted behind, while the two trolley wallahs ran with bare feet on the steel rails, pushing the trolley before them.

The track was a single line cut in a wide path through the jungle, and the village lay a little distance on one side, situated on the bank of a small stream.

The place was in a state of fear, so that no one dare go out of their houses after sunset.

"Why do not the Indian Government exterminate these savage creatures by offering a big bounty on every one killed? Eighty thousand people are killed by tigers every year in India, but of course they are mostly poor country natives."

Imagine a common occurrence, one which often happens. A young woman going down to the stream for water, in the early morning; she must go, even if it is known that there is a tiger in the district, for it would put shame on her husband to perform so menial a task, or even to accompany her.

She goes in fear and trembling, casting looks of apprehension to right and left.

A great striped shape appears silently from the jungle. She drops her jar, and tries to run, almost suffocated with terror, when with a bound the tiger is upon her. Its terrible claws are ripping her vitals, and its fangs are sinking into her flesh.

"Who can realise the agony and terror of such a death?" "What would we do, if this occurred often in England?" "What an outcry there would be."

We would probably organise wholesale extermination, as we would organise for war.

Those who have only seen a tiger in a cage, in some zoo or circus, can have no idea of what a tiger in its wild state in the jungle looks like. The docile and well fed appearance of the former, which reminds one of a great tame cat, is very different from the other, with its ferocious expression, its alertness, and quickness of movement. The one inspires curiosity, and the other a feeling of repulsion, and a sense of its enormous power and cruelty.

The old head man of the village conducted us to a hut, where we deposited our things, and then some of the villagers preceded us to the spot where the carcase of the cow was lying. Each man carried with him a "Dao" – a long knife useful as a chopper.

After proceeding some distance, I noticed Simpson sniffing. "Phoo, what a horrible stink."

"Yes," I said, "we must be getting near to the place now."

The dead cow was lying in some long grass, on one side of the roadway. Its belly and entrails had been partly eaten, as also had been part of its lips and nostrils. Its head was pointing up to the sky, at right angles to its body, as its neck was broken; the tiger had probably sprung on to its back, and jerked up its head with its paw. The thing was alive with vermin and insects, and clouds of flies were buzzing round it. The smell was disgusting.

The next job was to search for a tree with a suitable fork, for building a chang on. It would have to be high enough to be beyond the tiger's spring. Simpson was edging round to the windward side of the carcase.

"Here," I said, "that won't do, we will have to be on this side, or the tiger will get our scent."

"If we smell any stronger than that thing, it is about time we had a bath," said Simpson.

"I am not quite sure whether a tiger has a keen sense of smell or not," I said.

"Well, it would have to be pretty nifty if it could smell me when it has its nose down in that mess."

I thought for a moment, and then came to the conclusion that the tiger is not a keen-scented animal, judging by how it had behaved when I was in the boiler; and I have since found out that I was right. It does not need to be; it has powerful weapons of offence and defence. It has not had to develop its scent, to be constantly on guard from being eaten by other wild animals, nor is it like the rhinoceros, so blind as to be hardly able to see 100 feet away, and therefore has developed a marvellously keen scent, on which it depends more than it does on its eyesight.

We selected a suitable tree, and left the natives to build a platform, while we returned to the village to have a feed and a sleep in the head man's hut, remembering that we would probably have to be awake all night.

The village consisted of about thirty families, who supported themselves by weaving, by hand, a cloth of many colours. They are light skinned, with a slight Mongolian slant of the eyes; a happy, care-free people.

Now all was changed; a state of panic existed in the village. Somewhere in the jungle lurked a foul thing which might at any moment pounce with teeth and claws, even on a little child. No woman would venture to go down to the stream for water, alone. All the water for the village was brought at one time under an escort of the men armed with spears. They had no silly ideas about dignity, they are not Indians.

After sunset the night comes quickly, and then the village would be silent and in darkness, and the people barricaded in their huts, ever on the alert for the hoarse, deep-chested cough, to indicate that the man eater was prowling round near to the village.

Just before sunset we set off, after first making sure that we had everything that we would require; our rifles cleaned and loaded; the lantern, matches, and a couple of flasks of spirits; while I had a pocket torch.

The sun was just setting as we climbed into the tree, and after fixing the lantern to a branch, ready for lighting, we settled ourselves down on the platform.

"Now is the time to get a smoke, because afterwards we will have to do without and remain quite silent."

"Do you think the tiger will eat that stinking carcase," asked Simpson.

"Sure to," I said, "don't we hang game up until it's rotten, and eat Gorgonzola cheese when it is full of maggots? Besides, I have smelt its breath."

The sun had gone down, but there was sufficient light in the sky to make out the dead cow, which looked, in the half light, with its twisted head like some strange prehistoric monster.

Now the mosquitoes began to come out in shoals, and we tied some pieces of netting round our helmets, and put on gloves, but still they bit us through our linen suits. The night was still, and there was hardly any sound, except the croaking of frogs, and the occasional wail of a jackal.

We could see well enough, as there seemed to be a kind of glow everywhere, due to the fireflies, probably.

Simpson looked at his watch, and was just able to make out that it was 9.20; although we seemed to have been waiting hours.

I do not know how long we sat waiting, and I think that we must have dozed occasionally, when suddenly we were wide awake. There must have been a sound, although I was not conscious of it.

We listened, and strained our eyes into the surrounding bushes, and then we heard it.

It was a deep sniff, that seemed to come from some mighty lungs, and we waited tense and still, with our eyes fixed on the carcase. A moment or two passed, and then there was first a movement in the clump of bushes behind the kill, then two eyes appeared, and the unmistakable head of the tiger.

I saw Simpson slowly raise his rifle, and I put out my hand, and made a sign not to shoot yet, as the target was too uncertain – a head-on shot.

The tiger stood there, silent and terrible, with its head low down near the ground, crouching; the instinct of the wild to reduce its bulk; it was suspicious; some instinct had warned it that danger was near. Then it was gone, and we heard it moving about in the undergrowth on the opposite side of us, and in a minute all was silent.

We waited, alert and listening for the slightest indication of its presence, for what must have been an hour, and then Simpson spoke, and let off steam.

"Well, have we to sit up this blasted tree all night now?" he said.

"I suppose so, unless you want to walk back in the dark, with a tiger maybe prowling at your heels."

We could only make the best of a bad job, and wait for daylight. We got out our pipes, and made ourselves as comfortable as we could. It was about 2 a.m.

The hours seemed interminable, and to make matters worse, it started to rain. We were soon wet through and shivering, because the temperature had fallen many degrees, as it often does in Northern India, in the early morning.

"I've had enough of this," said Simpson. "Tiger or no tiger, I'm going. Come on, let's go."

In getting out of the tree, the hurricane lantern, which we had lighted some time before, crashed to the ground, and the glass broke.

Now we were in a fine mess. The question was, whether to sit in the tree for another two or three hours, wet through and shivering, or to proceed through the jungle in the dark, with nothing better than a flash lamp to guide us.

I had a suspicion that the tiger was not far off; perhaps it was watching us all the time.

However, we made up our minds to go. I went first carrying the torch in one hand, and my gun in the other. It was difficult to say which of us was in the most dangerous position. The torch could only throw a light on a small patch at a time. Attack might come from any direction.

We had to move along a narrow path, with the dense jungle on either side, and the tiger, if it was there, might spring out on us before we could raise our guns.

It might stalk us from behind. This idea seemed to strike Simpson, at the same time as it came into my mind, and we called a halt.

We stood silent, listening for a minute; a feeling of fear was taking possession of me.

"There." Distinctly we heard the cracking of twigs, in the bushes, just on our left.

"Fire a few shots in the surrounding bush, and reload quickly," I said.

The crash of the shots echoed through the jungle. The villagers would have heard them, and would be rejoicing that the terror was dead; it would descend on them again, with renewed force.

I flashed the torch round in every direction, but all was silent, yet I had a feeling of almost certainty that the thing was there, close to us; watching and stalking us. The position was an unnerving one, but we would have to keep cool. Any sign of panic would be fatal.

Now we moved forwards slowly, back to back, with Simpson walking backwards, with his face to the rear.

There were seventeen bullets in his rifle, but they were small ones; it would take perhaps several of them to stop a tiger. If only I could get one shot in fair, with either of the barrels of my gun, it would do the trick, for one barrel fired a heavy charge of large shot while the other was a rifle barrel firing the Martini-Henry cartridge.

We moved along for a few hundred yards, and then we heard a slight movement in the undergrowth on my right. Simpson quickly fired a couple of shots in that direction, which were followed by a loud crashing of breaking foliage as some creature made for the rear. It was hunting without giving tongue.

Our nerves were almost keyed up to breaking strain, but to hurry would be almost sure death for one of us at least.

Suddenly Simpson shouted, and I swung the torch round quickly, and there, not twenty paces behind us, was the tiger. The torch shone full in its face, as it crouched as though about to charge, revealing for an instant the twisted, and badly healed nose and lip, giving its face a peculiarly devilish appearance; when Simpson fired shot after shot in its direction, as fast as he could pull the lever of his gun.

For a moment the tiger staggered as though hit, and then with a roar of pain, made off, followed by both charges from my gun.

Even now we did not change our mode of progression; although we moved as fast as possible, and arrived at the village both exhausted and thankful.

Next day we searched the jungle, but although we found bloodstains, we did not find the tiger.

CHAPTER 8

The Healing of the Wound

Next morning I set off by trolley along the line to the workshops, which were situated several miles away. I was going to make arrangements about the fan, and the piping.

Although the line was a single track – and there were only two trains run on it a day, being a branch line – it was necessary to be on the look out, as there was always the possibility of a special coming down with some important official. However, I generally depended on the coolies. The track ahead was screened from view in many places by the jungle, wherever there was a slight curve, but the two coolies, running on the steel rails with their bare feet, could feel the vibrations of the rail if there was a train on the line, even if it was a long way off.

Moreover, they could tell whether it was in front or behind them, and whether it was approaching or receding. I never could understand how they did it. If the train was heard approaching the trolley would be quickly lifted off the track.

A gang of platelayers was working on the line, and my thoughts turned to the tiger. I wondered if it had been badly wounded, or if it would be heard of again. The jungle on each side of the track was not more than fifty yards away, and these coolies would be easy prey should it appear. I noticed that some of them had spears and daos lying near them, but I knew that, should the tiger come, they would all run.

The work must go on, in spite of tigers, and I would probably, some time, have to turn out through the night again.

The getting of the new boiler to the spot had been a long and difficult job; it had necessitated the use of elephants to get it along the jungle paths. In some places, where the track was wide enough, the boiler could be rolled along the ground by an elephant. The animal simply placed its head against the boiler and pushed, and it had intelligence enough to keep the boiler straight, but where the path was narrow, the boiler had to be dragged lengthwise on rollers. Where there was an incline, two elephants were required. Before I had got the elephants on the job, a hundred men and women, tailing on to a rope, had failed to move the boiler. One of the creatures was a magnificent tusker of colossal strength, and when the boiler had been finally got to its destination, and I had manoeuvred it into position with the base lying on the concrete bed, the elephant had placed its trunk under the other end and raised the boiler into a vertical position. It was amazing to see the strength and sagacity of the animal, and the gentle manner in which it picked knobs of sugar off the palm of my hand, when the job was done.

On arrival at the workshops, I immediately started some fitters cutting and making up the necessary piping for the hand fan, and was attending to some other work, when a telegram was brought to me from the station bungalow. It simply said, "Prepare brass coffin plate, William Lumley, age 27 years. Urgent."

I was stunned; I had seen Lumley well and hearty that very morning. I knew that bodies had to be buried the same day that death takes place, in this climate. I wondered what had happened. "Had there been a fall of the roof in the chamber for which the fan was intended?" This seemed to be the most likely explanation. I might have been working in the place myself, and would have been doing so on the morrow, when the piping was ready.

I hurried back to the mines, and there found that my surmise was correct; Lumley had been killed by a fall of coal; the chamber had caved in, burying Lumley and three coolies. Very peaceful he looked as I gazed down on the dead face, laid out in the room in which so many merry parties had been held. He was not crushed at all, he had evidently died of suffocation.

As I stood, along with the other Europeans, in the little fenced clearing in the jungle, and watched the coffin lowered deep into the ground, I thought of the many once familiar faces that had passed away, to be seen no more.

The earth is a great live thing, that wages a perpetual warfare, in its endeavour to kill off the living creatures on its surface, by means of disease, famine, floods, earthquakes, typhoons, explosions, fire and many other ways. From the day we are born, the earth begins to suck our lives away.

Every movement of the body has to be made against the resistance of the earth's gravitation. This means that a little of our life has been expended. Every movement produces a little heat, which the earth absorbs; heat energy which we have obtained chiefly from the sun, and which the earth sucks from us in an endeavour to prolong its life. It will die, as everything must die. Human and animal life will long since have passed away, but how?

"Will it be by some strange comet, of which we have no knowledge; whose path is so great that it only approaches the sun once in a million years? By head-on collision, or by contact with its tail, which may be a streamer of a million miles of poison gas?"

Perhaps it may be by flood, raised by the too near approach of some wandering dark body from the depths of space; to pass on to where it came from; or perhaps to meet us in head-on collision; fire following flood, leaving a new and larger red-hot earth.

Some great disturbance may take place in the sun; a portion of whose surface may collapse, to fill up a void below, formed by internal contraction. Then such fierce heat would be released, that all life here would be instantly scorched and burnt away.

"Will it be owing to the moon, whose speed, decreasing, approaches slowly towards us, until it appears to fill a quarter of the whole sky; producing enormous floods hundreds of feet deep; washing over the Continents, as they follow in the moon's wake? Approaching still nearer until tides of molten matter, from the earth's centre, burst through the crust and swamp the whole surface, killing all life thereon."

Nothing is more certain than that, sometime in the dim future, all life on this planet will come to an end. If we escape all the disasters already mentioned, then the human race may live on for hundreds of millions of years, until cold eventually brings about the final death.

Long before this occurs, the whole of mankind will be living at the equator, a land of ice and snow, and semi-darkness. They will be dressed in skins and the sun will appear as a purple-coloured ball in the sky.

By then all vegetation will have disappeared from the face of the earth, but man will have made great strides forward in science and invention; he will have invented new kinds of synthetic foods. He will burrow deep down into the earth for chemical means of producing heat, to replace the sun's. Great cities will be built underground, artificially heated and ventilated, and every aid of science will be made use of in an endeavour to prolong life a little longer, but the end will come.

CHAPTER 9

The Delights of Hashish

There is a drug which, with the exception of opium, is more popular among the drug-taking population of India than all others, and that is Indian hemp.

There are several preparations made from this plant, and perhaps the most delicate and pleasing in effect of any of them is "hashish."

This is the young shoots and buds of the plant, dried and prepared for smoking.

"Bhang" and "ganja" are much coarser and violent in their action. The former is a liquid extract or decoction, made from the roots of the plant, while "ganja" is simply the leaves dried and prepared for smoking. I have tried both "bhang" and "ganja," but I found them both too crude and violent in their action, besides leaving an unpleasant after-effect.

Even "hashish" is not a drug to continue with for long. The immediate effect of smoking hashish is a very peculiar form of intoxication. Under its influence all the senses will gradually become curiously distorted. One may appear to live a whole lifetime in a few minutes. Objects may appear to be enormously extended either in length or breadth, or both, or they may appear to be microscopic in size.

The faintest sound will sometimes appear to be a thunderous roar. At the same time the action of the drug is also stimulating and intoxicating, producing a feeling of strength and well-being.

Under the influence of a big dose, nothing will appear as it really is. Former periods of one's life will return to one, to be actually lived again, years seemingly passing, although the actual time may be only a few minutes.

Or again one may seem to have an entirely different personality. Under the influence of very large doses, combined with a certain proportion of cocaine, it is possible almost to experience anything one wishes, quite realistically.

A person may be in the heart of a London fog and yet it may appear to him as a beautiful tropical climate. This, of course, could only be produced by very large doses.

I do not mean to say that a beginner would experience all these effects, because it takes time to work up to the necessary quantities, but he would experience some of them in a minor degree.

The effect of the drug soon wears off, perhaps half an hour, yet this may appear as years of time. The most pleasing effect, I find, is produced by a mixture of cocaine and hashish, the cocaine injected followed by a dose of the other smoked. The hashish seems to improve the quality of the cocaine, and give it a strange intoxicating effect.

The Dr. Babu had initiated me into the joys of hashish smoking, and I had made several trials of it so far, but only in a small way; I intended, however, to have a regular binge with it. I was becoming very fascinated with my experiments, constantly trying new combinations, and noting their effects.

The Babu had a vast store of knowledge, on which I could draw, and I intended to learn all I could from him; also I made up my mind to visit as many countries as I could, and make a study of the drug habit thoroughly.

My idea was that there must be hundreds of roots and plants in the jungles of the Malay Archipelago which have unknown medicinal properties.

In the great islands of Borneo, Sumatra and New Guinea, there are thousands of square miles of unexplored territory. What secrets must there be hidden in those jungles. The Pharmacopoeia will never be complete until every plant and flower and root has been tested.

For the purpose of the binge which I have just mentioned, I intended going over into the hills for the week-end, and staying with some friendly Nagas, who frequently came to my bungalow to sell me rubber which they had collected, and which I used to send home for sale. Rubber at that time was selling, I believe, at about seven shillings a pound or more, and I had got as much as five shillings myself. I used to have it sold by auction in the Liverpool market; many cwt. of it.

The "Nagas" would come in Indian file. First would walk a buck, whose only costume would be a conical-shaped helmet made of fibre, decorated with two boar's tusks, and some coloured feathers; a kind of grass skirt round his middle; a spear, and a big shield made out of tough fibre and skins.

He would be followed by several women, carrying the rubber in baskets on their backs. Their only costume was three or four yards of cane bent into a spiral of several hoops which started at their hips, and just extended about a foot down, and when they walked, the canes lifted. They had no need to wear low neck blouses and openwork stockings to show their charms.

In payment for the rubber they would have to be given opium, tobacco, sugar, and one or two other things, which they could barter in their own territory for anything else they might require.

The bartering would all take place by pantomime. Abdul would pick out so many balls of rubber, and lay them down beside a pot of opium, or a package of sugar into which the bucks would stick a finger and then lick it, to make sure that it was sugar.

Each few balls had to be bartered for separately, as they could not count very many. All the time, no doubt, they were gloating over the idea that they were getting the better of the white man, on account of the stones in the centre. I would weigh the balls, and would notice the difference in weight between a ball of pure rubber that I had, with great labour, opened, and extracted the stones, and the ones offered for sale.

The women would be squatting on the verandah without any thought of modesty, as the canes were slack, and lifted more than ever; in fact they might just as well not be there at all, very often.

They were light skinned women, with slant eyes and in some cases were comely.

I took a coolie with me into the hills, because I wished to collect some orchids, and he would have to carry my things.

After spending the day in the jungle, I settled down in a hut the Nagas had put at my disposal.

I had been taking a good deal of cocaine during the day, and when night came, I started in earnest; I meant to test cocaine and hashish together, to see what curious dreams they would produce.

Up to this time, I had never had any idea of waking visions, and the experience I am about to describe came as a great shock to me; it was so startling and horrible.

In later years I came to enjoy this kind of vision, and no matter how horrible they were, I felt no fear, because I knew what they were and when to expect them; moreover, I could produce the kind I wished to see.

I started off, alternately injecting cocaine, and smoking hashish, continuing far into the night, until my senses became so acute that every problem in the universe seemed to be solved.

A strange, unexplainable sense stole over me; a sense of the presence of something near me; something horrible and menacing, and I suddenly felt afraid.

Expecting I know not what, I looked fearfully round.

The room was lighted only by a small, native coconut oil lamp, standing on the bamboo floor, and there, standing in the gloom in the corner of the room, I saw three figures. Two of them were tall Indians such as one sees in Northern India, dressed in the usual white coat and turban, while the third was naked with the exception of a loin cloth. He had a piece of cord in his hand, and his attitude was crouching, as though about to spring at me.

The expression on the faces of all three of them was murderous, and their eyes were fixed on me with unwinking intensity, and as I looked they seemed to be getting nearer, although I could not perceive the slightest movement on the part of any of them, not even their eyes. They seemed to glide or float.

As they approached, I seemed paralysed with fear, and I could feel drops of cold sweat trickling down underneath my armpits.

For a moment I was incapable of any movement at all, just as though I was in a trance. It was a mental agony. Slowly they were approaching. My eyes were fixed on the piece of cord. I seemed to know that they were "Thugs" who were about to strangle me with the cord, after the manner of their calling, two of them holding the victim, while the third one manipulates the cord.

Suddenly with an effort of will I sprang up, and the vision disappeared.

I then mixed myself a grain of morphia, and injected it. At once I felt calm and without fear, and I clearly realised that what I had seen was only a vision born of drugs.

I still felt extremely exhilarated but calm, with a tremendous sense of power and well being, this being the effect of just the right quantity of morphia following on top of the other drugs.

The night was lovely and the moon was shining. I walked along the runways leading from the village into the jungle, which was full of subdued sounds; the gentle murmur of the breeze through the trees; the croaking of frogs, and the wail of a jackal, which was immediately taken up and answered by others in the distance; the hoarse hooting of night birds, and once the loud crashing of some large animal in the undergrowth ahead; followed immediately by the excited chattering of monkeys in the tree tops where they had retired for the night.

Faces peeped out at me from behind trees, the branches of which would sometimes gradually change, as I looked at them, into animals or reptiles, of shapes something similar to the shape of the branch.

The three Indians glided without movement, close behind me, but I was no longer afraid, I knew that what I was seeing was only a vision born of drugs. The touch of morphia, had been just the right thing to complete the perfect combination. I felt only interested; exhilarated, but without the excitement which would have resulted from cocaine without the other drugs.

I found that with a concentration, or effort of will, any of the visions would disappear, only to return again.

I walked on seemingly in an enchanted world. Suddenly, when coming round a bend in the path, I saw a large striped shape standing facing me. The moonlight showed it very distinctly, and probably made it appear larger than it really was. I recognised it at once; I had seen it twice before in reality.

"Was it a vision only this time?" My heart-beats increased slightly. The tiger stood without movement, it could not understand why I was not afraid like every other creature in the Indian jungle, except only the rhinoceros, which fears nothing.

I had a revolver in my hip pocket, but I never thought of using it. I simply kept my eyes fixed on it.

We stood staring into each other's eyes for I don't know how long, as time had no meaning for me then. I felt no fear, only curiosity, and I seemed to be able to read its inmost thoughts. Who shall say that a tiger has not a brain that reasons? In its eyes I saw rage, cruelty, superstition, fear.

I took some steps forward, and then I noticed that it was still the same distance from me as before and I knew that it was a vision.

I relaxed and allowed my mind to become passive, and then I noticed that it seemed to be drawing nearer, without any perceptible movement, on its part.

With a concentrative effort, I banished the vision, and returned to my hut, where some pipes of opium brought me back to a normal condition, and I soon was sleeping soundly, to wake next morning no worse for my experience.

Sometimes I intended to test hashish by itself, as I had an idea that the cocaine somewhat changed the effect produced in this experiment.

CHAPTER 10

A Trip to Calcutta

Healy and I were going to have a month's holiday, and intended to spend it travelling in India, seeing all that we could in the time. I had always had a desire to see things that were new and strange; to look below the surface, and find out how the world lived; to have new thoughts, and see new places.

Drugs to me meant, not so much the bodily pleasures which they brought, as mental pleasures; the powerful stimulation of the imagination; the effacement of the present, so that I could live, almost in reality, in other scenes and periods of the world's history.

Healy was a foreman of one of the mines, a jolly good fellow, full of life and fun; a diamond in the rough. He had been a coal miner at home, who had worked his way up owing to force of character and intelligence, to be mine foreman.

I had just got home and finished bathing and changing, when he called in, on his way home from the mine. He was in his pit clothes, and his face looked like that of a nigger minstrel who hadn't blackened properly round the creases of the eyes and mouth, and parts where the sweat trickles. He was in high spirits about something.

"Well, old man, I've got a month's leave, and I'm off to Calcutta. Can you imagine the time I'm going to have?"

"When are you going?" I asked with envy. How I wished I was going too; I had never had a real holiday since I came out, and had seen little of India so far.

"Next week," said Healy. "Why not try and get leave and come along too? What a time the two of us could have in Calcutta; going alone is not so good."

"Oh, I couldn't get any leave yet; I haven't been here a year yet."

"How about trying to get round the M.O. and get him to put you down for sick leave?"

I laughed. "Sick leave, I look like a sick man, don't I? No, the doctor wouldn't do that, but I have a good mind to see the manager, and try and get some privilege leave; there are several things I want to do in Calcutta. Private business affairs, you know."

I at once became enthusiastic, and both of us began to plan and discuss the project. I decided to write off that very night, and to have a few words with the manager the first time he came down. The letter would prepare the way, and I would probably be able to get a definite answer when we met.

I got the leave all right, and then we started to make ready. I had plenty to do, and only a couple of days to do it in. I had to make a thorough inspection of all the machinery on the mine and give instructions to Lukai about the various repairs on hand. I was leaving Mulki behind, but arranged for her to have one of her friends to stay with her while I was away.

I impressed on her the importance of fastening all the doors and windows, and not to sit on the verandah after dark, and I tried to cheer her up by promising to bring her all sorts of pretty things from Calcutta.

I always had a pleasant feeling of adventure when going on a long journey. I remembered how, in my boyhood days, I had always had a hankering for adventure. First I had wanted to go to sea, and then to be a cowboy and, even when quite a little boy, I devoured every penny dreadful I could lay my hands on. I had been reading that bold and adventurous people, generally had prominent jaws, and often walked on the outer sides of their feet. I remembered walking down the road with my chin thrust forward, so that my lower teeth projected over the upper ones and at the same time trying to walk on the outsides of my feet, when a kindly old market woman had spoken to me, and said, "What's the matter, honey?" at the same time casting a glance down at the back of my pants.

Healy was the phlegmatic type, and it was difficult to tell when he was enjoying anything or otherwise; he had a poker face, but at the same time he had a keen sense of humour. Often he would speak in broad Lancashire dialect, and although well educated, he was often rough and uncouth in his manner. I liked him, and felt that he would be a jolly good companion to have with one in any tight corner.

At the railway station we found the usual crowd of natives camping on the platform, with their pots and drinking vessels, and their host of relations and friends come to see them off; a railway journey is generally a great event in their lives, and they become, for the time being, important people.

We managed to secure a compartment to ourselves, as there were seldom many Europeans on the train, and just before it started, a coolie came alongside and delivered several bottles of beer, which Healy had evidently ordered.

As the train moved out of the station I looked out of the window, and there I was surprised to see Mulki, and Healy's girl, waving their hands from behind a crowd of natives; they must have travelled among the coolies in the open trucks.

Poor girls, partings are sometimes very sad; I had seen one or two final partings, when the sahibs had been leaving the country for good. Generally the girl is given a little hut and a few hundred rupees, but even so, some of them had been almost heartbroken. I didn't like to think of the time when I would be leaving the country myself. I could not imagine what I could do. Best not think about it until the time came.

We went straight on board the river steamer, and that night I slept in my comfortable little deck cabin, with the cool breeze blowing past the open shutters, and listening to the chung chung of the paddles, as the boat made its way down the mighty Brahmapootra; a soothing sound charged with hints of slumber.

The steamer was tied up at Gauhatti, where it would remain a couple of hours or so, and I went round to Healy's cabin, where I found him stretched out on the divan with his pipe, and a bottle of lager beer.

"Come on, Healy, let's go ashore, I want to buy some silk."

"Well, can't you buy it on board? There are plenty of girls on the lower deck with silk for sale."

"I know that," I said, "but you will not get the best quality here; the best of it is sent to Calcutta; besides, we are tourists while on board, and will have to pay a good deal more for it than if we go ashore, and call at some place where it is made."

In coming back to the boat along the shady lanes we met a pretty Assamese girl, whom Healy persuaded to go for a walk. Afterwards the young lady offered to take me and show me round the place also, but I did not accept the invitation.

There were only five passengers on the boat in the first class, one of whom was a rather nice-looking girl, an English woman, tall and slender; an aristocrat in appearance, and Healy soon became very struck with her; moreover she was inclined to be friendly.

On arrival at Ghaut, we were in the saloon paying our accounts to the native purser, when she came in and handed a cheque to the latter.

"Cheque not taking, Mem Sahib," he said, in English.

"You must take a cheque," she said. "I haven't sufficient cash with me, and I can't get it until I get to Calcutta."

The purser firmly refused to take the cheque, and she turned a pair of appealing, innocent-looking blue eyes on Healy and me. "Whatever can I do?"

Quickly, before I could speak, Healy butted in, "Let me cash the cheque for you," he said.

"Oh, it is so kind of you; you are sure you don't mind?"

Healy did not mind, and said so; he was happy to oblige.

While we were speaking, I was looking on. I began to be a little suspicious. I noticed her business-like manner, and thought it queer that she had come in while we were paying our accounts, and offered her cheque while the purser was attending to us; so that I was not very much surprised, when we got to Calcutta, to hear Healy cursing one morning at post time. The cheque had been returned marked "No account," and we never heard tell of the young lady again.

We put up at "Spencer's Hotel," one of the most popular in Calcutta; getting bedrooms on the roof.

There were no electric fans in the Calcutta hotels in those days, and every guest employed a "punkah wallah," who sat outside the door pulling a string all night; a string which passed through a hole in the wall, and was connected to a "punkah," which swung backwards and forwards above the bed.

Frequently through the night, the coolie would drop off to sleep, and then the sahib would wake up drenched with perspiration. These punkah wallahs generally work somewhere during the daytime as well, so they have to depend on what sleep they can snatch at odd moments. They will come on duty at 6p.m., and of course most of the time, until perhaps 11 p.m. or later, the sahib will not be in his room, and the coolie will be curled up on the door-mat asleep. It is a curious sight to walk down the corridor of the big hotels in the early evening, and to see these punkah wallahs asleep on the mats; some of them, of course, will be working, if the owner of the room is in.

In many cases their only home is the hotel corridor and they get their meals in the bazaar or where they can.

We found that it was cool enough on the roof to do without punkahs, and we were lucky to get these rooms, as they were in great demand.

That evening, when the dinner bell rang, we went down into the big dining-room, and took our seats at one of the long tables. Most of the guests were in white evening dress, and the tables were beautifully set out and decorated. Bearers in white uniforms and turbans, flitted to and fro, bringing in and serving the many courses; while the big punkahs swung overhead.

Healy, who was always rather rough in his manner, was often inclined to be rougher still, when he found himself in polite company in a strange place, and as most of the company were silent and appeared to be strangers to each other, he started talking in a loud tone of voice to me, who sat next to him; moreover, he spoke in broad Lancashire dialect, which I had heard him use occasionally before. Healy hadn't an atom of self-consciousness in his make up, and seemed not to notice that he was attracting some attention.

The night was hot in spite of the punkahs, and sweat was trickling down the backs of our hands, and every now and then Healy would give his hand a flip, and drops of sweat would fly in all directions.

I saw a lady sitting next to him glance down at her dress.

I was beginning to feel uncomfortable; there were about twenty people at the table, and some of them, I thought, appeared to be looking on with fish eyes; observing but pretending not to.

Just then Healy spoke to a gentleman sitting opposite him; a shy young gentleman, seemingly. Instead of asking one of the bearers, he spoke across the table to the young man, asking him to pass the cruet. It was a very wide table and they both had to stand up and reach far over, and after a little exertion he succeeded in getting hold of the cruet; a large affair containing many kinds of chutneys, sauces, oils, and seasonings. Healy sat down and calmly took the stoppers out of the bottles one by one, and sniffed the contents, until he came to the olive oil; and then, with the eyes of the whole table on him, he placed the bottle to his lips, and drank half its contents.

At first there was a startled silence, and then someone laughed, but Healy immediately transferred the attention from himself by starting a long-distance conversation with the gentleman who laughed on the merits of olive oil.

Soon that condition of aloofness, so common to Englishmen in the presence of strangers, wore off, and the conversation became general. Healy even seemed to become friendly with everybody. Although he did some funny things sometimes, one could not help liking him.

CHAPTER 11

Investigating the Calcutta Underworld

It was late afternoon, and the sun, which had been blazing down all day with fierce intensity, was beginning to sink towards the horizon. The streets had a baked and parched appearance, and that peculiar smell of burnt clay, which is one of the first things to strike the newcomer to Calcutta. It was more noticeable than usual. Water carts had been traversing the main thoroughfares all day, only to leave the roads as dry as ever again, very soon after passing.

Soon the comparative cool of the evening would come, and the "Botanical Gardens" would be crowded with well-dressed people listening to the band, and the "Maidan" would be a lively scene; hundreds of Europeans and Eurasians strolling about on the grass, or playing games, while the seats on the beautifully level and well-kept paths would be mostly occupied.

Pretty Eurasian girls, strolling in couples or threes, keeping an eye open for possible adventures, and smart dogcarts with well-groomed horses, bowling along the roads, would give evidence of another day's work done. Many of the people would have been stewing all day in a moist state of perspiration, in offices and shops.

Healy and I, after having tea brought up to us on the roof, called a "gharri," and told the driver to drive round to "Radabazzar" and "Dhuramtollah"; we wanted to see the native quarters.

The gharri was a square-shaped structure, something like a great oblong packing case on wheels, with side doors and a flat wooden roof, but with comfortable seats inside.

Soon we were moving at a walking pace through crowded narrow roads, amidst a scene of colour and movement, with its crowds of humanity of many nations.

Portly "Babus" in snowy white "dhoties," which leave their legs bare; tall Afghans in voluminous dirty white garments; Persians, Arabs, Malays, Hindus, and giant Sikhs, were to be seen on every side.

Beggars with horribly distorted limbs, and self-inflicted injuries, and open running sores, whined alongside the gharri for baksheesh.

Here came a leper; his limbs corroded to the bone; his face a mass of corruption, covered in places, by a pinkish-white powder where the flesh was disintegrating.

45

Although there was a leper colony in Calcutta, and another in "Runnigunge," these people were allowed to walk the streets.

The disease is not infectious, but it is contagious, and twelve months after the disease is sown by contact, the first symptoms appear; a peculiar lion-like appearance of the forehead, produced by a swelling ridge between the eyes.

We told the gharriwallah that we wanted to go somewhere where we could see the "Can Can." He drove along "Dhuramtollah," and turned off along one of the side streets. The place was right in the heart of the native quarter.

The carriage stopped before a fairly large native type of house, having a stone-paved courtyard in front, with high walls all round.

After some knocking on the high wooden courtyard door, the latter was opened by an old woman, who after some talk from the driver, admitted us.

Seats were brought out and placed on the verandah for us by a native girl, and when I asked her in English whether there was anything to drink, she understood and brought out a bottle of whisky and glasses.

Presently three girls came out and squatted down on the floor and started to talk among themselves in a language which I knew was not Hindustani; it had a more guttural sound.

Their ages, I estimated, ranged between fourteen and eighteen years, probably. Their features and figures were quite different to those of the Hindustani or Bengali woman. Although beautiful in a way, there was a look about them which suggested cruelty and fierceness. I decided that they were probably Arab girls.

Healy was the first to speak to them, and he did so by asking them, in English, whether they would have anything to drink.

They understood and responded with a smile, which showed their sharp white teeth. Yes, they would have a drink, and one of them went away and presently returned with a square-faced bottle of some colourless liquid and a tumbler.

"What sort of drink is that?" I asked. I had a suspicion that it might be water.

"It is Arack, sahib," said one.

The girls rose and went inside, beckoning us to follow.

The room was a large one with a smooth stone floor, and comfortable basket chairs were arranged around the walls, and we sat down, making ourselves comfortable; we were becoming considerably interested.

We had seen plenty of native women of many different types in Calcutta and in the ports of call on the passage out, but we had not seen any like these girls before.

There was something about them which was very alluring while at the same time being repelling.

Presently three other girls came into the room, carrying some strange-looking musical instruments, including a kind of drum or "Tom Tom."

Then the dance commenced. Slowly at first the girls moved, gracefully swaying their bodies to the music, which was of a curious weird description, sad in effect.

Gradually the music changed; it became quicker and louder in tone, and the movement of the dancers followed suit; they danced with more abandon, while at every change of the music they cast off some garment.

The music became quicker still, and the girls were quite naked now. Their eyes gleamed, and their ivory white teeth showed in alluring smiles, while the dim light shone on their naked bodies, which gleamed like brown satin. They had bangles on their ankles and arms and these clicked in time to the music like castanets.

The shape of their bodies was a wonder of perfect anatomy, and their motions, swift and lithe; reminding one of the movements of some animal of the cat tribe.

The rhythmic motion of their bodies became almost a frenzy, and they were approaching nearer to both of us, until they were touching our knees.

Finally they came to rest, and each girl dropped, seemingly exhausted, in the arms of Healy and myself.

The markets present a strange and interesting sight when seen by a newcomer. Here there are hundreds of unfamiliar commodities exposed for sale; what some things really are, very few Europeans have any idea. Great piles of delicious-looking tropical fruits of many kinds; curious-looking sweetmeats, besides many nasty-looking heaps of stuff that smell abominably, are laid out for inspection and purchase.

We wandered about the city, seeing many strange sights, and in the cool of the evening, hired a "gharri" and drove round to the Botanical Gardens, where a military band played, and where the élite of Calcutta either sat in the gardens or drove round the Maidan in smart dogcarts and phaetons.

A smart carriage, containing four pretty girls, edged alongside of the one we were in, and a native servant who was standing on a small platform behind the carriage, jumped down and sprang on to the step beside us, handing to each of us a card.

Glancing across at the young ladies, we caught a smile and bow before their carriage drove off.

I looked at the card, and saw that it was just a private visiting card with an address, and I slipped it in my pocket.

After a good dinner at the hotel, we strolled out into the town, bent on seeing and learning everything we could of this great Capital, which was once claimed to be the second largest city in the world.

We strolled down by the Maidan, a large, open, green space, intersected by many paths; then along the river bank, and presently sat down on a seat.

Several times young Eurasian or half-caste girls passed in couples, giving us an inviting smile as they passed.

Many of these girls are engaged as assistants in the big stores, or as clerks during the day, while at night time they are not adverse to making a little extra income.

They are generally pretty in their own style; slender and delicate-looking, with pale complexions and jet black hair and eyes of the same colour; eyes which are large and beautiful. They speak a curious style of English, with an exaggerated perfection of grammar, and slow enunciation, and a peculiar "chee chee" in their accent.

The ambition of most of them is to pick up and become the regular sweetheart of a pure-blood European, and if they can become the wife of such, they have advanced many stages upwards in the social scale; standing high above their own class.

All this time I was using my drugs, by means of which life was a joy. The days spent without any feeling of fatigue, the body purring with ease and contentment, and the nights a pleasure to look forward to; to lie in a drowsy state, dreaming rosy dreams before dropping off into a sound sleep. To enjoy well-cooked meals of many courses, with a keen appetite.

One day we called a gharri, and again told the driver to drive round a bit. I spoke in English, thinking that we would be shown more if we were not taken for residents.

"What place sahib liking look see?" he asked.

I tried to explain in English, but it was difficult, so I told him to take us where we could get a drink; it would be interesting to see where he took us; these drivers are generally in the pay of somebody who has entertainment to offer.

Several natives began to collect and offer advice to the driver, who presently asked:

'Sahib liking go see "empty house"?'

What an empty house had to do with the matter, we did not know, but decided to find out.

"Yes. Empty house," I said, and I noticed some of the natives laughed.

The gharri drove along the Chowringee Road and turned off to the left, beyond the markets. Here the houses were mostly villas of the European type, many of them standing in their own grounds.

Presently the carriage stopped before a fairly large house, with a wide gate and a carriage drive.

The garden was a wilderness of weeds and rank vegetation, and the house itself looked dirty and neglected, with unwashed windows and without curtains, and looking closer we saw a bill pasted on a board in the garden; "House to let."

I cudgelled my brains to think what it all meant, and I began to have a suspicion of what was going to happen.

The driver got down from the box, and followed by Healy and me, he proceeded up the carriage drive until we came to the front porch. The coolie placed his hand in a recess under a loose flagstone and drew forth a key with which he opened the front door.

Proceeding inside with the driver we found ourselves in a large bare passage. The floor boards and the walls were covered with dust, and cobwebs hung from the ceiling. The place looked as though it had been standing empty for many months.

Going along the passage to the rear of the house, the coolie opened a door.

"Sahib waiting here little time," he said.

Now we found ourselves in a fair-sized room, the windows of which looked out into a back garden; a kind of orchard, overgrown with weeds, and enclosed by a high surrounding wall.

The room itself was perfectly clean but scantily furnished as a bed-sitting room, with woven grass matting on the floor, and a large bed. There were also comfortable chairs, a table and a few other things.

We looked round for the coolie, for an explanation, but he had gone, and returning to the front we were just in time to see the carriage driving away.

The question now was, whether to wait and see the thing out, or should we leave? Certainly we hadn't paid the gharriwallah, but then, he could easily find a European in Calcutta.

"This is a rum start," said Healy, "where do we get off? Has he gone to fetch a gang or what?"

"No, I don't think so," I said, "I think we will get our drinks all right." I was beginning to have an idea of what was coming. We took out our pipes and lighted up while we waited.

Just then we heard the gharri returning, and presently the front door opened, and there were footsteps coming along the bare boards of the passage. The footsteps were light ones; it was someone wearing shoes, a lady most likely.

We now began to wonder what we would say, and when the room door opened and a pretty young Eurasian girl came in, we just stared.

She came across the floor and held out her hand with a smile, and then stood waiting.

She was small and dark with a pale olive skin and refined features, and had, like most of the half-caste girls, very fine black eyes.

"I don't know how I can explain, but the gharriwallah brought us here, without us knowing that we were going to meet a young lady," I said. "I told him we wanted to drive round a little and that we wanted to get a drink also."

"I can get you a drink," she said, going to the cupboard and unlocking it, and disclosing several bottles on the shelves, with glasses, soda water, and one or two other things. "What would you like?"

We told her, and invited her to have something herself. She brought out the drink, with a glass of wine for herself, then sat down and looked at us expectantly. She appeared to be a very self-possessed young lady and I was feeling rather embarrassed.

"Excuse me asking you, but is this an idea of your own, and why do you have a room in an empty house?"

"No, it is not a new idea at all; there are many girls in Calcutta and even married women, doing the same thing. I myself am living at home, and I don't want my family to know what I am doing.

"There are a great many girls here who cannot get any employment; all domestic service in India is done by natives; men chiefly, and there are not sufficient jobs in shops and offices to go round among us girls. We have to do something. My parents are very poor, and I am trying to make a little extra money to help out. They think I make the money by giving music lessons, but pupils are few and far between."

"And how do you manage to hire a room in an empty house, specially in a large villa like this?"

"Well you see; many of these large houses are owned by natives, and when they are standing empty a long time, they are always willing to let a room on the quiet like this. I have to be very careful, so I have a room at the back of the house. I do not even use any gas, because the meter would register it, and there would be enquiries. That is why I use a lamp," she said, pointing to a lamp hanging on the wall.

"Don't you think that it is risky selling liquor?" asked Healy.

"Yes, it is a little risky; but then my clients always ask for something to drink, and I make a little extra that way. You see I have to charge rather a stiff price to cover the risk. I charge a rupee a drink."

We produced three rupees, and also a ten-rupee note, as a present, telling her that we would call some other time and see her again. I felt sorry for the little girl who could not have been more than eighteen or twenty years of age.

She appeared to be a very nice little girl, and very friendly and natural in her manner. She begged us not to recognise her, should we happen to meet her outside any time.

We took our leave of her, kissing her as we did so, which she returned as though she meant it.

Later on I investigated this empty house dodge. It seemed to be a well-known institution in Calcutta, and there were many similar.

Some of the ladies were bold and coarse, and smelt of drink, while others were quite young girls in their teens. All were not Eurasians, however, for there were Continental women among them.

Sometimes these would try to enlist one's sympathy by telling a hard tale about the effort they were making to give up the life, and save enough money to pay their passage home.

Of course, this may have been true, or then it may not. Then there were the fine villas on the outskirts of "Chowringee," in which about half a dozen high-toned young ladies shared. The house, generally sumptuously furnished, would be run by one of them, ostentatiously as a boarding house, and the others were supposed to be boarders.

Here champagne and expensive liquors flowed freely, and prices were according.

A great many of the inmates smoked opium, which they would offer to the guests, too.

Hardly any other drugs were used, and in the empty house business, perhaps none at all, because the girls who engaged in this were of a simpler type.

As far as I could make out, cocaine was very little used in Calcutta, nor was hashish, except among a few better class natives.

CHAPTER 12

We Travel by Night

Healy and I wanted to see as much of India as we could before going back to Assam, so we decided to have a trip up country for a few days, to see something of the famous cities of Mutiny fame.

We proceeded across the river to Howrah, and booked berths in the night train for Benares.

When we got to the railway station we found a great crowd chiefly of natives, who, when they intend to go anywhere by train, generally go to the station many hours before train time, and camp on the platform among their many bundles and evil-smelling parcels; their cooking and drinking utensils. Some of them will arrive in the early morning to wait for an evening train.

The train was not yet in the station; it was still in the sheds, as this was a terminus, and although it still wanted half an hour to train time, the station was a babel of sound and motion.

We had an all night journey by train before us, and were curious to see what the train would be like; we hoped that it would be comfortable.

There were four classes of tickets, first, second, intermediate and third, but Europeans rarely travelled other than first or second class.

The long, heavy train came slowly into the station, and there was an immediate rush and scramble, but chiefly round the third class carriages, and we had no difficulty in obtaining full length seats each in a first class carriage.

The carriage was nearly as large as a small sized bedroom, and the seats, upholstered in leather, were arranged lengthwise and crosswise, with bunks above them which would be let down at night time; and the cushions of the seats themselves were flat and stuffed with hair like mattresses. The windows of the carriage were almost covered by wooden louvres or shutters of venetian style; to keep out the sun.

We settled ourselves down, after arranging the luggage and spreading rugs on the seat.

The only other passengers in the carriage were two missionaries, and the wife of one of them, who were going several hundred miles up country. They were going, as they informed us, to teach the Gospel to the poor natives. How absurd, I thought.

51

No man, no matter how learned he is, knows anything whatever about the mystery of life after death.

I am not an atheist, but I do not agree with religion as it is taught at the present day.

It is foolish to imagine that sin can be forgiven by repenting on one's death-bed. It is impossible to repent thus, it is only fear, and if there was no fear of punishment there would be no repentance, in most cases.

Repentance means something quite different; it requires an entire change of heart; which can only come about gradually, by constantly putting into practice all the good qualities; like charity, pity, mercy, and banishing the bad ones: hate, cruelty, spite, malice, selfishness, etc.

"Is it not time that some rational religion was introduced?"

"Are we to continue pretending to believe all the religious fairy tales which were taught to our ancestors a thousand years ago?" These may have been suitable to the intelligence of those days, but now we are more advanced, and science has disproved a good deal of these stories.

Religion is a profession which was originally introduced and carried on almost solely with the object of providing a fat living for those who professed to teach that which no man can know.

If one reflects back through the ages, one realises that religion has been responsible for more bloodshed and murder than any other cause. The Church devised and carried on for hundreds of years, the most fiendish and horrible tortures, in the name of Christ, who taught gentleness, lowliness, charity, mercy and pity.

It is easy to see that the real object of the Church in the past was not to teach real Christianity, but to obtain affluence and power by means of terrorism.

The human body is a living organism, with heart, lungs, liver, and other organs, and a brain to control them. We imagine that we are individual in ourselves, but we may be just a minute portion of the universe as a whole, just as a single cell is to our bodies; or as a tooth in one of the many wheels of a watch, is to the watch.

For all we know to the contrary, the universe may also be a living organism, whose organs are its nebulae, suns, planets and other bodies, all in motion and performing their allotted functions, and having a superintelligence to guide and control; an intelligence as far above human intelligence as the size of the universe is to that of the human body.

"Do the germs in our blood know that the body they live on is alive, or is it to them the entire universe?"

All religions must in time, according to the Evolutionary Law, join together and form one. It will become reconciled to science, and then it will become the greatest and most honoured profession in the world, and the true meaning of Christianity will be taught, even in our schools.

The various attributes which are called sins will, as indicated by the Law of Evolution, come together, and there will be only one sin: "The doing of an injury or an injustice to another," and the magnitude of the sin will be the injury intended, not that inflicted.

It is not possible to sin against God, and to imagine this is possible is to attribute to him our own human passions.

"Is it reasonable to believe that God can be cajoled, by flattery and prayer, into granting individuals some favour beyond their fellows, or is it not more reasonable to believe that just as all the natural laws of the universe are unchangeable and automatic in action, so the judging of our souls, and the determination of their destination, is automatic; and whether a person is a believer or unbeliever; or whatever his religion may be, the only factor is the quality of the soul?"

Perhaps each good or bad action of ours alters the quality of the soul slightly, and finally it is weighed and judged automatically by some law of attraction in the universe, of which as yet, we have no knowledge.

There may be many stages of life; life on other worlds; each one a little better than the last, or a little worse, if the soul is descending the scale.

But it is useless speculating, because no man on this earth can ever know the truth about the matter.

We know nothing. Even that which we see with our own eyes, and hear with our ears, is not as it really is.

"What is your real weight?"

Suppose you test it. Imagine yourself standing on a spring balance. You are in a pit cage, about to descend, but the cage is at rest and the spring balance shows that you are supposed to weigh twelve stones.

Now the cage starts to descend, and the pointer of the scales will show for a moment that you have no weight at all. If the cage could descend with a constantly increasing velocity like that of a falling stone, you would continue to apparently have no weight. On your reverse journey upwards, your weight will be indicated as much more than twelve stones.

We have no absolute knowledge of direction.

Imagine yourself walking from the stem to the stern of a ship at the rate of four miles an hour, while the ship is moving at ten miles an hour towards the west.

"Are you travelling at six miles an hour towards the west?"

"No, because the earth's surface is moving eastwards at about a thousand miles an hour."

You may next conclude that you are travelling at about 994 miles per hour eastwards.

But then you realise that the earth is revolving round the sun, and the latter, along with us and all its planets, is moving in the direction of the constellation of "Hercules," as already mentioned in a previous chapter.

"Then which direction are you travelling?"

"Can you believe your own eyes?"

Suppose you look through one of the giant telescopes; say the one in California, and fix your gaze on one of the stars in the great "Nebulae" of the "Andromeda," you may be looking at a star which is no longer there.

Although you see it with your own eyes, it may have disappeared entirely 800,000 years ago, because light travelling at a velocity which would take it seven times round the earth in a second, or about ten million miles a minute, takes 800,000 years to travel here from that star.

We use the words large and small, fast and slow, but they have no real meaning in the absolute.

A grain of sand is large when compared with the atom, and small when compared with our sun, and the sun in turn becomes small when compared with suns like "Vega" or "Betelgeuse," which, if placed where our sun is, would blot out the earth's whole path or orbit.

Everything can be large and small at the same time. A snail's pace is slow when compared with the speed of a rifle bullet, but if compared with the movement of an avalanche, the snail's pace becomes fast.

There may be velocities which exceed the speed of light, of which we know nothing as yet, and until we know the maximum and minimum of the size it is possible for matter to exist in, and the greatest and least velocity possible, the words fast, slow, large, and small, have no real meaning.

When we think of the mysteries of the universe, we are like blind men groping in the dark.

"Is space finite or infinite?" Whichever way you think of it, the answer seems an impossibility when you try to visualise. The same difficulty appears when you try to consider whether time had a beginning or was always in existence. "The Unknowable."

Imagine that portion of the universe that we know something of, constructed to a scale model.

It will have to be a very small scale.

Draw a circle the size of a penny and let it represent the earth's path round the sun, say, 186,000,000 miles across.

Place on the edge a minute speck of dust and let it represent the earth, and a grain of sand in the centre, for the sun.

Now, at a distance of a mile, place another grain of sand, and this will be the nearest star.

At various distances of a mile and upwards, scatter grains of sand, peas, marbles, and globes ranging up to the size of a tennis ball, until several thousand miles in every direction is covered.

Here we have an approximate scale model of the "Galectic Universe," our universe.

At a distance of about 300,000 miles we start again on another: "The Extra Galectic Universe."

Beyond this, there are many others, extending into space beyond the limits of our telescopes.

If space is infinite, then the number of universes extending into space must be infinite, which is unthinkable.

If space is finite, the mind immediately seeks to know what is beyond, which is a contradiction.

"May there not be such a quality as nothingness?"

It is true that the human mind cannot conceive such a condition, but that is because we have no experience of such.

Everything in nature, whose atoms are free to move in any direction, and not being confined by some force, other than their own gravitational attraction, will take the shape of a globe.

Space then would be globular in shape, and be bounded by nothingness.

Take a cubic inch of some solid substance, and imagine that it is composed of every substance in existence in the universe. Melt it first into a liquid and then by means of further heat, turn it into gaseous matter. Now expand this quantity of gas, until it fills, in imagination, a thousand cubic miles, and we will have something like the condition of space.

The total amount of heat expended on the cubic inch of matter, now is distributed throughout the thousand cubic miles, consequently space is the absolute zero of cold. Let us imagine that there was once a time, so far back that it is unexpressible in figures, when there existed nothing but space. No stars or bodies of any description.

We have now the right condition for the formation by natural laws of the universe, as it exists to-day.

At various points in space, the atoms in this attenuated matter began to concentrate by their own gravitational properties; and according to the Law of Evolution.

As time went on, and the size of these accumulations increased, the atoms near the centre became tremendously compressed, becoming a glowing white hot mass.

In the course of unimaginable time, a great nebula was formed, with a glowing and incandescent centre; a nebula so large that it would take many thousands of years for light to travel from its centre to the outer edge.

Because the shape was irregular as yet, there was more pressure on one side than on the other, and the whole mass began to revolve about its centre of gravity; imperceptibly at first, then faster and faster.

Eventually, when this portion of space had been practically denuded of matter, the shape became first a spiral, and then a revolving disc, which eventually, owing to the increased velocity of rotation, broke up into many separate portions.

These in turn gradually assumed the form of globes. They still retained their circular motion round a common centre, and they began to revolve on their own axis also, in the same way as the nebula did.

They are stars, or in other words suns.

It will be seen that the atom contains no stored energy, unless it contains chemical energy like coal and some other kinds of matter, and this is only stored sun's energy. Only when the atoms are diffused and able to contract closer together, is energy or heat generated; and once they have come together into a solid and cooled down, they will produce no more energy.

Scientists are wasting their time when they talk about releasing the energy of the atom. The only energy in nature is gravitation, in one form or another.

The absolute foundation of every kind of power, motion, heat, light, etc., is the attraction of one atom for another.

Every star in the universe has its fixed place in relation to the whole, and it can only move when every other one moves; they are constantly in motion trying to keep in a state of equilibrium.

Let us in imagination construct a model to illustrate the principle.

We take a football to represent a star.

We fix to it all round its surface, say, a dozen strings, and we lead these strings in all directions and angles; to the ceiling, the walls, and the floor of a room; passing each string over a fixed pulley wheel, and suspending a weight on the end. The weights can vary, it makes no difference.

Now when the football is released, it will move to a certain position, and it will remain fixed there.

The weights will have descended and there will be a pull of various intensities in every string. The pulls will all balance each other, and the ball will be in a state of rest; it is in equilibrium.

Now if you move the ball a little with your hand, you will find that, when released, it will return to its former position; suspended in space, under the pull of all the strings.

Substitute for the ball, a star, and for the strings, the gravitational pull of other stars, and we have the explanation of the equilibrium of the stars.

Suppose one of the strings is removed, or another added, then the ball will move slightly to another position, and come to rest there.

No star in the universe can change its position without every other star doing the same, although the movement of the far distant ones would be imperceptible.

One might ask, what action is it which keeps the extreme outermost stars from moving in on the others, seeing that there are none on the far side of them to exert a pull in that direction.

The only explanation there can be, is that the whole mass must be moving in a circle round a common centre; in various planes, so as to set up centrifugal force.

CHAPTER 13

The Mutiny Cities of India

Benares at last, the sacred city of India; a city of strange contrasts; of beautiful palaces, and temples, and squalid hovels. Of dirt and disease, and cleanliness to a degree that becomes grotesque. Of costumes of more colours than there are in the rainbow, and almost nakedness.

One minute you might rub shoulders with a nabob in gorgeous silks and jewels, and the next with a leper in rags, or a human being whose feet and legs are almost identical in shape to those of an elephant (Elephantiasis disease).

Here in this city, we saw human rabbit warrens; wooden houses four stories high, built in continuous galleries round a central court, in which natives, packed like rabbits in a warren, worked at making brass and copper ware, filigree silver, and other arts and crafts, eating and sleeping alongside their work bench or floor space.

Extremely beautiful work is turned out with a few wretched and primitive hand tools, for a price which barely keeps them in rice and a few rags to wrap round their bodies, even by working far into the night.

Next day we took a trip by boat along the Ganges, along the banks of which are miles of magnificent palaces belonging to the various rajahs and nabobs, from all parts of India. It seemed as though luxury and self-indulgence had gone mad.

We also saw some of the so-called Indian magic; the basket trick and the Mango tree trick, and I was very disappointed.

Since then I have seen so-called magic in many countries of the world, and never yet have I seen anything which was not crude, or could not be better done by our own magicians. The Indian rope trick is a fable, and never has been done, and never will be done, and the man who says he has seen it is a foolish person.

Next evening we left on the East Indian railway to see some of the famous cities which recall the great Mutiny of 1857.

Allahabad, Cawnpore, and Lucknow. What interested me most was the "Secundra Bargh."

It is a large walled garden of about 500 feet long on every face, with walls of massive thickness, and 20 feet high. The stonework is falling into decay, and the garden is a tangled wilderness of rank vegetation.

57

In the centre of the garden is a ruined palace with its numerous courts and outbuildings; in each of which some mighty deed was done.

Along one side of the wall runs a wide mound, which covers a trench where rot the bones of 2,500 Sepoys.

The building was strongly fortified in 1857 by three mutinous Sepoy regiments.

It barred the passage of Sir Colin Campbell, who was marching to the relief of Lucknow.

Campbell's force consisted of about 4,700 men, mostly of composite regiments, the only complete unit being the 93rd Highlanders, 1,100 strong.

The troops surrounded the palace, while the guns breached the wall.

The Highlanders and other units then poured in through the breach, and a hand to hand fight took place in the garden and the buildings.

There was no quarter given, on account of the horrible massacre of our women and children at Cawnpore. The fighting lasted two hours, and its desperate nature can be discerned in every bit of brick and wood.

Before the sun went down that day, every man of the 2,500 Sepoys was slain; three complete regiments were wiped out.

Now all that remains to their memory is this long, low mound.

At Allahabad we saw the place where General Neill carried out his wholesale executions of captured mutineers.

Many of the worst offenders were first made, with whips, to clean up with their tongues a portion of the floor on which was the blood of murdered women and children – afterwards the prisoners were blown away from guns.

A battery of nine-pounder guns would be drawn up on the roadside at sunset, and placed "Action Front."

A Sepoy was then led forward and his hands strapped to the wheels of each gun. No ball was placed in the gun, only a blank charge, and the muzzle was depressed until it pointed at the pit of the man's stomach.

At a signal, the whole battery would be fired.

I have heard it said in India that it rained a fine drizzle of blood from the sky, until the white uniforms of the gunners were red.

This, of course, may be a legend, but it is believed by many old natives in India to-day.

At Cawnpore there took place the most stirring events of any in the whole history of India.

The name of Cawnpore is known to almost everyone, and it is associated with a deed as foul as any which has ever taken place in the history of the world.

Here on this open patch of ground or common, just outside the city, was entrenched a company of 1,000 English people, soldiers and civilians, more than half of them being women and children.

Day and night for weeks they were pelted from every angle, by more than a hundred cannon of all calibres, from 9- to 24-pounders.

The trenches they occupied were so shallow that they afforded little protection. They had hardly any water, and they were exposed to the fierce rays of the Indian summer sun. Death must have come to them as a great relief.

Here stood the "Bebe Ghar," that house of sad memory. A large square single storey bungalow of many rooms, into which 212 English women and children were crowded prisoners, after the massacre of the men at the "Murder Ghat."

In imagination one can picture the two troopers of the 2nd Bengal Cavalry, entering the bungalow with drawn swords, accompanied by a butcher from the bazaar with a cleaver.

The doors were locked.

After a long time, one of the troopers came out for a fresh sword.

It was night, and the murderers had gone, their work done, and all was silent except rustlings inside the darkened rooms.

At sunrise next morning, sweepers came to clean out the bungalow, and the mutilated bodies of women and children were dragged out and cast down a deep well in the compound.

The well is still there, but it is covered over, and a beautiful monument of an angel is built on top of it.

We did not have time to go to Delhi, but we visited Lucknow, that beautiful city of palaces.

Here is the old Residency in which the British withstood the siege. It is a ruin now, in exactly the same state as it was in '58, with its walls and towers, and buildings scarred and broken by shot. Weeds and tangled grass grow everywhere.

Here is the main gate, the "Bailie Guard," which was the scene of a tragedy of another kind, yet still sad.

In Sir Colin Campbell's force there was a regiment of Sikhs, who had remained loyal.

After going through weeks of incredible hardships on the relief march, and fighting many battles alongside of the British, they won their way to Lucknow, losing more than half their number.

The Residency was in front of them, and they were overjoyed; and, ever in the front, they rushed forward to greet the defenders, when they were met by a volley which killed and wounded many of them.

The British garrison saw only their black faces, and mistook them for the rebels, never thinking that natives would be in the van of the relieving force.

I was astonished at the enormous number of natives who eat opium, in small pellets. It seemed to be grown and manufactured throughout the whole of this district. There were miles and miles of poppy fields, the flowers of which are pressed, and the juice collected.

This is then dried and thickened to the consistency of thick black treacle for smoking, or to a solid for eating.

Eating opium is a very crude habit, it soon plays havoc with the stomach and bowels.

CHAPTER 14

The Death of Healy

I was generally an early riser. Soon after sunrise I would get up and go out on to the verandah, and lie in a long cane chair. At that time in the morning the air was generally cool, and the view of the jungle in the valley below was very fine; with the thick white mist, like clouds of steam, hanging in the hollows, and the bright sunshine beating on the tree tops, turning the foliage to gold. The forest was alive with sound. "Living creatures everywhere, each with their own joys and sorrows, living in a world of their own."

After smoking one of my really good brand of Indian cigars, which only cost me about five shillings a hundred, I would go in and have a bath.

Mulki was generally asleep. She looked very childish and innocent then with her face nestled into the pillow, and an arm thrown out, and hanging down over the side of the bed.

This morning, soon after I had finished dressing, a coolie came for me. Something had gone wrong with the boiler at the low level mine. It was a long, horizontal boiler of the Lancashire type, built into a brick seating. It was used for supplying steam for the pumps.

Passing along the loading sidings, and through a small tunnel in the hill into a further valley, I came to the mine entrance, and there was the boiler; steam was blowing off at the safety valve, and my first glance was at the water gauge glass. It was empty. I next tried the lower test cock. Still no signs of any water. This was serious.

I opened the fire door to withdraw the fire, when a sight met my eyes which almost froze my blood.

The furnace crown was red hot, and was bulging downwards with the pressure of steam, with a bulge almost the size of a bath tub.

My first instinct was to turn and run; then I saw numbers of women moving about or working quite close. Little children sitting and playing in the heaps of loose coal, and infants, rolled up in bundles, asleep under the shade of near-by trees.

The boiler might be on the point of bursting this very minute. "How much longer would the weakened, red-hot furnace crown withstand the terrific pressure of the steam above?"

Although I was almost sick with the fear of a horrible death, I waved and shouted to the coolies to get away, but they did not understand; they only stood staring.

60

Quickly I climbed on to the boiler and wedged up the weight of the safety valve.

The steam roared out from the valve opening with a thunderous noise; a roar which only those who have heard high pressure steam blowing free and unchecked by a valve can understand.

All the coolies within earshot scuttled like rabbits. The mothers snatched up their infants, and ran as though a tiger was after them.

Now, leaving the valve open, I proceeded to take out the fire. Each minute I expected to be my last.

I kept my eyes on the steam gauge as I worked. Slowly the pointer moved round as the steam pressure fell, pound by pound. Each minute the danger was becoming less.

At last the roar was becoming less fierce, then milder and milder, until only a gentle hiss could be heard, and the pointer had come back to zero almost.

I looked round and saw the coolies coming back again. Poor, simple creatures; they did not know that they had been on the brink of death.

Soon the little brown babies were playing in the coal again, and work was going on as before.

The pumps were stopped, and I had to see about getting a temporary portable boiler sent up, to carry on until a proper repair could be made to the other.

I fixed a pulsometer pump in the little stream for pumping water to the boiler, and this was a never-failing source of wonder to the native fitters. To see a strange-looking monster, pumping water without any sign of moving parts. To listen to its sighs and gurgles, and to feel its belly as they called it, go first scalding hot, and then suddenly go cold. The coolies feared it as some strange and evil spirit.

While sitting in my bungalow at tiffin one day, a coolie came over from Healy's bungalow with a chit from the Dr. Babu, and when I got over there I found him dressing a nasty wound. Healy's arm had been cut through right to the bone, just above the elbow.

A fall of stone had occurred in the mine, and he had only been saved from being killed by a coal tub taking the weight. Unfortunately he had his arm over the edge.

Fever set in, and although everything possible was done for him, including the calling in of another doctor, a European, he died.

We, his friends, took turns in sitting up with him through the night. Sometimes he was delirious, but early one morning, just before daylight, he seemed better and was conscious, but he complained of pins and needles in his legs, and would have me scratch them with a hair brush. I was doing this frequently until the next man arrived. I never saw him alive again.

We buried him beside Lumley in the little cemetery. It is nearly forty years ago.

"Where are all the young fellows that I once knew? Then so full of life and spirits. Or the pretty young girls; Chinese, Indian, Japanese, Malay or white, of those days. Most will be dead, and the rest old."

CHAPTER 15

I Go to the Malay Archipelago

I was making preparations for my voyage home, and the giving up of drugs on the way.

At the present time I had no regular dose, or fixed time of taking, such as is the custom of most drug users. For days, sometimes, I would use just the minimum combination of drugs, which would make me feel just right, with perfect comfort in mind and body; then I would have a regular binge with some particular drug, selecting one which I had not been using much for some time, so that it would have all its finer effects.

Not being able to smoke opium or hashish on the voyage, I would have to cut them out.

The first thing to be done was to cut out all drugs, except cocaine and morphia injections, and these I gradually wangled, until I was using an equal quantity of each.

In a bottle, I mixed up 12 grains of morphia and 12 grains of cocaine with 480 minims of distilled water. This was six days' supply of four injections per day; using 20 minims per injection. The syringe was graduated with the number of minims, in lines on the glass barrel.

For some days before leaving I was using the mixture, and the day's supply was of course 2 grains of morphia and 2 grains of cocaine.

I was leaving Mulki in India for the time being, intending to send for her when I got out to some other country.

I found a small hut for her, in a place about sixty miles away.

I sold my furniture to a new arrival, and said "Good-bye" to my friends, then set off for Calcutta and home; first making arrangements for Mulki's support.

I had come to be very fond of her. Not only was she beautiful in appearance, but she was beautiful in disposition. She had not learned to use drugs, although she had begged many times for me to allow her, and I was afraid that when I was away she would start with opium, as everywhere around there were natives using it.

The voyage home to England was not marked by any unusual incident, except that there was a young medical student on board, who shared my cabin.

Soon he discovered that I was using drugs, and he gave me a lecture on the terrible consequences of the habit. I asked him if he had ever taken any himself, and he confessed that he had not, and that he was going on what he had heard.

Shortly afterwards I missed my syringe.

I did not mention it to him, I just quietly observed, and soon I had more than a suspicion where the syringe had gone to.

However, this did not trouble me, because I had syringes of all kinds in my main baggage; syringes of the best makes, ranging in size from 20 minims, up to 60 minims.

After I had got settled down on board, I started my system in earnest.

I was using 2 grains of morphia, and 2 grains of cocaine per day, as before mentioned.

Without any trouble, I easily got down to 1 grain of each.

Now I mixed up 6 grains of each drug in separate bottles; each with 240 minims of water, and still keeping to the four injections per day, I started by drawing up into the syringe 9 minims of morphia, and 10 minims of cocaine.

Next day the morphia was reduced by another minim and so on until the fourth day my dose was 6 minims of morphia and 10 minims of cocaine.

Now I was beginning to feel slightly the need of a little more morphia.

Instead of taking more, I started reducing the cocaine 1 minim per day until on the eighth day my injection consisted of 6 minims of each drug.

Now I felt that I was getting enough morphia again.

Decreasing the cocaine had the same effect as though I had increased the morphia.

This may be difficult to believe, yet it is true. The explanation is, that these two drugs are in a certain way an antidote to each other, yet when taken together, they both seem to act independently, and one gets the full effect of each drug.

When I had got down to 5 minims of each drug per injection, I marked time for three days.

I was now getting half a grain of each drug per day.

I now commenced afresh, but instead of reducing the quantity of the liquid, I kept to the 10 minims per injection, first mixing up some fresh drugs, as it is not good to keep them mixed long.

Now for four days I added to the morphia solution, an equivalent quantity of distilled water every time I injected, that is to say:

Every time I drew out 5 minims of solution, I added afterwards 5 minims of water. The total quantity of liquid always remained the same in the bottle, but it was getting gradually weaker, and the dilution was taking place on a diminishing scale, as it should do.

Soon the mixture became pretty weak, and I stopped adding more water, and concentrated on reducing the actual number of minims used, until I was down to 5 minims of mixture ($\frac{1}{4}$ syringe full) per injection, and then I recommenced diluting as before.

A few weeks after my arrival in England, I was able to stop using drugs entirely.

I admit that at the end I had a little craving, but it was nothing really, and I was getting freer of it every day. Still, I decided that the system was not perfect, and I meant to continue experimenting and searching, until I found a cure which was fool proof and easy.

I have seen, in China, many years later, opium smokers trying to give up the habit.

They would start by getting a cylindrical pot made of hard wood, and $\frac{3}{4}$ in. inside diameter and of just sufficient length to hold their day's supply.

Every day they would file a little off the length of the pot.

This kind of system is no good; the craving becomes intense, and few have the will power to carry it out.

In England I had the chance of more than one good position, because I had good technical qualifications, with practical experience also. I wanted to get out to the Malay Archipelago or China to continue my experiments, and to make a study of the drug habit in these countries, so did not accept any work in England.

After about three months, I got a position as engine-wright for a new coal-mining concern in the Island of Sumatra, in the Malay Archipelago.

The salary was only £18 per month, but I would have accepted anything, to be able to get out there.

The voyage out to Singapore in the Glen line *Glen Farg* was uneventful. I had not used any drugs at all for over four months. I was in perfect health, but I longed to start using drugs again, because I found that it was the only way to be really happy; to get away from the deadly sameness of life in this world.

Arriving at Singapore, the first thing I did was to visit a chemist and buy some $\frac{1}{2}$-grain tabloids of both morphia and cocaine. Later I sent an order off to England for 6 doz. tubes (864) of 1-grain tabloids of morphia. Cocaine I could buy in plenty locally, as well as other drugs.

Morphia was more difficult to get; that is, the kind I required; in tabloids made by a certain famous firm for injection purposes.

I put up at the Hotel de la Paix along with some of the ship's passengers; a small but very comfortable place. After getting settled down, and having a good dinner, I took my first dose of drugs, $\frac{1}{2}$ grain of cocaine, and $\frac{1}{8}$ grain of morphia injection.

Life immediately took on a fresh meaning. I was in a happy care-free world again. All small difficulties and doubts, which life is full of, were gone, and I felt that no happening whatever could be a hurt.

I spent a happy time in Singapore during the next two days before leaving for Sumatra.

Singapore was in a state of excitement, because the Americans had just captured Manila, and most of the Manila-bound boats and passengers were held up.

First buying as large a stock of drugs as I could get in Singapore, I went aboard the small Chinese steamer, which took me across the straits, the whole journey including several hours up the Indragiri River, taking about twenty-four hours.

When I arrived at my disembarkation place, I thought that I had come to the most miserable place I had ever seen. It was at the mouth of a small tributary called the Tjenako.

The place consisted of a large bamboo platform, built on piles in the river, and on it stood a single wood and bamboo one-storey building. It was a house and store belonging to a Chinaman.

There was no dry land to be seen anywhere, only trees standing out of the water on both sides, where the river banks should have been.

For miles around me, the whole country was under water. There were, of course, no roads or railways, and the only traffic consisted of a few Malay sampans going up or down the river. This was the only shop within a day's journey by sampan, and then the only things sold appeared to be rice, salt fish and opium, with a few Malay requirements, which the old Chinaman supplied in return for rubber.

He had an assistant and a coolie to whom he mostly left the work, while he spent nearly all his time smoking opium and sleeping.

I became very friendly with him later, but this time I just saw him for a few minutes, when the company's manager, an Englishman, who had come to meet me in a small steam launch, introduced me.

Almost immediately we proceeded up the main river Indragiri, to visit Ringat, where the Dutch Resident lived. Some Malay coolies were being taken there to be birched for trying to escape. They were contract labourers.

After being introduced to the Resident and his assistant we were conducted to a large room, half office and half sitting-room, where we were given tea.

Presently in came one of the prisoners in charge of three native police, and after a few words, which I did not understand then, from the Resident, the Malay was held down by two of the men, while the other applied a rattan.

The victim was screaming and foaming at the mouth, while we were supposed to be drinking tea and having a friendly talk. It was a nasty experience and it nearly turned me sick.

We left after the coolies had been birched and a batch of about a dozen new Malays, who had come in with me from Singapore, had been signed on at the Resident's.

Back at Kwala Tjenako again.

The company was a newly-incorporated Dutch concern.

Coal had been found in the higher lands, about six days' journey by sampan, up the small tributary, the Tjenako, an uncharted river, passing through virgin jungle.

It was proposed to build a light railway from the coal field, to a site about halfway, where a loading wharf would be built and the coal would be there loaded into lighters and towed to the mouth of the Tjenako; then out along the broad Indragiri River, on to Singapore.

The Tjenako was so obstructed by snags and sandbanks that only flat-bottomed sampans could get up it to the site of the coal bed. It was proposed to clear the river up to the loading wharf, which would be the terminus of the railway.

The manager proceeded up-stream to headquarters, Pia Tarantang, where the coal was, and left me at the Kwala with a dozen coolies to build a small jetty and a store. This was to act as a receiving station for landing stores, and also the hundreds of Malay and Chinese coolies who would arrive from time to time from Singapore, for work on the railway, and the mine.

I was left alone on Towler, the Chinaman's jetty, and I surveyed the scene.

A single rickety bamboo jetty with a plaited bamboo platform for a top, and a wooden structure, half shed, and half bungalow built on it.

The muddy river flowed silently and swiftly always in one direction, and there was jungle everywhere, but no dry land.

Not twenty feet behind the store was the jungle, unknown, and almost impenetrable. Practically all of this district was unknown to the white man, and even the river, Tjenako, was not shown on the map.

The Malays that were with me were some of the old hands, and one spoke a little English.

They camped on the jetty, and Towler gave me a room in his store to live in. It contained a massive carved blackwood bed with canopy, the whole covered with Chinese dragons and curious carvings. There was nothing else in the room, and through the cracks in the floor I could see the river running underneath.

The bathroom consisted of two large tree trunks, floating in the stream, and connected together by a platform. There was a square hole in the floor, for an obvious reason.

CHAPTER 16

In the Jungles of Sumatra

Towler was a Chinaman of about thirty-five years of age, although he looked to be sixty. He was wizened and shrunken, and he spent most of his time in the little room behind his store, smoking pipe after pipe of opium. In the mornings he would be fairly normal, and then he would be bewailing his fate, and cursing opium.

"Banya Sussa Tuan," he would say, "Tida mow Mukan, Tida mow Binni, Tida buli buong aya," meaning that he did not want to eat, he did not want a wife, nor could he empty his bowels.

He would be groaning and pitying himself all the morning, then in the afternoon, when he had got stretched out on his mat, with the opium pipe by his side and several pipes smoked, he would be as jolly as could be. Life was beautiful again.

Often did I join him, and smoke his opium, and listen to his stories of China. I meant to go there some time.

The Malays would take the sampans, and go off into the jungle in search of timber for the building of the jetty and store, and as it was not necessary for me to go with them, I left them to it; they knew how to go on. I was keeping my eyes open and learning. I had already learned sufficient Malay, one of the simplest languages in the world, to make myself understood, as I had studied it on the voyage out. I could not yet understand when spoken to.

Towler had tried to give opium up more than once, and had failed, and now he was hopeless. He had sent his Malay girl away because he had no more use for her, he told me, and although well off, with a large store in Singapore, he lived here for opium. A living death.

I introduced him to some of my drugs, and soon he was like a new man; full of life and happiness; eating well; and then he sent over to Singapore for another wife. He ordered her as he would a bale of goods – by letter. He was never tired of thanking me for what I had done for him.

A difficulty which had to be overcome, I found, was the water. There was none but that from the muddy river, and although it was all right for drinking after it had settled, it was no good for injections.

Luckily I had some distilled water, and later, I constructed a small apparatus for making my own, so as to get it freshly distilled.

The building and the jetty were now completed, and I took leave of Towler, and proceeded up the river towards my destination; seven days' journey.

The sampan was a large affair, having a covered portion at the back, under which I sat on my mattress.

The deck was boarded over, and on it lived the coolies I was taking back with me, and the three sampan men who poled the boat up stream, against the tide. My boy did the cooking on deck on a little charcoal stove.

I was now fairly started on drugs again; I was using large quantities of all kinds, as I sat in my little shelter while the coolies poled the boat.

At night we tied up to the bank and after cooking and eating their rice, the coolies would stretch themselves out on deck and wrap themselves up in a sarong beside the smoke of the fire.

I was alone, with my drugs and my thoughts.

The night was cool, like most nights here, and the trees were simply alive with monkeys of all shapes and sizes. This was the home of the Orang-Utan, and the jungle abounded in more and greater variety of wild animals than any country in the world. A sportsman's paradise, but few know of it.

To-night, sitting alone in my covered cabin, I had nothing to do but think. Through the open sides I saw the swift-running water, on which the moonlight was shining, turning to patches of silver the ripples wherever there was an obstruction, and showing in feathery outline the outer foliage of the dark jungle.

I wondered what this place would be like a million years hence. What was it like a hundred million years ago?

This river would not be here, probably there would be no rivers anywhere.

The earth's crust would still be thin; the internal heat had not cooled much, and in the earth's bulk there had been little contraction, so that mountain ranges had not yet risen out of the water.

There would be no dry land, only slime.

A considerable portion of the water would still be enveloping the earth as vapour or steam, of such a depth that the sun's rays never penetrated through it, and therefore, everywhere there would be gloom; almost darkness.

The water was spread almost over the whole surface of the globe, because the ocean beds had not yet sunk to form deep seas, neither was the water salt. What sort of animals lived here then?

There is a skeleton of an animal in the Natural History Museum in London which appears to be most suitable for existence under these conditions.

It is enormous in size, having a neck fifty or sixty feet long, with a tail even longer.

It must have been able to wade in water sixty feet deep and still keep its head above water. It could swing its head round in a great sweep, and reach down to the bottom, searching for food.

To do this under water, it must have a tail of great length; to balance the movement of its neck against the water pressure, otherwise its body would upset. No creature could have been better designed for life under these conditions.

Its body was massive, with enormous bones, enabling it to stay down under water easily.

I don't know whether this animal or rather reptile lived in those times, but it seems probable.

Evolution goes on, atoms or units, concentrating or coming closer together, until they form one.

Prehistoric men each had their own hut, separated from his neighbour.

Next we have the Victorian type of dwellings; long lines of small houses in closely-packed streets, each house joining the next, yet still a separate house. Now we have the great blocks of flats in which a single building houses many families.

Next will come the roofed-in and centrally-heated cities, housing the whole population under one roof.

Finally, when the Earth's surface becomes too cold for human life to live on it, man who then, millions of years hence, will have made enormous strides in invention, and mechanical power will burrow deep down into the earth towards the heat, and there construct his cities, artificially lighted and ventilated.

The entire population of the world will then be under one roof. One house.

Language, and colour, will long ago have become one, as also will government, means of travel, distribution, ventilation, heating, education, and a list of others too numerous to mention.

Mankind will have become one family.

War will have passed through the evolutionary and then the dissolutionary stages, and will long have passed away.

The human family will then be in its dissolutionary stage, and be also passing.

I woke with a start; there was pandemonium on board; the coolies were shouting, and some had rolled off the deck into the river, and were struggling to reach the bank.

A big tree trunk had come swirling down with the stream, and caught the side of the boat, tilting it over to an alarming angle.

The Malays were pushing with their poles, and working one against another in their excitement, when I crawled out from under the roof, and cut the mooring rope, and the sampan floated free and righted itself.

CHAPTER 17

A Railway Terminus in the Jungle

After several months' work at the mine headquarters, I was sent down to commence work on the railway terminus at a place we called the Loading Wharf.

I was to be in charge of all the work, as I had been promoted to be chief mechanical engineer, in place of a Dutchman who had left. Two other Europeans were to help me in the work.

The first thing to be done was to clear a large area of the jungle on the river bank, and build temporary bungalows for ourselves, and permanent bongsals, or huts, for the hundred Malay and Chinese coolies with us, and for the hundreds that were soon to arrive from Singapore. Each bongsal was to hold a hundred coolies. Long, low buildings built of bamboo framework, with roof thatched with tough grass, and walls of "attep," a tough sun-dried leaf from the jungle.

A long bamboo platform ran the full length of the building on each side, for the coolies to sleep on. There were no windows, as plenty of light and ventilation would be obtained from the space between the top of the walls and the roof.

Time passed quickly and several months soon went by.

I now had about 600 Chinese coolies working on the line, of which I had completed about five miles. A light railway of narrow gauge, with bridges of timber.

The workshops and sawmills were up and working, and I had cut down trees and sawn up many thousands of sleepers, steeping them in creosote. I was burning large kilns of clay for breaking up to make ballast.

The loading wharf was beginning to take shape, too, and many Chinese carpenters were at work on it, fashioning the timber which gangs of Malays had cut and brought from the jungle. It was close to my bungalow, and I could hear the thud, thud, of the pile driver in the early morning.

The Chinese coolies were divided into kongsis, or gangs, of about a hundred men each, under a tandil, or foreman, and each kongsi lived in its own bongsal.

We went forward like an army on the march.

First would go forward about fifty Malays, cutting down the undergrowth and foliage with their parangs, in a wide lane through the jungle; making the cutting follow the pegs put in when the survey was made.

Next came a large gang of experienced Chinese axemen, who followed on, cutting down all the trees which were in the section. These in turn were followed by gangs of sawyers, cutting up the fallen trees into convenient lengths, so that they could be removed by others.

Timber was so plentiful here that we did not bother to save any, except what we required for bridges and sleepers, etc.

Now followed the biggest gang; three whole kongsis; about three hundred Chinese coolies. They were engaged in building up the earthwork embankments, and cutting through where the land was higher than was required.

Other gangs were building timber bridges over small water courses, the gang working under the direction of a Chinese carpenter.

The last gang was composed of the most intelligent coolies, working under a Chinese mechanic.

They were laying down the sleepers, and placing on and spiking down the rails, connecting fish plates, and levelling up the track.

Following behind all, and continually advancing further as the track was laid, was the locomotive.

It would look like a toy alongside of one of the main line English engines, yet it was doing valuable service, as it brought up the steel rails, sleepers, and all materials required, and took the coolies home at night.

To keep all these coolies fed was a great undertaking, because, if we ran short of rice and salt fish, which was their food, the matter would be serious. There would probably be riot and bloodshed. Luckily the river had been cleared up to here, and a steam launch with a lighter in tow, could get up this far. Several hundred coolies take a lot of feeding. Of course I got a good supply of fish from the river; it was only necessary to throw in a dynamite cartridge, and after the explosion fish for hundreds of feet around came up stunned.

The explosion was transmitted through the whole of the water. I have been in a boat a hundred yards away and felt it, like the blow of a hammer, on the bottom of the boat.

Occasionally we got wild boar from the jungle, and the Chinese love pork.

They are, I think, the best workers in the world. For less than £1 a month they will work from sunrise to sunset, with only one break for food.

Their wants are few, their clothes are a short pair of blue cotton pants, reaching to the knees, and a conical-shaped straw hat, and rope sandals. They have had to struggle for existence so long, that work has become second nature to them.

How different the natives of this country.

These people work for no one. They live in the same state of civilisation that their forefathers did before them, hundreds of years ago. They are a thousand years behind the times.

"Has civilisation really advanced with us?"

"I wonder."

These natives are their own masters, and they are perfectly free from almost all laws and restrictions. They are happy and contented, and have few wants.

They live in their own little huts, which they have built themselves, from material out of the jungle. Each has a large family, whose simple wants are easily provided for from his surroundings.

There is fruit of many kinds growing wild, and plenty of flesh and fowl to be had for the killing. As many fish as he wants can be got from the river, and he grows his own tobacco, and if he wants a piece of cloth or some opium, then a day's work in the jungle collecting rubber will supply his wants for weeks to come.

On the reverse side, our own boasted civilisation has brought us what?

The greater part of our population are wage slaves, at the beck and call of their masters. Living a life of privation and constant fear of unemployment and the workhouse; in a world where a man is too old to be employed at fifty and therefore is left to starve, practically.

They must drag themselves to work, no matter how they feel. To live crowded in slums. To be the makers and creators of all the fine palaces, luxurious yachts and expensive clothing, for someone else; and then to build for themselves – workhouses.

To be employed in sweat shops, or stand behind a counter in someone's great store, until their feet are aching, and they are ready to drop with fatigue on a long, hot day. Not to be able to sit down for a minute for fear of the jealous eye of the slave driver.

These and hundreds of worse things are the results of our boasted civilisation.

Think of the hundreds of worries and small troubles and annoyances our "civilisation" has brought us. The petty jealousies, and the constant striving to keep up appearances; the scraping and cheeseparing.

These things, the natives of this country know nothing of. Only when they become more "civilised," will they experience them, as also will they experience the host of bodily ills, which are chiefly due to our unnatural mode of living.

Of what benefit is our civilisation to ninety per cent of the people, if it brings them barely enough of the coarsest food and the cheapest shoddy clothing? Of what benefit are all the wonderful machines and inventions to us, if we do not make proper use of them, except to put some extra profits in the pockets of a few?

If our resources of production and distribution were properly organised for the benefit of humanity, there could be more than abundance for all, even if we utilised labour of only the able-bodied men and women between the ages of eighteen and thirty-eight.

There is not the slightest doubt that a standard of living equivalent to that of £1,000 a year could be enjoyed by all, with an abundance of leisure and travel and easy hours of labour for the workers. This could easily be done with proper organisation. All our requirements could be supplied within the British Empire.

First we would require to find out – and an adequate staff of experts could do so – the total needs of the entire population, taking separately every class of food, clothes, dwellings, amusements, travel, and in fact everything that a £1,000 a year man is now able to afford. Knowing this, it would not be difficult to arrive at the man power required.

Everything necessary in the way of plant, machinery, factories, railways, mines, steamships, etc., could be taken over by the Government by compensating the present owners by means of credits which could be spent on the higher forms of luxuries.

After a person reached the age of thirty-eight years, he or she would be free to engage in any private enterprise, in the higher forms of luxury trades, for his extra benefit, or if content to live on the same scale as the workers, he could spend his time in travel, sport, or on some hobby.

This only could we call civilisation.

War would disappear, because there would be no struggle for existence.

All the petty jealousies, envy, theft, and many other crimes would soon be almost unknown. A real civilisation.

CHAPTER 18

In the Chinese "Bongsals"

Now that I had got settled down for the next few years as I expected, and had got a decent bungalow built for myself, I thought it was time that I sent for Mulki.

I had had several letters, written for her by some native, to which she had put her name in an awful scrawl, the only word of English which I had been able to teach her to write.

In each letter almost the first sentence was one asking when I was going to send for her, so I wrote to Simpson in Assam, and asked him to see her off for Calcutta. There she would be met by a friend of mine and put on board of the steamer for Singapore, where I would meet her. I had booked her passage through a shipping agent and sent her some money for expenses. I longed to see her again.

There has been a murder here. The Chief Tandil has been murdered. At first we had no suspicion that anything was wrong; he simply disappeared, and the coolies said that he had gone into the jungle and never come back; they even showed us the spot where he had gone from, but we could find no trace of him. The other tandils all maintained the same story.

A few days afterwards we noticed that there seemed to be a state of tension and even terror in the camp among the Chinese, and none of the other tandils seemed to want the job as chief, although the pay was higher and the opportunities for squeeze much greater.

I had previously noticed that some of the small boys appeared to be sick, and one had run off into the jungle, but I could find nothing out. The Chinaman is as secret as the grave.

Queer happenings, one after another, began to awaken my suspicions, and we got in one or two of the small boys, and by skilful questioning got the truth out of them.

A terrible state of affairs was revealed.

The No. 2 Tandil was a cunning and brutal ruffian; an ex-hatchet man of the Chinese Tongs. He had collected into his clique a few of the most powerful and brutal coolies, and they had become horrible tyrants, and no one dare speak of it, as it meant sure death to do so.

They were extorting money from all, in many ways; even selling the young and good looking boys.

The kongsi houses at night time had become sinks of iniquity, where orgies of the worst kind were openly carried on.

We now understood the reason why some of the youngsters were nearly dead.

The No. 1, or Chief Tandil, had come to loggerheads with the ringleaders; perhaps because he was not getting a big enough cut, or perhaps he saw his authority disappearing, and the gang had set on him when at work on the line, and hacked him to pieces with their axes and hoes.

Most of the parts were burnt in the jungle; but we recovered several half burnt pieces – enough to identify him.

The first thing we did was to take a party of the Malays with us and seize the whole gang, and lock them up in the rice store – the strongest building on the site – placing the Malays on guard while we thoroughly investigated the matter.

Now everything came out quite freely when we questioned the other tandils and some of the coolies; each one privately.

The enquiry revealed that the No. 2 Tandil, and two of the coolies, were the chief culprits, so we sent them down to the Resident, with all the evidence and witnesses, who forwarded them to Java for trial and execution.

The terror had been lifted from the Chinese kongsis, but I found that the horrible orgies in the bongsals at night took place just the same. The only difference was that the young and good looking boys were not slaves any longer. It was just the opposite; some of them were beginning to put on side. They had become the aristocracy of the gangs.

Many of them were effeminate-looking boys of sixteen or so.

"Where did they get the money to buy Chinese silk coats and various luxuries stocked by the old Chinaman who ran a store here?"

They went about with their pigtails neatly plaited, and tied with silk, and their heads freshly shaved. All this costs money which the ordinary coolie could not afford. I had noticed that most of them came in for light jobs; as cooks and sweepers and sick house attendants. No more hard labouring work with hoe or basket for them.

The Chinese worked in one way only, and it was useless trying to alter their method. They got through an astonishing amount of work in a primitive manner, just the same.

A long line of men with big hoes would cut into the bank. Other coolies, each carrying two baskets suspended from a wooden saddle across their shoulders, by three strings to each basket, so that the baskets almost touched the ground when the man was walking, approached and slightly stooped. The baskets were quickly filled with loose earth by a coolie with a hoe, and then they were carried away and dumped by simply giving a jerk to one of the strings, and canting the basket.

Simple but very efficient.

The coolie did not have to stoop; he simply bent his knee about a couple of inches, and the basket was touching the ground, and being filled by one scrape of the hoe of the other.

There was a good deal of sickness among the Chinese here, chiefly "beriberi." The first sign of this disease is a slight swelling of the foot. The swelling is different from any other kind. There is no pain or tenderness, but when a finger is pressed on the part the depression remains as though the flesh was putty.

There is no cure, except to get away from the country, and of course the company could not afford to send coolies away; also it was doubtful if they would be allowed to land at Singapore.

We had no doctor now. The one we had before was a half-caste Chinaman. What his qualifications were I do not know, but he hardly ever attended to the sick; he spent his time mostly insensible through opium smoking. Often a bucket of cold water would not wake him.

I felt sorry for him, and did his work, but when the manager came down and happened to want him we could not wake him, so he had to go.

I tried to teach him a few things about drugs, but he stood on the dignity of his position and I gave it up, but still I shielded him as long as I could, specially as we only used stock medicines. I liked to see that the sick were attended to personally.

For the beriberi I could only give the poor sufferers the stock medicine, and see that they were made as comfortable as possible.

It was terrible to see them every day a little more swollen. Every part finally swells; even the face. The toes and fingers looked as though they were one toe, and one finger. Death was not far off when they were swollen so big that they had to be turned on to their backs.

A foul kind of skin disease had broken out among the Chinese. I did not know what it was, although I had a suspicion of the cause.

I knew that it was not like anything I had ever seen or heard of.

A dozen or more coolies who had it I lined up naked, and watered them all over with a solution of permanganate of potassium from a watering can sprinkler. They seemed to have great faith in my treatment. I had tried to put a stop to the carrying on which occurred nightly in the bongsals.

I had seen with my own eyes; by the simple method of putting my finger through the attep wall and then applying my eye. I certainly got an eyeful.

There were about a hundred coolies in a bongsal, and they varied in characteristics, from the brutal ruffian with massive muscles, to the meek and gentle and effeminate.

They were the pig-face type, the lantern-jawed, and the hatchet-faced; the intelligent-looking, and the idiotic types. There were faces showing every kind of abnormality, also many with really good looking and fine faces. They were nearly all well made bodily; strong and muscular, although some might almost be mistaken for girls.

It was certainly going to be a difficult job, though why I should bother I do not know. If only I felt sure that none were being coerced.

Well, I had started a couple of Malay night watchmen, to patrol all the bongsals at intervals through the night. Did it answer?

I thought so at first, until I noticed that they both now seemed to have plenty of money to buy all sorts of Malay luxuries at the store, then I started some investigations myself.

I found out that the watchmen were not only being well paid to keep their mouths shut, but that they had been initiated by the Chinese into many of their revels.

Finally, I stopped all interference; I had so much advice from the other Europeans.

The German who had charge of one of the two camps on river cleaning operations, said, "You never can. You never will. You never should," this being a favourite expression of his.

Several causes operated to produce this state of affairs, the chief of which were, that we were right away from civilisation; that there were no women here in the jungle, and that several hundred young men and boys of various races – Malays, Indians, Chinese, Javanese, and Singapore nondescripts – were congregated together.

Although the Malays were Mohammedans, many of them drank arack, and smoked opium.

They were learning to drink the fiery spirit called "sumsu," which the Chinese maddened themselves with. It was made from rice, and a quart bottle could be had at the store for a few coppers.

Is there another place on this earth where depravity is carried on on such a gigantic scale? I have never seen or heard of any.

What I have seen in this place I am not able to put into print. There were harems here that contained no women.

Gambling was rife, and the player would sometimes gamble himself into bondage for a month or more.

Public shows in depravity were sometimes held in one of the bongsals, and admission charged for, I believe, while some experts in beastliness exercised their ingenuity in providing the entertainment. Conditions like this were to be expected somewhat.

When the coolies came in from work at night there were no amusements. We were isolated in the heart of the jungle. There were no theatres, libraries, shops, or busy streets here. Nothing to do except sit in your bungalow or sleep.

For myself, I had plenty of books, and my drugs and experiments.

News travelled in this country in a mysterious way. I had let it be known that I would pay for curious specimens of plants, and natives passing down river often brought me specimens, as they knew that I would pay in opium.

I had just had a very peculiar plant brought me. The decoction I made from it I first tried on some rats I kept for the purpose; great, voracious creatures, that would eat anything.

I next tried a small dose on myself, without any effects except a slight intoxication, and a feeling of lightness and increased energy. Taking a larger dose next time I found that it had a very curious effect.

At first it made me quite drunk, as far as my movements were concerned, but clear mentally, and later when I tried it in combination with cocaine injected, I had a very peculiar experience which I will try to describe.

CHAPTER 19

A Strange Waking Vision

Sitting on my mattress under the grass roof of the sampan, I was journeying down the Tjenako with the stream; gliding swiftly along, without any effort from the two coolies who were sprawled on deck. Only the steersman, with his long oar, at the stern, was standing, and my Chinese boy was busy with the clay stove, cooking my evening meal; a chicken curry.

The sun had set, and the jungle was beginning to fall into shadow; soon it would be dark, and we would pull into the river edge for the night. Already the steersman was looking round for a sandy shoal, on which he could run the sampan.

I had been steadily taking the new drug during the afternoon, and I was intoxicated in an entirely new and strange manner. I had a voracious appetite, and would enjoy my curry. Afterwards I would start with cocaine injections. I meant to have a regular binge, and was looking forward to some new experience in the Spirit World.

"Would it be a vision which was beautiful, or would it be something horrible? No matter, even the latter would be interesting, and I was no longer scared; no matter what I saw."

It was now quite dark, and the sampan was moored on a sand bank near the edge of the jungle, the coolies being stretched out on deck. They were completely enveloped in their spare sarongs, and looked like corpses stretched out. Their heads were wrapped in cloths.

The smoke from the wood fire forward, drifted through my shelter; it was rather pleasant than otherwise.

I started with $\frac{1}{2}$ grain of cocaine, and in ten minutes 1 grain more, then gradually increased the strength of the injections to about 2 grains, continuing these every quarter of an hour or twenty minutes.

This method prevents any undue shock on the heart, which would occur if an extra large dose was taken at once.

When I felt my breathing accelerating too much, I corrected it with a small dose of morphia, mixed with my next injection.

Soon I was Absolute, All powerful; nothing was impossible to me, it seemed. I wished to get some more drugs out of my box, and I willed the box to come to me. I saw the box moving towards me slowly and distinctly, until it was there beneath my hand; yet when I stretched out to open it the box was not there, it was back where it was at first.

I cannot explain how this happened, it may have been a case of perfect self-hypnosis, and when I stretched out my hand the condition was temporarily interrupted; just as on other occasions similar to the present, I have willed a door to close, and have seen it moving distinctly, until it was closed, and then when I have got up from my seat and walked towards it, I have found it still open.

I continued injecting cocaine, with an occasional dose of the new drug.

My cabin had become the size of a large room, and the whole of the space was peopled with living shapes; some of them were beautiful, and some horrible, while others were merely grotesque.

There were no animals or reptiles among them, all were humans. They floated about all around me; each one was alive, and the expression of their eyes was intense; they seemed to be trying to tell me some great secret.

Spirit-like faces and forms of many nations, and of all periods; men and women of noble and beautiful appearance passed before me. Their faces only seemed to be alive, for although they approached or receded, I could distinguish no movement of their limbs. Further in the background were others, whose faces and forms were ghastly and horrible, like denizens of a lower world.

As time went on, these latter type seemed to be increasing in number and getting closer, and the beautiful ones were receding and their number getting less.

Slowly approaching me, and getting nearer every minute, were a group of Indian lepers. Their appearance was revolting, and would be terrifying, were it not that I was interested, and that I knew they were only visions.

I had seen many lepers, in the flesh, but never had I seen such awful sights as these before me now.

Some of them had hardly any face left; there were only holes where their noses should be, and what flesh there was left on their faces, was of a pinkish white colour, livid, with here and there a patch of their natural brown colour, where the flesh was not diseased. There was a pinkish white powder on the surface of the skin, which indicated the disintegration or corruption of the flesh.

Their eyes fixed on me with an unwinking stare, which seemed to be full of malice and hate.

They were so close to me now that they seemed to be almost touching me, and I shrank back, and then they were gone.

I now stopped taking any more cocaine, or the other drug, and started smoking some hashish.

I must have dozed for a minute or so, for I remembered nothing in the interval. When I opened my eyes I was sitting in a large dimly-lit room.

There was a musty smell of corruption and death, and a faint sound of running water.

Along one wall, arranged and laid out on marble or stone slabs, were many corpses. Some lay peaceful in death, while others were bloated and swollen; with starting eyes, and a horrible intensity of expression; while some had started to decay, and I now saw that it was on these that the water was dripping.

As I looked, I saw that they all were rising into a sitting position, although I could see no distinct movement of their limbs. Now they were off the slabs, and were facing me; they were moving towards me.

I looked towards the end of the room, and saw that the wall appeared to be receding, and there were more slabs. Soon the wall had disappeared in the distance, and as far as the eye could see, there was slab after slab, each with its corpse rising and coming towards me.

The first one, which was nearest, was swollen and becoming decayed in parts. It was that of a drowned man who had been in the water a long time, and had been partly eaten in places.

It was now quite close, almost touching me, when it began to swell and increase in size, until almost everything else was blotted out.

The smell was becoming overpowering, and the light was growing dim, when with an effort of will I started up, and the whole scene disappeared, and I was back in the sampan, sitting on my mattress.

As soon as I relaxed, familiar objects again commenced to disappear. I no longer saw the cabin, the boat, or the sleeping coolies stretched on the deck.

The space around me seemed to be filled with faintly luminous globes, which some curious instinct told me were the souls of unborn children, waiting for their turn to be born. Everything around me seemed to be weird and unreal.

The trees in the jungle alongside assumed grotesque shapes, and faces peered out at me from the foliage.

The moon, which had risen, shed an unearthly light on the branches, which, as I looked, took the shapes of animals or reptiles.

If I shut my eyes, I heard the sound of what seemed to be the continuous ringing of bells in the distance. I was living through years of time, and former periods of my life returned, and I lived them again, not only as a memory but actually, with every long-forgotten detail returning with startling clearness.

I must have slept, for when I opened my eyes it was broad daylight, and the boat was in motion.

I was lying on my mattress, and as I looked out, I saw my boy making my morning coffee.

I was little the worse for my last night's experience; a slight headache, which I easily removed at once with an injection of morphia.

Every detail of my experience was clearly remembered, and I thought over each detail. It is true that many times I had lived former periods of my life over again, but so far I had never been able to take on another personality, and go back and live in earlier periods of the world's history, but the time was to come; but many years later.

As time went on, the experiences seemed to become more and more realistic.

The new drug, I decided, had a more curious effect than even hashish, and I was preparing a large stock of it in a more concentrated form.

I had bought a proper laboratory evaporating pan. I first boiled the roots until there was a thick brown liquor, and then I evaporated this in the pan, until there remained a dry sediment, which I collected and made into a powder, and stored in bottles and sealed, labelling it No. 1.

I was exploring the jungle on each side of the river bank.

There was a path, or runway, close beside where the sampan was moored for the night, and I climbed up the bank.

I was not afraid, I had an unbounded sense of confidence and power; I was well primed with cocaine.

I had my revolver with me, but I never thought of it. I always carried it in my hip pocket. A neat Smith & Wesson, which I bought in Singapore for fifty dollars.

I smile when I think of my first going out to India, with the great R.I.C. revolver, with a barrel about 8 inches long, and a bore of .450, with belt and enormous leather holster with buttoned flap, and cartridge pouch on the other side.

I was proud of it at the time, but I soon got rid of it.

Although I had no idea where this path led to, I set off along it. It was fairly light, because a certain amount of moonlight streamed down through the trees, and when the moon was obscured by clouds, there was light from the sky, owing to the almost continuous flashes of sheet lightning in the distance, without sound of thunder.

At both sides of the path the undergrowth seemed to be impenetrable. Great ferns, and young tree trunks, with a matted growth of tangled grass and curious weeds, all seemed to be struggling to find space to live. Long streamers of monkey ropes hung down from high up the great trees, reaching right down to the ground.

The croaking of frogs everywhere was like a band gone mad, and every now and then I felt a sharp sting from a mosquito. There were many other noises around me, which I could not identify.

The path which I followed was not more than half-a-dozen feet in width, and in some places I had to push my way through newly-grown bush, while the ground was littered with fallen leaves and twigs, and creepers stretched like great snakes along the ground.

While passing under the branches of a large tree I was startled by an appalling burst of noise overhead. Roars and shrieks in various keys came down from high up among the thick foliage.

That they came from monkeys I knew, but from what species I was uncertain; perhaps it was a tribe of Orang-Utans that I had disturbed. This is the Malay pronunciation, Orang for Man, and Utan for jungle.

Only now did I begin to realise my danger, because if the creatures overhead were Orang-Utans, the position was full of uncertainty, as they are extremely vindictive when disturbed; besides they are so full of cunning and wisdom, that the Malays give them a wide berth. They stick together, and the whole tribe attacks. They have been known to wait in the vicinity of a village and wreak their revenge when opportunity occurs.

The native house is built on stilts, but even when the ladder is drawn up there is nothing to prevent one of the tribe from climbing up one of the poles, entering the house, and tearing the inmates to pieces.

I did not turn back, I walked on along the winding path. I came to a fallen tree which lay across the path, and further on some large bird flew out of a tree with a loud squawking and took a snap at me.

I was feeling just nicely lit up, and right for any adventure, but I had not had sufficient drugs to produce fancies or visions; I was walking on air, as one might say.

Presently I came to an open space, a clearing in the jungle, and in it I saw, through the trees, a native village.

The place was silent, and might have been deserted for any sign of life there was. Then I remembered that it was somewhere about midnight.

The moonlight was now no longer obscured by the trees, and the village stood out clearly; each curiously-shaped house, with its high, steep-angled grass roof, and bamboo platform in front, looking ghost-like, in the silver radiance.

The ladders had been drawn up, and I was about to steal silently away when suddenly a loud hollow, booming clatter broke out and echoed seemingly from all round the silent forest.

Immediately pandemonium broke out, women screaming, and men shouting, and the booming, which was caused by a hollow piece of tree trunk suspended by a cord and beaten with a wooden club, increased.

Evidently there had been some one on watch.

Soon I was surrounded by native Malays with "krisses" and "parangs."

As I was a white man, and appeared to be unarmed, their excitement soon subsided, and an old man came forward and greeted me.

"Tabek Tuan. Tuan mana piggi. Tuan apa mow?

I explained that I did not want anything, but was on my way by sampan to Kwala Tjenako, and was just taking a walk through the jungle.

He guided me to the largest house, followed by one or two of the men, who I noticed had discarded their parangs.

Squatting on the floor we were soon holding a general "chukup," or talk, for by this time I was able to speak Malay fairly well.

Opium was brought out, with lamp and skewer, and soon the chief and I were lying on mats, with the lamp between us, cooking the opium, fixing it in the pipe, and passing it in turns.

We lay talking and smoking many pipes, and the others had gone, and presently we talked no more.

When I awakened I saw that it was morning. The village was astir, and I could hear the sound of women and children's voices and the old chief was sitting hunched over a small charcoal fire. He and all of them were extremely friendly; perhaps I was the first white man who ever smoked opium with any of them.

They pressed on me all kinds of fruits, as well as chickens, and native cultivations, and sent a man with me to carry them. In return I sent the chief a large tin of opium.

Among the fruit were some durians, which I believe is the most delicious fruit in the world.

About the size of a large grape fruit, it is green in colour outside, but the pulp, which is eaten with a spoon, has a flavour of many things; almonds, sugar, brandy, petroleum, ripe pears, vanilla, and other things.

CHAPTER 20

Singapore

I was on my way down to Kwala Tjenako, to receive a fresh batch of coolies, and forward them on to the camp, and from there I was going to Singapore.

Mulki was with me. She had not been so happy lately. She had been worrying about her family in India, whom she had not seen or heard of since she ran away from home. She did not even know from what part of the country she came. Only that the name of her village was Chickalda, and that it was near a town called Mungeli.

I was sending her off to India with a letter to a friend of mine in Calcutta, asking him to find out where her village was and to see her on the train. At the same time I was going to make arrangements with a shipping agent so that she could get a return passage.

I needed a change of air badly, as I had noticed signs of beriberi in myself. I pressed my finger on my foot, and the depression caused by the finger remained there for a few minutes.

My heart was very sad for the poor coolies who were dying of the disease and could not get away from the country, but I could do nothing. It seemed cowardly for me to go away, but it would not benefit them by my staying. Many of them would probably be dead when I returned.

Arrived at Tjenako, I found the large batch of Chinese and Malays that had arrived from Singapore. They were sitting like lost sheep on the jetty surrounded by their bundles and boxes, waiting for they did not know what. They must have thought that they had come to a queer place. Water everywhere, with jungle growing out of it, and enormous trees whose lower part seemingly disappeared in the river.

Many of them were young boys of fifteen and sixteen; probably they had come from China, with high hopes of making their fortune. The Malays were different, they knew the ropes, and most of them had knocked about among the islands. Besides they spoke a language one could understand.

Some of these Chinese were tough-looking customers; bandits, hatchet men, pirates, and what not, while others were merely tame country men. I noticed one or two effeminate-looking boys among the crowd, both Malays and Chinese.

They did not know yet what they had come to. In a little while they would be smartly dressed, and mostly have easy jobs. No hard labouring work for them.

Some of the Malay boys had beautiful eyes, and skins like brown silk; later they would have their hair cut with a neat fringe and a patch of the crown shaved. The little Chinese boys would have their heads shaved, and their pigtails plaited afresh and tied with black silk.

Every Chinaman had a pigtail, for the time had not yet come when it would be abolished by order; when soldiers would stand on most of the bridges leading into the cities in China, and when a poor, simple country man came along, he would be seized by two of them, and another, producing a big pair of shears, would snip off the pigtail before the country man had got over his astonishment. They have a high-handed way in China. I will tell a few things about China in later chapters.

I proceeded out into the main river, the broad Indragiri. I was visiting a large fishing village called Preegi, a village of many houses and native shops, built in the river on a big bamboo platform.

Here they caught and cured large quantities of fish for export to Singapore, and manufactured that horrid stuff called "blatschan," beloved by the Chinese and Malays, and even some Europeans; but then I had seen it made.

First they pile up the fish in a heap and leave it until it is rotten. Then they pound it up into paste, mixing it with many biting and spicy seasonings, with plenty of salt. It is put in pots and exported, and I have seen it on the table of many of the best hotels in the Far East.

Here in Preegi there was a perpetual struggle between two smells: opium and fish, and I decided that opium had it. Practically everyone here, and of course there were no Europeans, smoked opium.

This is the country of the head hunters; the savage "Batacks," who live in the interior, and have been known on more than one occasion to make raids into the surrounding country.

Although no one seemed to worry about it, we always had the thought of these.

A white man's head is valuable, so I meant to take care of mine if possible, specially as Towler told me that mine would bring a big price, as I was very fair-haired.

Not far from here in direct line, although many days' journey actually, a European lost his head. Some one came into his bungalow in the night and took it, and the trunk portion of his body was found in bed next morning.

The Resident offered a reward of one hundred Singapore dollars for the return of the head, and shortly afterwards a sampan came down river from the interior, containing two natives and a box.

When the box was opened it was shown to contain the head even with the poor fellow's spectacles on it. The whole was packed in salt, to prevent insects eating it on the journey down the river.

I had heard that these people were real artists in the head curing business, and that their speciality was the shrinking of the head until it was little bigger than a large orange.

To do this, they take all the bone out, and the head, when shrunk, is almost lifelike, but in miniature. The shrinking prevents the flesh from becoming emaciated and withered-looking.

The little Chinese steamer was moored at the jetty when I got back to Tjenako and Mulki and I and the Chinese boy, A'Fah, went on board. The boat, which was less than the size of a small tug boat, was piled up with deck cargo almost as high as the bridge, so that it was almost impossible to move about. There were only two small cabins, little bigger than a good-sized cupboard, the bunks being about five feet long. However, as the journey was only one of about twenty-four hours, we camped on the bridge, the Malay skipper kindly allowing us to use his "charpoy."

All through the night we camped there as we threaded our way through the tiny islands, with the cool, spice-laden breeze blowing gently on us.

Singapore at last. We dropped anchor in the roadstead among craft of every description and of all nations, all gently rising and falling with the swell.

We drove to our hotel, through streets which seemed to contain people of every nationality on earth. Singapore is truly the meeting place of the world.

I felt very sad; Mulki would soon be gone.

"Would I ever see her again?" I was reluctant to let her go, but she had been fretting so much that I had finally consented, and now, at the last minute, when all arrangements had been made, and her passage booked, she changed her mind.

I knew that if I let her stay she would only be fretting again, so I insisted.

I took her on board of the steamer, and saw her safely installed in her cabin, and then when the final bell rang went ashore.

I had a pair of glasses lent me by a friend, and I saw her standing on the deck of the steamer long after she had lost sight of me. The tears were streaming down her face. For a long time I stood there watching the steamer slowly fade into the distance, and then she was gone.

Now I felt very miserable. I knew that I had the power to banish the feeling with my drugs, but somehow I seemed not to want to banish it.

"Can it be possible for one to enjoy suffering and unhappiness, or is it that because I knew that Mulki would be suffering my inner consciousness told me that I should share it with her?" I do not know; I was not able to analyse myself.

What a contrast between my mode of life here now, and my state only a few days ago.

Now I was staying at one of the best hotels, the Hotel de Europe, and I was dressed in a freshly-laundered white suit, sitting in a large, cool lounge, with its marble floor and palms and ferns.

Overhead were whirling the silently running fan blades. I was sitting in a cane chair, the arms of which were prolonged to serve as rests for the legs, and looking out on the scene outside.

It was evening just before dinner, and the élite of Singapore were driving past in many different kinds of turnouts.

I called "Boy."

One of the many Chinese waiters in snow-white costumes, who were noiselessly flitting to and fro in their padded-soled slippers, approached, and I said "Brandy Stingah."

He brought me an iced brandy and soda. A sparkling and tingling coolness.

I revelled in a real shower bath, and slept between sheets which were snow white, on a real spring mattress. It was past belief.

In contrast I recalled a morning I spent quite recently. I was with the advance party of Malays, who were cutting a passage through the jungle. We had come to a particularly bad section, swampy and very dense in undergrowth, with many sharp thorns.

Leeches were clinging to everything, and there were clouds of mosquitoes and sand flies; tiny little specks which stung like the prick of a needle.

The Malays looked as though they had just come from a sanguinary battle. Their bodies, which were bare to the waist, were smeared with blood, and small trickles of the same were running down their bodies in every part. They had wrapped their feet and legs with large leaves, bound with rattan, and with their parangs and their bloody condition, they looked a fierce crowd. My white cotton shirt was stained red nearly all over in patches, and so were my trousers, because there were many leeches in both.

When I got back to my bungalow I found that even the flannel strips which I wore wrapped on my feet, puttee wise, instead of socks, were soaked with blood also, although I had top boots on.

These were full of mud and blood, because I had many times been up to the knees in swamp.

My shirt and pants were in rags, torn by the sharp thorns which had left long scratches on my skin.

Death might leap out on one any moment in such places as this, in the form of a snake bite.

Although the probability was not great, the possibility was always there, and could not be guarded against, because a snake might be hanging from a branch in the thick undergrowth, and not seen in time.

Now I had just had a first class dinner of many courses, with coffee and liqueurs to finish off, and I was lolling in a rickshaw riding along the Tanjong Pagar road.

There was a cool breeze coming in from the sea, and I was feeling kind to all mankind, when suddenly my new hat, which I had just paid ten dollars for, was snatched from my head from behind.

It was no good giving chase because this was a road with plenty of hiding places, and the thief had already disappeared. Life is full of jokes.

I found, afterwards, that this hat snatching was quite a profession for many enterprising Malays, trained runners, who operated in lonely roads.

I had just received a letter from Mulki from Penang, written by a lady passenger on board, and she was well, and now I was taking more interest in Singapore.

I was now confining my drug indulgence almost entirely to morphia, having a proper rest, lounging and dreaming the days away.

Every time I changed over to morphia, it had regained its original charm and potency. I was its master; it was my servant.

Although it is a drug which, beyond all others, one must be on their guard of, I was using it singly. But not for long; soon I would begin to combine it with others. Never again would I allow it to affect my health, or use it long enough to impair its fine effect. Always was I using large quantities of drugs, but in combinations, increasing and decreasing them systematically, and changing their nature. Only thus could life be made a happiness beyond description.

The drug habit was prevalent among all classes in Singapore.

It was chiefly opium that was used, the Chinese smoking it, and the Indians and Malays often eating it.

Not much cocaine was used except in the Red Light quarters, and many Europeans drugged secretly, but in a very crude and timid manner.

Opium has a very powerful and pungent smell when cooked and smoked, and practically every street in the Chinese quarter smelled strongly of it. In fact one could see through the open doors of the Chinese shops and houses men lying smoking the drug.

Most of the women in Malay Street used both opium and cocaine.

I visited many of the better class Chinese houses. The room where the smoking was done was generally furnished with massive blackwood furniture, beautifully carved with dragons and grotesque figures, and the bed was a tremendously heavy affair, with canopy and curtains of silk. The mattress was part of the bed, being woven fibre, and the pillows were small and hard.

The opium pipe, lamp and tools stood on a lacquered tray on the centre of the mattress.

They generally rationed themselves to a fixed daily allowance. This means to say that they had become slaves to opium. This daily allowance being a fixed quantity, must soon become of just sufficient effect to bring them to a normal condition. Without it they were irritable and uncomfortable until the time came for their smoke.

CHAPTER 21

The Loading Wharf

Here in this place, situated, as we were, almost directly on the equator, there were practically no seasons; the temperature and the climate generally remained nearly always the same.

It was a lovely place to live in, at this part where the land was above the level of the river; always cool in the evening and not too hot during the day like India.

The jungle was teeming with wildlife of almost every kind, and many varieties of fruit, and lovely orchids and other flowers could be had for the picking. Bananas grew in great clusters, and the "durian," for which many Chinamen in that country would pay big prices, grew everywhere.

Little native villages were scattered about the country, but many miles apart; villages of a dozen or so families, generally perched on the river bank or even built in the river on piles, with roadways of bamboo, and roomy bamboo houses with high, steep-angled roofs.

My house at the loading wharf, I had built to my own requirements, on the river's edge. It was a three-roomed structure built of some hard wood like teak, with boarded floors cut by the sawmill, and furniture made by the Chinese carpenters, just as I designed it.

About 6 a.m. my Chinese boy, A'Fah, would come into the room with early morning tea, and if I was not awake, he would shuffle his feet, and rattle the window shutter.

He would have his pigtail coiled round his head at this time in the morning, and, with a bland smile on his face, would say,

"Towkay, tea have got. Six clock belong," then he would go out on to the verandah and beat with a piece of steel, a length of steel rail, which was suspended by a wire from the verandah roof. He would continue beating until the whistle blew in the little wooden workshops I had built.

After having a cup of tea and some bananas, I would get up and go down a bamboo platform to the "Tempat Mandi," the little floating bath house, where I would ladle river water up through a hole in the floor, and pour it over myself with a gourd.

By this time the jungle opposite would be full of sound, chiefly coming from the hosts of monkeys of great variety, springing and gambolling in the tree tops, and chattering with excitement when chased.

Sometimes I could see dozens of them going up hand over hand on one of the monkey ropes, or long streamers. Often there would be twenty or thirty on one rope, moving up with incredible speed. I wondered whether the rope ever broke. The top monkey might be fifty feet up when the bottom one was just leaving the ground.

The jungle on the opposite bank had never been explored, in fact nothing was known of the country round here, except the narrow strip located for the railway track. Even the river, no one seemed to know where it came from, it swirled along forever in one direction.

An unknown land of mystery, as primitive as it was a thousand years ago.

Work had fairly started for the day, when I set off on my rounds.

First I would visit the hospital, because I wished to make sure that the poor souls who were condemned to die, the "beriberi" sufferers, were properly fed and cared for, and their suffering relieved as much as possible. They would be left to die if I did not keep my eye on them.

The hospital was a long, low hut about 50 feet long, built of bamboo and attep. There was a door in one end but no windows. There was plenty of light and ventilation, however.

Along each wall there was a springy bamboo platform on which each patient lay stretched out or sat up if they were able. Each had a blanket, and a grass-stuffed pillow, and there was a shelf of bamboo running along the wall above the head, on which his few belongings were kept.

As soon as I entered the patients would brighten up; they feared death, and looked on me as their last hope.

The place was in the charge of a Chinaman who had had a little experience as attendant in a hospital; a man who had knocked about the islands and spoke a little South Sea pidgin English which he was never tired of airing.

I examined the patients. Here was a man who was so far gone with "beriberi" that he was swollen up like a balloon, so that he could hardly move.

"Him live for die, short time little bit," said the attendant.

I could only give him stock medicine which was ready put up for the disease, and see that he was made as comfortable as possible. Many of them were lying on their Tempat Tidor, or sleeping place, smoking opium.

Another man lay groaning and rubbing his stomach.

"What is the matter with this man?" I asked.

"Him belly belong walk about too much." I examined him and took his temperature, looked at his tongue, and felt his pulse, but could not find much the matter with him, so I gave him a dose of castor oil, and ordered him to lay up until I saw him again.

The next man had a nasty wound on his leg which he had covered with a foul mess of pig dung and let it dry on. I ordered it to be properly cleaned with permanganate of potassium solution, and bandaged.

After seeing the out-patients attended to, I visited the workshops, and set the day's work; then the sawmill, where I examined the logs selected for cutting up for sleepers, bridge and other work, rejecting some and chalking others with distinctive letters to indicate the job they had to be used for.

By this time it was 8 o'clock, and I would go for my breakfast, which was generally coffee and some York ham fried, which I got from Singapore.

I tried boiling one once; a 20-lb. one, but it was not a success. Instead of the fat being white, it was dark brown, and it tasted horrid, because my boy had boiled it without cleaning it first, or changing the water.

I gave it to the Chinese and they thought it was delicious.

The only bread I had was made by my boy, but it was generally sour; he had no yeast and so used a bit of sour paste. The water was from the river direct; it was a muddy colour and had to be allowed to settle. In spite of all this, I enjoyed my food, and was in fine health.

After breakfast I would be on the go all the time until 12 o'clock, which was my tiffin time.

I had all the bongsals to visit, and see that they were clean, and that there were no skulkers hanging around. There was also the storehouse to visit, and stores accounts to examine. Sometimes I would make a surprise visit to the hospital again to see that the rations had been issued, and that all the sick were getting properly fed.

There was always work being done round about, such as road making, bungalow building, stores and coolies arriving by lighter, and I had all this to attend to.

After tiffin and a sleep, I turned out at 2 o'clock.

The afternoon I would put in on the railway work in rough jungle kit. There were the embankments and cuttings, the small bridges and culverts, the tree felling and sawing, also the jungle cutting party of Malays ahead to visit.

More important still was the laying and levelling up the track. The curves, where any occurred, required careful bending with the Jim Crow, and sighting to make sure that the rails were bent in a true curve without kinks. One part of the track had for some time been steadily subsiding; about 50 feet of it sinking a little every day. We had packed it up and reballasted it several times, so we decided there was probably a quicksand or a bog lower down, and we started to uncover a portion of it.

Deep down we came upon marshy ground under the upper strata. In it we found an ancient dug-out boat made out of a tree trunk. It was quite unlike anything seen before, and must have been there hundreds of years.

To make good the track I had to uncover the embankment for about 70 feet along, and drive rough piles, using straight lengths of tree about 30 feet long and 8 inches thick, with a sharpened point. These we spaced about 6 feet apart under the rails, with cap pieces for the sleepers to rest on, and built the embankment around the whole.

Work ceased at 5 o'clock, but I was not finished yet. After the coolies had all had their food, the tandils and mandors had to come round to my bungalow and report, and take orders for next day's work.

Then after a good dinner I was free, and turned to my drugs.

First I would scheme out the many problems concerning the work. It was no easy job I had. Here I was far removed from any law or order, right in the heart of the jungle, in charge of several hundred Chinese coolies and many Malays.

Many of the Chinese were powerful and brutal, of the lowest type, most of them carrying keen-edged axes or hoes, and other implements, while the Malays, a naturally bold and fierce race, were armed with parangs, and "krisses."

It was no use trying to control them by force, only guile was any good.

There were various cliques and combinations among them, and rivalry between the different kongsis, and I had to balance one against another. Moreover, the Malays never sided with the Chinese, and although there were only about two hundred of the former, they were the more formidable party.

I had made real friends of some of the Hadjies, this being an honourable title and indicating that the bearer of it had made a pilgrimage to Mecca, and seen the Prophet's tomb. The Hadjies had great influence over the rest. Control the Hadjies, and I controlled the rest through them.

Moreover, I had the control of the rice, and of more importance than all, I had the opium.

The Chinese feared the Malays. The Malays were guided by the Hadjies, and the Hadjies respected and obeyed me without question.

I was particular to be absolutely just and fair to all, and I could speak Malay and Hindustani fluently. Only by these various factors was I able to remain in control.

The forward progress of the work varied considerably, and a lot of wangling had to be done to balance the progress of the various gangs.

Perhaps the tree-cutting gang might be lagging behind owing to one or two giants of the forest which they had to cut and remove, and then more men must be put on, or the Malays might be getting too far ahead, and I had to put some of them on to other work for a time.

It made me sad to see one of these monsters of the forest come down. It had been standing a sentinel of the jungle for perhaps a thousand years.

What sunsets and sunrises it had seen. What storms it had weathered. It was there when William the Conqueror landed and when the Inquisition was in operation in Spain. It was born long before this part of the world was known to white men.

It was a living thing, with an intelligence of its own. See how it extends out most of its branches on the sunny side; how it extends its roots deep into the ground, and spreads them out in a hundred tiny tendrils, through each of which it sucks its nutriment from the earth. It has a circulation like all living things, pulsing through every part of it, and even its leaves have a myriad of tiny veins, through which the sap flows just as blood flows in our veins.

Its leaves are tiny cups for catching the rain drops, which give life to its branches, and at the same time serving as a shade against a too powerful sun. In the winter it casts its leaves because it then wants what sunshine there is, and does not require so much water, as the evaporation is less.

Even its bark is rough and ribbed, to obtain maximum strength with lightness, and the ribs also catch and hold the rain drops.

See how the tree leans over so as to obtain a perfect balance, if its branches are heavier on one side than on the other, and how the tapering branches are perfectly proportioned at every part, so that the strain is equal at any distance from the trunk.

If two trees are growing close to each other, their branches will leave room for each other, by growing out on the opposite side.

It drops its seed to take root in the ground so that a young tree may spring up. A few hours of man's destructiveness and it will be no more.

Sometimes one of these trees was crowded with monkeys, who would not leave it until they felt it falling, there would be a wailing cry, almost like a human one. They would spring incredible distances through the air to a nearby tree. I do not ever remember one being hurt.

Mulki was coming back; I had a letter from some native postmaster. Her village was in the Central provinces of India, near Nagpur. She found that her father had died, and her mother gone, and only a sister and brother were living in the village.

She wanted to bring her young sister with her; a girl of fifteen years of age, but I was very sorry at not being able to agree; she would have been welcome but for the tongues of the world.

Before the world can be a happy place to live in, we must get rid of the scandal mongers and nosey parkers, and the old men who govern us.

Old men in Parliament will make laws which rob the young of all their joys and freedoms, because, being past many of the joys of life themselves, they will try and prevent others from having them.

Whoever does any act which is the means of robbing another of some happiness, is making the world a little less perfect; a world in which they and their children have to live.

Not only that. The exact equivalent of their action, whether it is a cruelty or a kindness, will be returned to themselves.

There is a natural law which never varies.

Action and Reaction are equal and opposite, and this applies not only to mechanical force, it applies to our conduct, our actions and even our thoughts. It applies to every motion in the universe.

Press your hand on anything, and the pressure will be returned. Throw a stone, and the effort put forward will be impressed on your body. There is no such thing as a straight line; a beam of light would, if it could travel far enough, return to its starting point; and this applies to every piece of matter in the universe, atoms, planets, suns and comets – they all return.

Every action, whether it is a cruelty or a kindness, is returned, and felt by the doer in its exact equivalent. The reaction may be a minimum, extended over a long period of time and hardly noticed, but the sum total of the effect or reaction will be equal to the action.

Man-made laws will, as Evolution proceeds, become unnecessary.

They will all merge into this one law.

CHAPTER 22

I Discover the Elixir of Life

I was still having many strange plants and roots brought to me by the Malays from the interior, and I had collected many myself, but so far I had not found anything special.

I had certainly found some which might be useful. One which produced a violent perspiration, and another which would slow the heart's action, and lower the temperature – producing a sensation of cold.

Then I discovered the perfect antidote.

One evening as I was sitting on my platform or verandah facing the river, some strange native Malays arrived in a sampan. They were people belonging further inland, and they had brought me some plants and roots, in the hope that I would take them in exchange for opium.

Most of them were no use, I had had them before; but there were one or two that I decided to try.

One plant in particular I was struck with. It was a plant carrying many pods, which were full of seed.

Later on I collected the seed and boiled them for a long time.

The decoction I obtained I strained off and found to be of a dark brown colour, with a strong aromatic flavour when applied to the tongue.

I next evaporated the liquor in the evaporating pan, leaving a sediment.

From this I prepared a dry powder, very concentrated in strength.

I tried a little of it on my rats, mixed in their food, and carefully took note of results.

As nothing happened which I could notice, I continued to give it to them for a few days, and then, as they seemed quite well and healthy, I took a little myself.

If you have ever experimented on yourself with some new kind of medicine from which you were hoping to get results, and waited for its first effects to appear, you will have some slight idea of my sensations.

In your case you have the knowledge that what you are taking has been tried before, and that at least you are not likely to suffer any ill effects.

In my case, I was trying an unknown drug; a very small quantity it is true, but still I had no idea what its effect would be, and I was waiting, imagining all kinds of sensations.

Finally I came to the conclusion that I could not be sure that it had had any effect at all.

Next day, I took a larger dose.

Now I was sure that the drug had some effect on me, but I could not exactly define what it was. I felt different somehow; more sedate and deliberate in my thoughts and actions, perhaps, with a great calm and peaceful feeling.

The following day I took a little larger dose, about a grain of the powder, and then the effect was quite noticeable. The effect was not like morphia, because it did not produce that delightful dreamy feeling of luxurious ease, in which the imagination is extremely fertile, through a pleasant kind of haze.

Neither had it the fascinating exhilarating effect of cocaine, nor the grotesque distorting and intoxicating effect of hashish. It was unlike any other drug that I knew of. It simply produced a feeling of great vitality, the absolute perfection of mental and bodily health.

It was only after taking it on several occasions that I discovered its real properties.

It was when I decided to try it in conjunction with cocaine, and for this purpose I first injected $\frac{1}{2}$ grain of the latter, and continued with 1-grain doses until I was well under the influence of the drug.

Now I mixed a grain of the new drug, which I will call No. 2, and drank it.

An amazing thing happened.

In almost the time it takes a person to feel the effects of a glass of whisky I was in a normal condition again; just as though I had never had any cocaine or any other drug.

I was just normal in every respect.

I took note of my heart-beats, my respirations, and my temperature, and they were just right; also the dilation of the pupils had disappeared.

The drug had entirely nullified the effect of the cocaine. Again next day I tried it with morphia, and I found it act in the same way, although I had to take a second dose. It did not seem to have so much power over morphia.

Its effect with hashish was even more powerful and complete than with cocaine.

Since then I have tried it with wines and spirits, and even absinthe, which I used for some time in later years.

Not only would this drug remove all forms of intoxication, exhilaration, and narcotic effects, but it would remove pain of most kinds. It would reduce the temperature if too hot, produce a feeling of warmth when too cold, and remove fatigue.

It seemed to have the power of bringing the bodily condition back to normal in every case, and producing a feeling of perfect happiness and content.

Of course cocaine will remove pain, if injected locally where the pain is, but the effect does not last long.

Morphia injected will make the body so comfortable that most pain will disappear, and the effect is lasting, but not permanent.

I intended to obtain more of these plants, and prepare as large a stock of this drug No. 2 as I could, putting it up in sealed bottles for future use. I did not know how long I might be in Sumatra.

CHAPTER 23

Lost in the Jungle of Sumatra

I rose early, I had work in the jungle to-day. I was going to search further in for straight lengths of hard wood to be used as piles for the jetty.

It was 4 a.m. and Ali-Bin-Mohamet, one of the Malay mandors, was waiting on my verandah; he was going with me.

If I had any luck, I could be back in time for breakfast.

"Tuan ambil mukan, sya peckir lambat?" asked Ali.

"No, I am not taking any food, we will be back early," I answered.

We crossed to the opposite bank of the river where the jungle was practically untouched, and any trees I selected we would mark, and the Malays would come in later, cut them down and get them across the river.

The jungle was almost silent and shrouded in a thick mist; which, however, would clear away when the sun came up, and as we entered I half regretted that I had not brought my rifle and an extra Malay to carry it, but I reflected that we were not going in far, and would be back in a few hours.

Proceeding ahead, and forcing my way through the thick undergrowth, I was soon wet through and black with mud. Ali followed me making a chop with his parang on the trunks of the trees we passed, as a guide when we returned.

Pushing on, we came to more than one open space, where there was nothing but stiff long grass, and weeds, and once we came to a swamp of thick black bubbling mud, into which I pushed a pole and found no bottom. Now the sun was beginning to rise and the mist was clearing away I could see around me better. The trees were now full of monkeys, making a terrible chatter, and many strange sounds could be heard all around me; mostly birds, I think, and small animals.

Beautiful orchids hung from the trees, clinging to them, like the parasites they were, and great flowers and ferns could be seen in the undergrowth.

Suddenly there was a loud crashing just ahead; it was approaching. Some large animal would be upon us in a minute.

Quickly Ali led the way, and turned off at right angles and I followed, forcing our way into the thick foliage, where we crouched and waited.

A great animal appeared, one of the most curious I have ever seen. It was shaped partly like a pig and partly like a deer. The "Babi Rus-a." I did not know much about the animal, and was uncertain whether it was dangerous or not, and Ali was not a native Malay, he was a Singapore man, so we waited silently until it had passed.

It must now have been somewhere about 8 o'clock judging by the sun, and as I had found and marked many fine pieces of timber, I was thinking of returning, when we heard a peculiar sound. It was some little way off, and listening carefully, I could hear grunts and squeals for all the world like one would expect to hear from a great drove of pigs.

"Babi Utan," said Ali.

The wild pig is a vicious and dangerous animal, and a person caught by a drove of these would be ripped to pieces in a few minutes, so we turned tail and scrambled through the foliage and bush as quickly as we could, meaning to find a tree we could climb.

"Seeni," called Ali who was ahead, pointing to a medium-sized tree whose branches started low enough for us to reach. He scrambled up it easily, using his toes like a monkey, but I had more difficulty, and he had to reach down and give me a pull up.

They were nearly on us. Whether they sensed our presence and were coming for us, or whether it was chance that they came our way or not, I cannot say, but just then the head of the drove came in sight. There were dozens of them, fierce-looking brutes, the boars with enormously powerful heads and wicked-looking tusks.

We kept quiet until they were well past, and then we descended.

"Where are we?" I asked Ali in Malay.

In our hurry we had not taken note of our direction, and we started to hunt around for our path.

The sun was now almost vertical, and it was impossible to obtain any help by observing its angle.

I was cut and scratched in several places; my clothes were torn, and I was bitten by mosquitoes and sand flies; altogether thoroughly uncomfortable. We wandered through the jungle for hours, searching, stumbling into pools, sometimes having to almost creep on our hands and knees through the dense growth.

To make matters worse, I was beginning to feel hungry and exhausted, and I expect Ali was the same although he was a Malay; we had gone through a rough time.

I was beginning to feel thoroughly miserable, not to say scared, because I knew what a serious thing it was to be lost in the jungle without camp equipment.

Just then I noticed Ali take out of his waist band a little tin box, open it and take something out which he put into his mouth.

"What is that?" I asked.

"Opium, Tuan, "he said.

I did not eat opium as long as I could smoke it or get morphia injection, but just at the moment it was a great boon.

Taking a piece the size of a large pill and swallowing it, my troubles all seemed to fade away.

All fatigue and discomfort vanished in a few minutes, moreover my frame of mind had changed.

I was now full of hope, and felt quite confident that we would soon find our way out, and even my hunger had become a pleasant anticipation.

Now we proceeded quite calmly, and studied our surroundings more.

With another pellet or so, I felt that I could lie down comfortably in the undergrowth and have a sleep.

Ali climbed a tall palm tree and threw down some coconuts, which we cut open with the parang. The milk was deliciously cool and refreshing.

While he was up the tree I called to him to look round and see if he could tell in which direction the river lay, but there was no sign of it.

We struggled on for hours, but we were in a better frame of mind and more comfortable in our bodies, owing to the opium, and we had had a rest and some durians we found. As the afternoon began to wear away, the sun sinking almost due west, I was able to take my direction.

We struck off on another course, and after a long time we made the river and recognised the place.

Scrambling along the river bank through thick mud and jungle in about an hour we reached our sampan. The camp was right opposite.

How glorious to get my torn and mud-soaked clothes off, a bathe and a change, then an injection of my favourite combination, followed by a good dinner.

The experience seemed worthwhile just to revel in the contrast. But for Ali's opium we might never have got back, because such a position calls for the best of the mind and body; calmness, keen perception, staying power, and this opium will supply when wanted.

Now, under such a situation, cocaine would not have been so good, it might even have been a disadvantage if used alone. It would not produce calmness and deliberation. It would produce a feeling of great vitality, but there would be the liability to hurry, and not to be cautious enough.

The ideal drug to have with one in such circumstances would be my discovery No. 2.

Going into thick, unknown and unexplored jungle, is like going into the catacombs; you must leave a trail behind you which you can easily recognise on your return, and the reason we lost our way was that we ran without noting our direction when the wild pigs appeared, and we could not find our tree notchings.

I had been experimenting on myself with the drug No. 2 for some days, and I had not used any other drugs at all, stopping every kind suddenly and only taking this one drug three times a day.

I felt perfect, without the least trace of the usual adverse symptoms; which would be expected otherwise.

Next I started diminishing the amount of the drug daily, and in a fortnight I was quite free.

I had no suffering or craving at all, and I had been without drugs of any description for over a week. I have proved the power of this drug conclusively to my own satisfaction.

No matter what drug I was using, with the aid of No. 2 I could give it up quite easily.

I was no worse for my experience in the jungle, beyond a slight stiffness, and some cuts and scratches.

The nightly orgies in the bongsals were still going on, and nothing could stop them. The Chinese were very close and secret, and some of them seemed to have a peculiar sense of humour.

A Chinese coolie appeared with his face tattooed; an obscene picture had been tattooed on his cheeks and I could not find out anything about it. The victim seemed to look upon it as a joke, and whenever he came in view of the crowd, there were ribald remarks and pleasantries, which he appeared to enjoy. It had brought him into the limelight, and he strutted about as though he was an important character.

CHAPTER 24

The Rhinoceros

As I sat in the sampan, moving slowly up the river against the tide, keeping near to the bank so that the Malays could use their poles, I felt very lonely. Mulki, who had arrived back from India, was asleep under the covered portion at the back. She was a little hurt because I would not allow her to have her new monkey, which one of the Malays had caught in the jungle, and which was now tame, in our sampan. I had relegated it to the small one which was following with our personal belongings.

It would take about five days before we would arrive at Pia Tarantang, the headquarters, where we were going. There was plenty of work waiting for me to start there, and I could be spared from the loading wharf now.

The night was cool and still, and far over to the west, there was a beautiful light of many tints in the sky. A hollow booming sound floated on the air, sounding as though it came from a great distance. It was a hollow piece of tree trunk being beaten in some native village deep in the jungle. The sound was strange, resembling some sort of primitive tune.

I thought of the crowds of well-dressed people that would be moving along the Strand and Oxford Street, the busy restaurants and hotels, and I wondered how many of them ever thought of the lonely places on the earth, where white men sometimes have to live.

Over in the direction from which the sound was coming, but further inland, was the country of the Head Hunters. I shuddered to think of leaving my head in this country, and having it hung up as a decoration in some village, yet really our lives on this earth are but a very brief span, and about as much importance in relation to the universe as a germ in a drop of water in the sea is, and even the earth itself is of no more account among the billions of suns, planets and other bodies in space, than a grain of sand is to the sea shore.

Yet we see the heads of the many different religious bodies, squabbling among themselves as to which is the true one, and whether it is right to burn incense in the churches, or whether unbaptised babies will go to an imaginary place called Hell.

A true sense of proportion seems to be wanting.

If the size of the universe is, as some scientists estimate, two hundred million light years in diameter, it is difficult to realise the insignificance of our earth.

Let us in imagination lay it down to scale; it will have to be a very small one.

100

Lay off a straight line about two and a half miles in length, and let it represent the extent of the universe.

Now imagine a miniature railway train travelling along this line at a speed of sixty miles an hour, for two hundred million years, keeping to the same scale. Then at the end of that time it would have moved along the line only a distance of one sixty-fourth part of an inch; about the thickness of a sheet of thick paper. It has been travelling for two hundred million years, yet on the scale it has hardly moved.

What must have been the thoughts of the first astronomer who tried to find the distance of one of those stars – which are a million light years or more away – by triangulation. First he would probably lay off two points on the earth's surface as far from each other as possible, to serve as a base line, and then observe the star from each point. He would find the lines to the star apparently running parallel to each other, and he decided that the base line wasn't long enough.

Then he had a bright idea. He clamped his telescope on the star, with the centre, where the hair lines cross, exactly on the mark. Now he waited six months, until the earth had moved away to the opposite side of the sun, about 186,000,000 miles across, and then looked through the telescope again. Imagine his surprise when he found that it was still on the centre of the star. The 186,000,000 miles was so small a distance in comparison with that of the star that it was negligible. Light would travel the former distance in about eighteen and a half minutes while the other would require a million years to do the journey.

"This being the case, where is Heaven they preach about, and how long does it take us to get there? What happens to the person who is just not quite good enough for Heaven; does he go to the same place as the cold-blooded murderer?"

Of course there may be many stages of life on other worlds, between the highest and the lowest. The soul may have some changeable quality, some affinity of attraction, which takes it automatically to the world it is destined for; a happier world, or a more cruel one, just according to the quality of the soul.

It may travel through space with a constantly-increasing velocity, like that of a falling body, invisible, and insensible of time or anything else, until born again, on a new world.

This is a strange idea, but there may be many natural laws in the universe of which, as yet, we have no knowledge. Who, a hundred years ago, would have believed that wireless and television were possible?

I always enjoyed these river trips; the long rest, reclining on my mattress in the shade of the attep roof of the sampan, dreaming, living other lives, in other places, made life a thing of joy. I always had something to look forward to; always was I on the eve of a new and fascinating experience.

The scenery and the jungle on the river banks was constantly changing; it was full of life, sound and beauty.

Frequently we passed strange animals drinking at the edge, and the river was teeming with fish.

Giant crocodiles lay basking on the sandbanks, or came floating down the stream like logs of wood.

Beautiful orchids and strange flowers everywhere, with tall palm trees, and ferns, making the scene one of beauty and colour.

The river was getting narrower, and the banks higher, while sometimes we passed stretches of almost open country where we could see hills in the distance.

Arrived at the spot where we had to leave the sampan, it was a job to get our stuff as well as ourselves ashore, for the bank was high and the water shallow near the edge, and deep in mud into which I sank up to my knees.

We had about a couple of miles to walk to get to the camp, but a rough road had been made through the jungle.

There had been a great change here since my last visit. Four good-sized European bungalows, with wide verandahs all round, raised high above the ground, had been built, and a large area cleared and roads made.

The number of coolies was not many yet, as the mine would not be started until we got a lot of the other work done; probably there were a hundred Malays and Chinese altogether.

My first job was to scheme out a water supply for drinking and domestic purposes, making provision for the large number of coolies and others who would arrive later.

The settlement was built on a hill, so that made the problem of the water supply more difficult; there was no way of getting a steam boiler here, and petrol motors were hardly known in those days.

Searching the near-by jungle, I found a small stream flowing down the side of a high hill. It was beautifully clear water as it flowed over rocks and pebbles, and wound its way down to the valley below where the coal seam outcropped.

Having made my calculations, I ordered from Singapore all the necessary piping of various sizes from 2-inch diameter down to $\frac{1}{2}$-inch diameter, with valves, bends, etc., and the tools required, including a portable forge and riveter's outfit.

I also ordered twelve wrought iron tanks, 5 feet square, to be made with $\frac{3}{16}$-inch plate, all ready bent and with holes drilled ready for riveting up here.

Having got off my order for all requirements, I started to build, at a convenient place in the settlement, a platform of timber, about 2 feet high, for the tanks to sit on, allowing for four rows of three tanks, with a space of 2 feet between each; all being connected together by a 2-inch pipe at the bottom of each.

When the material arrived, I riveted up the tanks with the assistance of a Chinese fitter and some coolies, put them in position, and connected them up on the platform.

Next I ran a 2-inch pipe from a stop cock on the tanks, up the stream to a higher level, where I constructed a small settling tank of cement concrete.

From the iron tanks I ran a 2-inch pipe through the settlement with branches of 1-inch pipe off it, to the bungalows, and coolie houses.

Everyone had to be content with a simple pipe standing up out of the ground near their house, with a stop cock on it. No expensive plumbing here.

The erection of the heapstead was a bigger job. The building would be about 40 feet in height. I had several Chinese carpenters working on it. The best carpenters in the world are the Chinese, I think, if they have someone to do the thinking part for them.

Meanwhile we were pushing on with the railway from this end, to join up with the other section from the loading wharf.

Of course it was more difficult working here, as we had no locomotive, nor could we lay any steel rails; we could not get them up this far. We were only clearing the jungle along the survey line and preparing the embankments and cuttings and bridges.

But for the abundance of fine timber right on the spot, this railway would cost about twice as much to build.

No steam launch or lighter could get up this far and each sampan load of rice and food took about five days' poling by four Malays. There were parts of the river, even, where the coolies had to get out and push it over a sandbank.

Transport was a big problem until we got the railway completed.

My bungalow was not quite ready, so Mulki and I had a room in the bungalow of a Dutchman, whom I will call "Otto." He was a very decent sort of chap; somehow I have always found Germans and the Dutch fine people, and good to get on with.

He was of a scientific turn of mind and had a large trunk full of books, so we spent some pleasant evenings together, and I had tried his favourite beverage "bols," a Dutch drink like gin.

We were sitting in Otto's room which was at the front. It was nearly midnight and Mulki was in bed and asleep in our room, which was on the other side of the passage. There were two back rooms also which were used as a dining-room and a storeroom.

Behind the bungalow, situated about 20 yards away, was the cook house and a room for our Chinese boys.

The floor of our bungalow was raised a good six feet above the ground, and there was a verandah at both back and front.

Outside everything was so quiet that we could hear our servants talking in their hut; it was practically the only sound with the exception of the eternal croaking of frogs. The bungalow was isolated, well away from the coolie bongsals and the other European houses. I was thinking of turning in, and I got up to go to the window, which was simply a shutter. It was a dark night but the sky was frequently lighted up by flashes of sheet lightning in the distance – the silent kind.

As I looked out on the jungle, my first warning that there was anything unusual was a shaking of the ground as though some giant footsteps were treading it.

Otto stopped speaking and looked at me to see if I had noticed anything.

"What is that?" he said.

I put my hand up, to indicate silence, and I noticed that the servants at the back had also stopped talking.

The footsteps approached, fairly shaking the bungalow; some large animal weighing many tons must have been approaching.

Otto slipped off his shoes and crept silently into the back room for his gun, but I saw at once that if it came to shooting, my Cape gun would be the only one of any use, because he had in his hand a Winchester repeater of small bore.

I got my gun as quietly as possible and put a cartridge in each barrel.

Tiptoeing silently to the window we looked out.

Just then the whole bungalow gave a lurch, and we heard some great animal moving under the floor; it had most likely brushed against one of the piles in passing. Now it seemed to be almost under our feet, then it passed round to the back.

From the servants' hut there was not a sound, and I could picture them all sitting in terror in the dark, in a room right on the ground, and with nothing between them and the animal but a thin bamboo partition, which it could easily walk through.

Our position was different, because we were raised over six feet above the ground, with a good floor under our feet, and both of us well armed with rifles; whereas the coolies only had knives, and perhaps a kitchen axe. Worse than useless.

Now we could hear it at the back of the house, so we crept silently into the back room and peeped out of the open window.

It was quite dark, but we could make out a great black shadow, and we could hear it breathing in snorts.

Just then another flash of lightning occurred in the distance, and the whole compound became plainly visible, and there, standing sideways to us, with its head raised slightly, trying to get the scent, was a large rhinoceros, the creature with almost the keenest scent and hearing of all animals.

It was puzzled because it was getting two different scents from directly opposite directions; one from us, and one from the coolies in the cookhouse. It had not the brain to puzzle this problem out.

We knew that there was not much likelihood of it seeing us; it is a very short-sighted animal.

"If we fire we might hit the coolies," whispered Otto to me.

Quiet as the sound was, the creature heard, and the sound confirming his scent he charged.

"Crash!" went one of the piles, while the whole bungalow rocked, and a scream came from Mulki, who had been awakened.

We could now hear it snorting in the front of the house, and we hurried round to that side.

"Never mind the noise now," I said. "It has located us."

The next flash of light showed it quite distinctly; it was just getting ready for another charge.

We both fired together, and then it was dark again.

Straining our eyes, trying to pierce the gloom, we could just make out its dark bulk moving slowly about, when Otto started pumping bullets in a steady stream, and I fired both barrels.

The ground vibrated and the bungalow shook, there was a sound as of some heavy body falling, and the next flash of lightning showed it lying stretched out on the ground.

We did not go out at once, but waited some time, watching it every time we could see.

When we finally ventured out we found it quite dead. I always regret having to shoot any animal, and I would not have shot it if it had not charged.

In the case of a man-eating tiger it is different, and I would kill it with pleasure.

This was a dangerous jungle, even the tiger was more fierce than its Indian brother.

The Chinese working on the line never strayed away from their gang, but the Malays were bold and fearless, and three or four of them together would stand up to a tiger with their parangs.

When maddened by arack, they are bloodthirsty, and will cut and slash right and left at anything or anybody.

I myself had a still which I made, and I could make spirit of many different kinds.

Many kinds of vegetation contain some volatile essence, and this is the first to be turned into vapour when heat is applied. This vapour is then condensed.

We are all drug addicts in some form or other. What is tobacco smoking, tea and coffee drinking, liquor drinking and many other forms, but drugging?

The South African war was on, and I had noticed a great difference in the bearing of the Dutch and German assistants towards me and all Englishmen. There was none of the former friendliness, and I found the half-castes were the worst, but I took no notice of them.

These islands, and even Singapore, were simply swarming with half-castes, who were bubbling over with delight. One saw them in twos and threes gloating over a newspaper in the bars in Singapore; reading with wide grins and excited chatter, an account of some fresh British reverse.

The stock of the Englishman had gone down in this part of the world.

CHAPTER 25

The Beachcomber

The coolies had knocked off work for the day, and crowds of them were bathing naked in the little stream which ran in a series of levels and falls down the hillside, into the valley below, where it formed a large still pool in the shade of the jungle, the water being cool and clear as crystal.

There was much horse play, specially among the Chinese, who are naturally more boisterous than the Malays; a grave and dignified race.

In the coolie lines the cooks were cooking the great coppers full of rice, boiling it with a perfection that is rarely seen in England. Other coppers contained a greasy kind of soup, made out of salt fish and many other things, which smelt horribly.

I was sitting on the verandah when the manager came along with three Europeans to whom he introduced me. There was an old Irishman, a German, and a magnificent specimen of manhood, something after the build of Jack Dempsey, an Englishman.

They were all dressed in dirty white linen suits, unshaved, with long ragged hair and a general unkempt appearance.

They had, I heard, been on the beach in Singapore, down and out, hanging about the water front during the day, and at night sleeping where they could, in warehouses and timber yards. They had been given a passage over here by the company's agents, on the chance that there might be some work for them, seeing that our coolies were fast increasing in number and the mine would soon be commenced.

Two of them were going to be kept on, but the Englishman was returning to Singapore, to my surprise, because he was the best of the bunch.

Afterwards I said to the manager: "What is the matter with the big fellow?"

"Oh, he looks too much like a prize fighter," he replied.

It happened that I was proceeding down to the Kwala next morning, and it was decided that he should come with me in the sampan.

He had an order for his return passage to Singapore by the Chinese steamer.

During the four days he was with me in the sampan I learned a good deal about him, and found him to be a very decent fellow, and a well-educated one. I could tell he was of good family.

"I think your boss did not like the look of me," he said. "I know my appearance is against me, but take any one, let them sleep out on the waterfront for a week or two without a shave or change of clothes, and what will they look like?"

I gave him what money I could spare, with a clean linen suit and a change of underwear, and while in the sampan my boy cut his hair and I lent him my razor.

The change in him was astonishing, he looked like a gentleman.

When we got down to the loading wharf we stayed overnight and I introduced him to the assistants there and privately told them of his hard case, with the result that he did not leave empty handed.

At Kwala Tjenako we found the Singapore boat just arrived, and after going to Ringat, would return and leave at 4 a.m.

Going aboard the boat I took him to see the chinchu or purser, and got him fixed up, then the chinchu turned to me and said:

"Tuan, have got one bag dollars belong you. Bring Singapore office. You takee now?"

I was quite aware that I had to collect 4,000 dollars, which was mostly in silver and was for paying the coolies.

"Should I take delivery of it now?" I had nowhere to keep it except a kit bag in which I kept my things, and there were many strange coolies about from the boat, the steamer's crew and passengers, and I would have to cart it about with me all the time. I decided to wait until the boat returned.

That night, after saying "Good-bye" to the Englishman and watching him go aboard the little steamer, I turned in to the room at the back of the wharf, which Towler had lent me.

The room was quite bare with the exception of an enormous bed, hung all round with curtains.

The floor was boarded, but the river could be seen flowing underneath, through the spaces between the boards. There was no fastening of any kind on the door, and nothing to put against it, so I decided to put the bag under my head and let my boy sleep inside the room, on the floor against the door.

I took no morphia nor smoked any opium, although Towler had invited me to join him.

I had only some injections of cocaine, as I intended to keep awake all night, or at least until the boat had left.

The time passed quickly and I had no desire for sleep.

About midnight I sent my boy, A'Fah, for some water from the river to make coffee, and then stepped on to the wharf and stood looking out into the night.

With the exception of a faint light in the Englishman's cabin, all was in darkness on board the boat. The sky was faintly illuminated by stars, and I could see the dark and silent jungle across the river, which flowed past me to join the broad river Indragiri just round the bend.

I went back to the room, and with the point of my knife pushed up the wick of the coconut-oil lamp which stood on the floor, and then sat on the great bed waiting for A'Fah coming with the coffee which he was making in the sampan.

Having drunk the coffee I got into bed and sat in the gloom of the hanging curtains, while the Chinese boy closed the door and lay down beside it.

A strange thing happened; I must have dozed, in spite of the fact that I had taken cocaine only, and a minute ago I was feeling very wakeful.

If someone had drugged my coffee they evidently did not know my capacity for drugs, for I was wide awake in a minute and feeling for the money.

Yes, it was there all right.

The lamp was still burning, and I looked at the door and saw that it was open, and that the boy was not in the room.

Was that a slight sound I heard or was I mistaken?

I listened intently, and was now certain that I heard voices; softly spoken, and they seemed to come from outside on the wharf.

Now there was dead silence, while I listened and waited for I did not know what.

I felt that I was in an advantageous position; my revolver was in my hand, and while being hidden by the bed curtains myself I could see through them, and anyone entering the door would be in full view.

Presently there were footsteps outside, and into the doorway stepped the Englishman, where he stood looking into the room.

All was quiet and I did not speak, but my eyes were fixed on him.

There was nothing furtive or guilty about his manner, and after standing and looking at the bed a minute, he spoke.

"Are you awake?"

I did not reply. I knew that he could not see me, although I could see him.

After waiting a minute he turned to go, and I called out.

"I saw your door open," he said, "and I thought you must be up, so I came round for a chat; it is too hot and stuffy to sleep in that cabin."

I began to think that I had misjudged him, and then I thought of the coolie's absence, and the open door, and I was puzzled.

Just then the coolie came in, and I said, "You go what side?"

"Go tempat mandi, Tuan," he replied, meaning that he had been to the bathing place which is also the lavatory.

Well, I brought out some brandy, and we yarned until it was sailing time, when I saw him off.

Some months after I was in Singapore, when who should come round to my hotel but this fellow.

He was well dressed and well kept and he told me that he had got a job, thanks to the clothes I had given him and the money we subscribed. He insisted on paying this back, and altogether he proved to be a very decent fellow.

Since then I have several times tried to puzzle the matter out, and the most likely explanation, I decided, was that some of the steamer coolies had planned to drug and rob me, and that the Englishman, coming when he did, frustrated the attempt.

Meanwhile I had discovered signs of beriberi in myself again, and as it would be dangerous to remain any longer in the country, I decided to return to England, first getting a good stock of Drugs Nos. 1 and 2 prepared and put in sealed bottles.

Mulki had never been in England before, and she was delighted with it, specially with the shops, in which she spent hours having them show her a great part of their stock without any intention of buying, as she had already bought a good outfit. She seemed to think it quite in order to go and examine all the pretty things they had. Whenever she saw anything she liked in a shop window, she would go in and ask to see it. It was a great excitement. Her beautiful face drew a great deal of attention wherever she went, and her childish chatter in pidgin English, which had now become a mixture of the Indian and Chinese varieties, sounded very quaint.

One day, when we were visiting the British Museum, we came to a case containing the weapons, dress, and other things pertaining to the "Nagas"; she became quite excited at the incident, and started explaining in her quaint English all about them to a young fellow with a girl, who were gazing in the case.

Soon more people stopped and listened, and very soon she had a crowd round. Her tongue never stopped. I was gradually edging to the outskirts as I hate being in the public gaze, but Mulki was right in her element.

Suddenly she stopped and looked round for me, and called out my name, and seeing me hid in the background, she pushed her way through. She would have me explain to the crowd all about the "Nagas," but I managed to escape with her.

She had not the slightest particle of shyness, and sometimes in a bus she would address perfect strangers, and hold forth about some subject or other, gradually embracing the whole bus full of people in her talk.

She would ask them the most intimate questions about themselves and family. She made instant friendships, and everyone seemed to like her.

Important events occurred in England about that time; Queen Victoria died, and the South African War came to an end.

Mulki cried a great deal when the great White Queen died. The Queen had talked to her in London.

It happened that we were lodging at the house of a musician employed at the Palace, and Mulki had many times begged him to take her to see the Queen.

One day he took her to the Palace, in the hope that she might get a glimpse of the Queen if lucky.

Queen Victoria, wheeled in a chair and accompanied by some Indian retainers, happened to pass near where Mulki was standing, and the Queen saw her and sent one of the Indians to bring her across.

Queen Victoria spoke to her in Hindustani, and asked all particulars. She talked quite a while with the Queen, who finally ordered one of the attendants to give Mulki a five-shilling piece, and told her to make it into a brooch.

Shortly after this, Mulki was in St. Thomas's Hospital with liver abscess.

CHAPTER 26

The Underworld of the Ports

We were living in Sheffield at the time when I got my opportunity for a third trip abroad. I had been about a year acting as chief draughtsman for a firm of Consulting Engineers in High Street. All this time I had been keeping my eyes open for a chance to get out to the Far East again, specially China. It was a country of which I had read so many strange things, I wanted to see them for myself; to delve below the surface, and to find out all I could about the drug habit there, the greatest drug using country in the world.

I was getting fed up with life in England. There was too much sameness about it; a place where there is little real freedom, and where one had to do just as the next fellow did. To wear the same kind of clothes with a collar and tie, and talk about football and horse-racing, or be considered no sport; making conversation for the sake of talking, whether one had anything to say or not; to be considered shabby if there was no crease in one's trousers and one preferred comfortable well worn clothes. These were just some of the things that I found irksome.

As the opportunity of getting to China did not seem to occur, and I had a chance of going to India again, I took it, chiefly owing to Mulki's persuasions.

I had been constantly using drugs all this time. I found that I could use large quantities of an evening, and more at week-ends, without showing any trace next day, owing to the drug I had brought home from Sumatra.

I forget the name of the P. & O. steamer that I went out to Calcutta on, but at the station, after I had taken leave of Mulki, who was remaining in England until I got settled down and sent for her, a young fellow got into the carriage. Probably he had seen my labelled luggage, for he got into conversation and soon made it known that he was travelling out to Calcutta on the same boat.

At Tilbury he was met by a stout, horsey-looking individual, whom he introduced as his agent, and the latter, after talking a few minutes, said, "Well, your luggage is all on board, and the charge is £1 15s." The young man, who had previously informed me that his name was Mr. Wilson, felt in his pocket and produced a wad of notes, and after going through them discovered that he had nothing less than £50, which the horsey-looking one could not change.

Mr. Wilson appeared to consider a moment, wrinkling his brow at the inconvenience of the situation, and turning to me asked if I could change it for him. I could not and said so. Then a bright idea struck him.

"I hardly like to ask you," he said, "but if you will pay the man, I can give it to you when we get on board."

Unfortunately I had nothing less than a £50 note myself, a strange coincidence, and I told him so, and the last I saw of them, they were going to seek change somewhere else.

"Tell the steward that my luggage is in the gangway, will you," he said.

"Certainly I will," I replied. "By the way, what is the number of your cabin, then the steward can have the luggage put in for you."

Mr. Wilson appeared to hesitate, and I said, "I suppose you are not in with me, No. 127."

It was a strange coincidence again, we were both to be in the same cabin, and we shook hands on it. He had a poker face, and I could not tell whether or not he knew that I was pulling his leg.

At Naples I went ashore with three other young fellows to see the sights, hiring a guide for the day to show us round. After seeing many, including cathedrals, museums and the cemeteries of which the guide seemed very proud, someone suggested a drink.

Whether any of the party had added any private instructions or not, I cannot say, but I had my suspicions.

He led us up a staircase in what looked like a private house. It struck me as being strange, but as I am always ready to learn anything that I can which seems to be out of the ordinary, I thought I would wait and see.

We went into a large room on the first floor and sat down; I was just starting to enquire of the guide, when a door at one side opened, and a tall, blond Continental girl came out, and after a glance round, seated herself, to my astonishment, on my knee.

She was quickly followed by several other girls, dark and fair, of various nationalities, who followed her example with regard to my friends.

Drinks were brought out, and soon the party became a merry one, the girls speaking quaint English, which easily identified their nationality, Slav, Latin or Saxon.

The young lady sitting near me took a small tube out of her satchel and shook out a little pellet, which she dropped into her drink.

"What is that?" I asked.

"I have got a leetle cold, I take the medicine."

I took the tube out of her hand, and looked at it; I saw that it was labelled cocaine, $\frac{1}{4}$ grain.

We had been knocking round for some hours, and I was feeling ready for a dose of any one of my favourite drugs, so I said, "Is this for a cold?" and being answered, I took out four of the $\frac{1}{4}$-grain tabloids, and put them in my mouth, immediately taking a drink.

My action seemed to cause a sensation, for she talked excitedly in Italian to the others. They all watched me, with scared faces, but a grain of cocaine taken by the mouth was only a very small dose for me, I could have easily taken more. After a while, when, in answer to her enquiries, I told her that the medicine did not seem to have much effect, she seemed astonished.

We spent a very pleasant afternoon there, with songs and dancing, etc.

We went ashore at Port Said, in those days a sink of iniquity which, for its size, rivalled any place in the world for beastliness of the worst kind. Here we did not require a guide, as it was a small place and I had been ashore before, but one tried to force himself on us.

He said his name was John Ferguson, from Aberdeen, although he was an Egyptian with a face as black as my boots. He even offered to fight any of us for half a crown, when we refused to employ him otherwise.

We walked along with John dancing behind us, shaking his fist and gradually reducing the stake, until he came down to a shilling. One of the party was about to fight him for nothing.

"Wait a bit," I said. "We don't want to have a row here, or we might end up in some foul-smelling and verminous jail and lose our passage; I know a better way."

Presently we came to a large Egyptian cigarette store that I knew, and going in we bought some cigarettes and explained the case to the manager. The latter said a few words to an assistant, and we had the pleasure of seeing John seized by the coat collar and booted several times.

Arab boys followed us, offering to take us to see the Can Can and worse things, and many shop windows had horribly indecent photographs exposed for sale.

The place seemed to be overrun with guides and touts, all eager to conduct us to questionable places; alongside of which, the Can Can is a mild and innocent spectacle. The outskirts of the place were swarming with Arab girls.

We started off back for the ship, to find that coaling was going on. It was being taken in at both sides, and when viewed from a little distance the whole ship seemed to be enveloped in clouds of coal dust.

When we arrived on board we found coal dust floating in clouds about the deck. All the ports and the companion doors, and even the passage and corridor doors were closed, and the air down below, in the saloons and cabins, was stifling, besides being stale and full of ship's smells, as these very soon become manifest below unless there is constant ventilation. The smell was chiefly of hot paint.

A few passengers were still on board, some in the smoke room with the doors shut, and a few hanging about disconsolately on deck, watching the coaling, and at the same time getting coal dust in their eyes and ears, and on their clothes.

Soon we were in the Suez Canal and then on to Aden and Colombo, where we went ashore.

Arrived at the jetty we proceeded along the main street, past the Grand Oriental Hotel, and the Bristol Hotel further along, but on the opposite side of the road.

The scene was a very animated one. Natives of many different countries passed to and fro: Sinhalese men who might be mistaken in some cases for women, with their long hair coiled on their heads and fastened with tortoiseshell combs, and their coloured sarongs or cloths wrapped round their waists, looking almost like skirts. Indians in white or coloured turbans and white dhoties wrapped between their legs. Malays and Chinese in their own distinctive costumes. Also in this part of the town there were many Europeans in the streets in white linen suits and sun helmets.

It was the business quarter of the town and there were many European shops and offices.

We called a gharri, and told the man to drive round Colombo.

Presently we left the European quarter of the town behind, and passed along through the native quarter.

Here the scene was very picturesque; no slums like there are to be seen in many Eastern towns.

The roads were lined with tall coconut palms and other tropical trees, forming a pleasant shady avenue; native houses, grass and bamboo-built structures, generally standing under some palm trees; picturesque little self-contained structures in their own little bamboo-fenced compounds.

Strange-looking clumsy bullock carts, drawn by two small hump-backed oxen passed now and then along the vividly green, grass-covered lanes.

Very few Europeans were to be seen here, but hundreds of natives everywhere.

Here came a man with Elephantiasis of the legs; his legs and feet for all the world like those of an elephant, the foot, ankle and calf being the same width right up, and the size of an elephant's foot. Further on we met a man with the disease in a different part of the body. Imagine what a sensation would be created if a man was seen walking down the Strand pushing a wheelbarrow in front of him in which rested an unmentionable part of his body swollen to such a size that only with the aid of a wheelbarrow could he get along.

Beautiful, sweet-smelling plantations of cinnamon and other spices met the eye, and almost every little native compound was almost hidden by fruit trees of all descriptions. Truly a lovely place is Colombo. It is said that sometimes when the wind is in the right direction, passing ships can smell the spices and fruits, which grow so profusely in the island, from twenty miles away.

Leaving Colombo, we turned north, and soon the ship was steaming slowly up the Hooghly, that treacherous passage of water that winds and twists its way among the many small islands of the Sundabunds, between the Bay of Bengal and Calcutta.

A Hooghly pilot was in charge, an important person, for the lives of everyone on board were in his keeping. Many a fine steamer in the past has got caught in the treacherous quicksands, and slowly sunk out of sight below the river bed.

Those of the passengers who had never been in India before were scanning the islands with much interest as they passed; islands of virgin jungle, the haunt of tigers and other wild animals, mysterious, menacing. What cruelties are perpetrated in its hidden recesses, where the law of the wild reigns supreme.

We steamed on, slowly and cautiously, and then we arrived at Garden Reach, opposite Calcutta.

Again I could smell the odour of baked clay, and again I was at Spencer's Hotel in a roof bedroom, looking out over the great city.

CHAPTER 27

Strange Thoughts and Visions

With the first few injections of cocaine, tempered with a little morphia, my thoughts became very clear, and my imagination very fertile, while at the same time remaining sensible and reasonable.

As I continued to take more and more of the drug my thoughts became more fantastic, and I seemed to be living them in actual fact.

Later, by continuing the injections about every twenty minutes, visions began to appear, and I actually saw what I was thinking about.

By now introducing hashish and minute additions of one or two other drugs, the visions which I saw, and the thoughts which accompanied them, began to change in character, and became grotesque and fantastic.

I started off by turning my thoughts to the mystery of the universe.

I felt that no reasonable person who had studied the things around him, and who had used his brains, could doubt the existence of God; perhaps not the God we have created in our minds, but a great intelligence, the Absolute and Ultimate of all power and knowledge.

The wonderful order and design of everything in nature throughout the whole universe impressed my reasoning faculties with the conviction that there must be a Creator. Order does not come out of Chaos by itself. When we see a watch or some wonderful piece of machinery, our reason tells us that there must have been a watchmaker or an engineer, so that when we contemplate the wonderful system of everything in nature the mind immediately deduces the Creator.

Is it reasonable to think that the design just happened?

I have read Atheist works in which the writer points to the many terrible disasters and happenings which take place in the world, such as wars, shipwrecks, explosions, etc., and argues that if there is a God he must either be cruel or unable to prevent them.

We have no knowledge of what purpose is served by these things, or even that they are calamities really in the Absolute, or that the victim has really suffered any injury on the whole.

They are assuming that this life here will be the only one, but for all we know there may be many stages, and many worlds which we have to pass through.

As I became more under the influence of the drug, I seemed to be able to see into the future, to know and follow the progress of humanity.

I realised that the Church, and religion generally, was an influence for the good, and that at present it was following the natural Law of Evolution. Its atoms and units were scattered and isolated, but they were concentrating, and coming together, and one religion would join up with another, until eventually there would be only one – the true one. The teaching of mankind to do right to his fellow man.

What teaching could be of more benefit to humanity if followed by all? The evil qualities of the human race would die out, and the world would be a beautiful place to live in.

Science and religion are coming closer together, and the time will come when they will be reconciled one to the other.

I saw the time when the profession of religion would become the most honoured one in the world, and then its ministers would teach people the true meaning of the word sin: "The doing of an injury or an injustice to another."

My faculties were now so powerfully stimulated that I could hear the tiniest sound, even the buzzing of a fly's wings as it flew across the room; or I could work out complicated problems in mathematics mentally, remembering, and even seeing, each previous figure.

As time went on, my thoughts began to change, and visions began to appear before me; visions which at the time I believed were always there, but could only be seen by one whose mental and nervous system was powerfully stimulated by drugs or otherwise.

Small luminous globes, which I believed were the souls of unborn children waiting to be born, floated before me. There were spirits hovering round, materialising before my eyes and then disappearing; spirits which I seemed to know were the souls of those dead who, while in the flesh, were neither too good nor too bad for this earth, and were therefore destined to be born here again, and also of those whose lives were cut short before their time, either by accident or design.

Scenes from many periods of the world's history passed before me, even to the time of prehistoric man.

These were massive creatures of enormous strength, which some curious instinct told me was due to the long hair which covered their bodies, each hair being a conductor which attracted the sun's magnetic rays and passed it into the body, producing vital energy.

"When Delilah cut off Sampson's hair, he lost his strength."

A wraith-like cloud, a luminous shape, arose out of the ground before me. It was constantly changing shape; it was an intelligence which had the power of guiding my thoughts, and communicating with me without spoken words. I felt that there was something evil about it; something which was now beginning to produce a horrible sensation of fear and repulsion in me.

I sought to know what it was, and then I knew.

It was trying to draw my soul away. It was the evil spirit of the earth which takes the souls of the wicked – those which are too earthly – down below into the internal fires, for cleansing and purifying.

Only by suffering or being actually in contact with much suffering, can the chief qualities of goodness be learnt – pity, charity, and mercy.

It was enveloping me, trying to suffocate me, or to stop the beating of my heart. It was changing into a gigantic flame, and I knew fear.

My fear passed, and I suddenly knew that it could not hurt me, yet I started up and moved away, and it was gone.

I tell this experience just as I remember it in detail, simply to show the strange manner in which drugs, if enough are used, can act on the imagination.

The sensations and imaginations produced are legion, and are never twice the same.

CHAPTER 28

Calcutta is Startled

There had been, I found, a good deal of change in Calcutta since my previous visit. For one thing, electric fans had been fitted up in the bedrooms of the big hotels, in the place of the old swinging punkahs.

No more did one wake up during the middle of the night in a bath of perspiration, to find that the punkah was stopped and the coolie asleep. Moreover, the fans were a great boon during the day, for it was no pleasant job working in Calcutta during the hot season, as a draughtsman, as I had to do. Even with fans, the perspiration would be continually trickling down one's wrists, and little beads standing on the backs of the hands.

It was just towards the end of the hot season that I saw the first motor cycle that I had ever seen.

The reader of this, to whom the motor cycle is as common a sight as that of an ordinary cycle almost, will fail to understand the sensation produced in Calcutta by the appearance of one of these in the streets.

Passing a large cycle shop one day, I saw a great crowd, chiefly of natives, round the door, and as I approached I heard sounds like a gatling gun, and the shop was full of smoke.

As I thought that something serious had happened, I went in and then I saw it.

It was a fearsome-looking monster, and must have weighed a couple of hundredweight. At the back, beneath the saddle, there was a gigantic case, bigger than a Foreign Legion knapsack. This contained four dry batteries for producing the spark.

To get it going one had to get on it and pedal along the road like mad until the engine fired, as there was no clutch or speed gear.

However, I was very much taken with it, and I bought it.

After a few days something went wrong with it, and I could not find anyone in Calcutta who understood anything about it. I sent it to two different engineering firms, and in each case it came back covered with tool marks but without being cured.

The only thing to do was to set myself to study the thing, so I took it all to pieces, and reasoned out each of their functions.

Finally I discovered that the spark plug had too wide a gap, so that it would not spark under pressure while in the cylinder, although when outside it did so properly.

That machine soon became notorious in Calcutta, and caused scores of people to gnash their teeth and curse.

In the cool of the evening, Chowringee Road and the Maidan and round by the Botanical Gardens was a promenade for smart turnouts, dogcarts and pairs chiefly, and when I came thundering along the road horses snorted and reared, and drivers cursed. I received so much abuse and bad language that it got my back up. There was no law to stop me being with my machine on the roads, but if the protests had been polite I would have confined myself to less frequented places.

Just about this time the cycle dealer got another one out from America, and I persuaded one of my friends to buy it.

Now there were two of us, and I felt greatly reinforced. We started riding out together; we never took any notice of the shouts and abuse that was heaped on us, we just rode straight on without any unnecessary blowing of horns or trying to annoy anyone. We went on our way just naturally, feeling that we had just as much right to use the road as the buggy wallahs.

Apparently they did not, so we meant to show them.

One evening we were riding along the road to the Botanical Gardens when who should we see coming along but the Viceroy in his carriage, with escort, and when passing the horses they started to shy.

Next day I heard that there had been a trooper at my friend's house with a complaint.

Even this did not stop us, as we reasoned that the motor cycle had come to stay, and that they would have to get used to it.

Now we began to notice that wherever we went there always happened to be a mounted police trooper not far away, and if we stopped anywhere we were immediately ordered on.

"This wants thinking out a bit," I said to my friend. "It is our next move, and it must be a good one."

"What can we do?" he said. "It is not very pleasant to have a police trooper following us wherever we go, and we can't stop them from using the road any more than they can stop us."

Well, I thought the matter over, and then I sent to England for two more machines.

I knew that I could sell them, because I had received several offers for mine.

The cycle dealer had also got another one out and sold it, and we sought the buyer out and now we were three.

Meanwhile I heard of a young lieutenant at the Fort who had got a motor cycle, so I sought him out too.

One afternoon, just before the busy time for the buggy drivers, I met him on the Maidan to try his machine.

We had just started up when a mounted trooper rode up to us and in a very officious manner ordered us off.

The trooper was just starting to lay down the law to us in a loud tone of voice, when the lieutenant, who was in civilian dress, said to me, "Here, let me deal with this fellow," and turning to the man he said, "I don't know what your authority is for giving orders the way you are doing, but if you have any complaint to make you will find me at the Fort any time, Lieutenant ————. Moreover, I take exception to your manner and tone of voice. You will hear more about it."

What a difference in manner; all the bluster was gone. It was like an officer speaking to a trooper on parade. The fellow was at "attention."

"I am sorry, sir," he said; "I haven't been rude, I had no intention of being."

"No, perhaps not, but I thought you might be, and in any case, we can manage quite well by ourselves; please do not follow us further."

All this was spoken by the lieutenant in a quiet but authoritative manner, and the trooper saluted and rode away.

From that time onwards we had hardly any more annoyances to put up with. More motor cycles began to appear, and the buggy contingent were made to understand that they had not the exclusive right to the road.

I started dealing in motor cycles, in my spare time, and sold many; I even sent machines as far away as Lahore.

There were some peculiar specimens in 1901, in the motor cycle line. Even my machine had no carburettor; there was simply a kind of clack valve which had a tiny hole in the seating for the petrol to squirt through every time the air rushed in.

The speed of the machine was regulated by a needle valve on the petrol pipe. It answered very well.

One machine I came across used no liquid petrol at all in the engine. In the petrol tank there hung a series of lamp wicks from the top, dipping into the petrol. Air was let in at one end of the tank, and sucked out of the other end by the engine, first having to pass through the hanging wicks, and thus becoming charged with petrol vapour. This machine worked well and smoothly, but its disadvantage was that on a rough road the engine got too much gas.

All this time Mulki and I had a small bungalow in Calcutta. It had only three rooms with stone floors, and a small cookhouse at the rear, with a room for a servant. I only kept one as I had to pay for him myself.

The bungalow had no gas, and of course there was no electric light.

There was one thing about the place I liked, and this was that, although in a busy street, it was entirely enclosed by high walls, and had a little garden. It cost me forty rupees a month rent.

Here I could indulge in my drugs privately, for in a city like Calcutta I had to be more careful than when in the jungle.

I was able to mix up my combinations of drugs for outside use in such a way that very few people suspected my habit. I could take morphia without it producing the pin head pupils of the eyes and the sleepy look which is most noticeable when used singly.

Also cocaine, when I wished, did not cause my pupils to enlarge.

The long summer was drawing to a close, and the cool weather was approaching. The nights were getting cooler, although there was not much change in the length of the day in this part of the world.

I was thinking of having my holidays, and had arranged with a friend, whom I will call "Hutchins," that we should spend our fortnight's holiday together.

He was an ardent motor cyclist like myself, so we had decided to go for a tour on our machines, our destination being Benares, the holy city of India.

We each had trailers to our machines. These were, in appearance, like comfortable arm chairs, nicely sprung on two wheels, and having a hood which could be put up.

The trailer was connected to the motor cycle by means of a single bent shaft fastened to the back of the machine by a pivot. Into the trailers we loaded our gear, consisting of our personal luggage, a camping outfit, and a small tent. We also took a good supply of tinned and other food.

I had previously made sure, by letters to friends and acquaintances in one or two towns on the route, that we could get petrol there.

Each of us had our revolvers, and in addition I decided to take my Cape gun, and we also bought a good supply of the jumping variety of Chinese crackers – the kind that crack several times. There is nothing more effective in scaring wild animals, unless it is a golden rain firework.

If you can see a wild animal and get a shot at it, then of course a gun is the best, but if you cannot see it, and only think that it is lurking about, a few Chinese crackers are very effective.

After my experience in Assam, when Simpson and I had to walk through the jungle in the dark with the tiger stalking us, I often thought how effective a few jumping crackers would have been.

Having had a light breakfast of tea and bananas and toast, we set off about 4 o'clock one fine morning, as we had loaded up the trailers the night before and everything was ready.

It was still dark, and there were hardly any people about as we came along the Chowringee Road, and turned off sharply after passing the Bristol Hotel.

Faint lights were beginning to appear in the sky, and it would soon be light, and as we roared through the native quarter there were already signs of people stirring. In some of the open-fronted shops could be seen dim coconut-oil lamps burning, and figures in dirty white cloths moving about, while in some of the others the owners were still stretched out on the floor asleep, wrapped up in a sheet, giving them the appearance of dead bodies.

The motor cycle had become a fairly common sight in Calcutta by this time, and we did not cause much curiosity among the natives.

Pariah dogs ran snapping and barking at our wheels, but as I had hitherto had a lot of trouble this way I had fitted up a little gadget of my own invention, which I had found very useful.

From the exhaust pipe before it runs into the silencer, I had fitted a branch pipe, with a cock that could be operated from the handle bar, while on the end of the pipe was a tee piece pointing outwards on either side.

All I had to do was just to open the cock, and there came a series of loud explosions, with hot gas and flame issuing out with a rush just somewhere near the dog's nose. It worked like a charm.

Hutchins was a young fellow of about my own age, employed in one of the big stores. He was slim and delicate-looking, and I was a little doubtful about his being able to stand the camping out, because camping out in the tropics is not like camping in England.

About 10 o'clock we halted by the wayside having covered about 120 miles. We set up our camp cooking stove and got out all the requirements, as we thought, for preparing a good meal.

We were halted on a grassy patch of ground, under some large trees, on the edge of the jungle. "Put the kettle on," I said to Hutchins.

Immediately a startled look came over his face.

"We have forgotten to bring any water," he said.

The question now was what to do. We had passed a small village about ten miles back, but how far ahead we would have to ride before coming to another I had no idea, so we decided to go back.

The village was off the road a little, and stood in a clearing near the jungle. It consisted of a few scattered huts. There was a small lake near, and a few paddy fields. Small, naked children, who were wallowing in the mud on the edge of the lake, scampered off with screams as we approached.

We marched into the village, leaving our machines on the roadside, but we could see no sign of any inhabitants. We shouted "Kohi Hai."

After shouting several times and going all round the village, an old man came out of one of the huts, with a shrinking and terrified expression, and I had a suspicion that he had been pushed out by stronger ones lurking inside, who were probably spying on us through the cracks of the bamboo.

Speaking in Hindustani, I asked him if we could buy any milk.

"Sahib. There is no milk. For many days I have not seen milk; we are very poor people, Huzoor. We have no rice, no dhall; I have not eaten this day."

After questioning him awhile, I made out that there was almost a famine in the village, because the crops had failed, and they were living on what they could get from the jungle and lake; and being an old man and unable to glean for himself, he came off badly.

"What do you think about it?" Hutchins asked.

"I feel sorry for the poor blighter," I replied.

"Let's give him something," said Hutchins, so I gave him four silver rupees.

His astonishment and gratitude were tremendous; he was fairly trembling and dithering in his excitement.

We were his fathers and mothers all in one, besides being great lords.

Now we could hear excited jabbering from inside the hut, and in a minute we had about a dozen of them round us; not only from that hut, but from others.

However, we had no more rupees to give away; all we wanted was some water, and this we finally got. The fellow who brought it in a large earthen jar stood waiting expectantly, so Hutchins gave him a rupee, and, believe me, he seemed not satisfied. Enough to keep him a week.

We squatted down under a nearby tree and set up our outfit, making a meal with nearly the whole village squatting or standing round, watching our every action, making comments among themselves.

After the meal, followed by coffee and a smoke, we tuned up our machines and set off.

We had made up our minds not to follow the main road but to get off the beaten track, and to pick our way so as to pass through Burdwan, Asansol, Gaya and Patna.

The scenery was wild in some parts, strange and primitive, and the people we saw or came in contact with, quite different from those we saw in big towns.

For the most part they were very poor, and they gazed at us as though we were some wild animals to be scared of.

The jungle seemed to be nothing nearly so thick as the Sumatra jungle, while, so far, I had seen no wild animals, not even any monkeys.

About 1 o'clock we camped in the shade and had tiffin, and afterwards we stretched out on our waterproof sheets for a sleep.

We rode on all the rest of the day, passing many interesting sights; fakirs covered with ashes, who cursed us, women who covered their faces, and pariah dogs who got a nose full of gas and went off with a yelp.

About 7 o'clock we made our camp for the night in a large village. Here there were native shops and a bazaar where we could buy fruit, milk and chickens, so we made a chicken curry which we had with Patna rice. The chickens cost about fourpence each.

The people were very friendly and staged a Nautch for our entertainment, accompanied with tom-toms. The dancers were not professional Nautch Wallahs, just some of the village maidens, but I preferred them, I think, to professionals.

Later on we were offered a hut to sleep in, but we preferred to sleep in our tent, for we thought it strange them offering us a hut, or even allowing us to enter one, in a place where caste prejudice is so strong. Moreover, we noticed that the hut seemed to be an abandoned one.

When we declined the use of it, one of the principal villagers said, "Sahib Log, dar nai hai? Jungle me bargh hai?" meaning were we not afraid to sleep out, as the jungle contained tigers.

I told him that we were not afraid of tigers; in fact, I said, we liked them, we ate them alive.

But I could see that he had no sense of humour, he just stared goggle-eyed at me, and I think he was beginning to regard us with awe, especially when we started tuning up our motors with back wheels raised from the ground to be ready for next day.

We fixed up our tent, and put a machine, with trailer, on each side of it, and it was only afterwards that I noticed that this proceeding was regarded by the villagers as a kind of rite. There must be some mysterious kind of protection in these strange monsters standing sentinels at our tent doorway.

Inside we spread our ground sheets and rugs, with our bags for pillows. We lighted our hurricane lamp and got our pipes going, then we were all hunky.

CHAPTER 29

Thugs and Dacoits

Next morning, we were up before sunrise, and the air was fresh and cool; we had had a big breakfast of fried ham and coffee, and we were feeling fine. I had had my morning combination of drugs, which produced a glorious feeling of happiness.

As we had not had any adventures out of the ordinary so far, Hutchins began to think I had been pulling his leg when I had impressed on him the fact that there might be some danger on our trip. I thought it as well to tell him this before we set out. We were much nearer to what might have turned out to be a tragedy than we knew.

With the exception of cocks crowing, the village was silent and wrapped in slumber when we left, and the jungle opposite seemed menacing in the dim half light. It was silent, and perhaps that accounted for the feeling. If there had been the croaking of frogs and the chattering of monkeys, such as I had been used to, it would have seemed more natural, but the silence seemed to turn the thoughts to the unseen and unheard that might be lurking in its depths.

However, as we rode along the sun gradually rose, and the light of day began to put a more friendly aspect on the scenery.

We rode all day, passing village and hamlets, and natives, men, women and children, working on their paddy fields, and when night came we still rode on, using our powerful gas lamps.

Suddenly my back tyre commenced to go flat, and I called a halt.

"I am afraid it means camping here," I said to Hutchins when he came up. "It will be too much of a job to make a good repair in the dark, besides I am tired and hungry."

"All right!" he replied, and we hunted round for a suitable spot on the roadside.

Having got our tent fixed up, and our bedding put down, we made coffee on our spirit stove; we had buttered ship biscuit and bloater paste spread thickly on it. It was a meal we thoroughly enjoyed because we were hungry. After getting our pipes going we lay down on our blankets, and talked.

"What about Dacoits and Thugs?" said Hutchins. "Of course I don't expect there are any Thugs left now, but Dacoits yes."

"There are plenty of Thugs still carrying on their business," I said, "although they now work more secretly and carefully, making sure that they leave no sign of their operations.

"Have you thought of what becomes of the thousands of people in India who simply disappear and are never heard of again? The cause is generally ascribed to wild animals, but Thugs are responsible for many of them. Thuggism is a religious sect; they are worshippers of the Goddess Kali, the Goddess of Destruction, and they believe that by killing as many people as possible, they are helping Kali, and thereby making sure of some extra benefit for themselves in the next world."

"It is a form of greed and selfishness. One hears people spouting religion on the street corner in England and elsewhere. Why do they do it?

"Because they have an idea that by this means they can obtain some reward hereafter, otherwise they would not bother. It is not that they wish to do anyone else a good turn. It is simply a kind of selfishness.

"With each killing by the Thugs there is a kind of ceremonial rite, in which a pickaxe and sugar plays a part.

"There are generally three operators, and while two of them seize the victim from behind by the arms, and force him down on his knees, the third, whose turn it is to acquire merit, slowly strangles him with a piece of cord or a handkerchief. They generally operate on lonely roads, often making friends with the victim first and winning his confidence by pretending to be also bona fide travellers."

"Brrr!" said Hutchins. "You are a nice, cheerful blighter, telling bedtime stories; I am sure to sleep soundly now."

We talked for a while and then blew out the light, and soon there was silence in the tent.

A wailing, mournful cry, broke out on the night, and was immediately taken up and repeated in the distance.

"Jackals," I said; "we have nothing to fear from them, anyway."

There was no reply from Hutchins, he was asleep.

I felt my revolver under my pillow with my hand, and then snuggled down into a more comfortable position, and soon followed his example.

I do not know how long I slept, but I awakened with a sense of impending evil. It may have been some kind of sixth sense that I had developed, by living in the jungle so close to nature, or there may have been some slight sound, although I was not aware of any.

The tent was in darkness, and I could hear Hutchins' regular breathing, and I knew that he was asleep.

Every one of my faculties seemed to be strained and in tension, yet I could not define the cause.

I listened. Was that some other breathing that I heard? Faint and suppressed. I could not be sure.

I put my hand under my pillow and took out my revolver, and lay straining my ears for some slight sound, trying to pierce the darkness with my eyes.

The thought came to me that if I struck a match it would advertise my position, and if it should happen to be a Dacoit he would have a knife, and throw it when I made such a good target.

Now I was certain that I saw a faint patch of blacker shadow near the entrance, and it moved.

Not the slightest sound, yet the shadow was coming nearer.

I knew that it was not a drug-induced vision, as I was not in the right condition for seeing these. I knew exactly when to expect waking visions, and could almost forecast their character, from the amount and kinds of drugs I had taken.

So far I had hardly stirred, so as not to give any warning of my position and that I was awake; I knew that if I called out to Hutchins he would sit up only half awake at first, and perhaps get a knife through his throat. A mistaken move now might and probably would mean death for one of us.

I released my hold on my revolver, as I was reluctant to shoot without knowing what I was shooting at; it might not be a Dacoit. Besides I could not shoot without warning. I tensed myself, and then sprang with all my speed and suddenness, and I gripped with both arms a naked body, slippery with grease.

It went down with a crash, and me on top of it, gripping its arms for all I was worth, and shouting to Hutchins to strike a light.

Meanwhile the fellow was struggling his utmost to release himself, and use his arms, which I had locked. Although slightly built he was incredibly strong and wiry, and covered with grease, so that, in spite of my strength, I had difficulty in holding him.

Hutchins wasn't long before he had a light, and came to my assistance. He twisted the fellow's wrist until he released a long and ugly knife he was holding. Hutchins placed his revolver against the Dacoit's ear, and told him to be still.

When we got him secured, we found that he was naked except for a small piece of rag tied tightly like a bandage round his fork, also smothered in grease.

"What are we going to do with him?" said Hutchins. "Shall we take him with us, and hand him over at the nearest Thana?"

"That would mean that we should have to hang around, to give evidence, and perhaps spoil our holiday," I replied. "Besides, how could we get him there; our trailers are quite full?"

Eventually, after taking the knife, we gave him a good leathering on his stern with Hutchins' belt, and kicked him out.

We did not go to sleep any more that night.

We cooked a good meal of fried ham and coffee, and then set to with the aid of my acetylene lamp to repair my back tyre.

"This rather takes the fun out of camping," said Hutchins. "I think we will have to take turns in keeping watch at night, and wherever possible put up at a Dak bungalow."

"I have an idea," I said, and I explained it to him; so when we got to Patna we bought a length of bare copper wire, and got four wooden stakes made;

about 12 inches long and $1\frac{1}{2}$ inches square, with sharpened points for driving into the ground. In the top of each stake I had a hole bored, $\frac{3}{4}$-inch diameter, and into this I fixed a piece of vulcanite with a small hole through the centre. This acted as an insulator for the copper wire to pass through.

Next time we camped, I drove one of the stakes into the ground, outside our tent at each corner, and passed the copper wire through them, thus encircling the tent, the wire being about 6 inches above the ground. To the wire I connected our dry batteries, eight of them, and our electric horn, in such a way that any animal or human coming in contact with the wire would sound the horn inside the tent, with a loud and continuous blare.

It was hardly any trouble to fix, and only took about five minutes, and we could sleep in safety.

From Patna we headed for Benares, where we put up at an hotel and stayed for some days, further investigating this famous city, where many arts and crafts are carried on, as I have described in another chapter.

We returned to Calcutta by train.

CHAPTER 30

Piccadilly

Shortly after returning from my motor cycle tour I met with a bad accident; my front wheel hit a dog which was running across the road, and caused me to somersault with my machine. I was picked up and taken to the hospital.

There, drugs were a godsend to me.

The three months or more that I was laid up were happy ones.

I underwent two serious operations, but I felt no pain to speak of. I lived in a happy, dreamy state, in which almost every minute was luxurious ease and contentment.

Mulki visited me daily, and brought me my drugs, mixed strictly according to directions and ready for injecting.

My syringe and a small phial I was easily able to conceal in my pillow.

Even so, some of the staff knew that I was taking drugs I think, although nothing was said.

I was content with small doses of drugs; just sufficient to produce a happy state of mind, and pleasant dreams, and the banishing of all pain or discomfort.

The time soon passed away, and I was well again and getting about, but not on my motor cycle. I found that I had developed a distinct distaste for this form of pastime, and I therefore sold my machine, and bought a pony and small dog cart. I joined the buggy brigade, and came in for a good deal of chaff from my motor-cycling friends.

My time in India was getting short now; my three years were nearly up, and I was returning to England.

I wondered if I would ever see India again; that land of mystery and enchantment, with its beautiful temples and palaces, its crowded bazaars and curious native customs. I doubted it.

Mulki had gone to the Central Provinces, to pay a final visit to her family. She was going to stay a month, and then come on to England later. I had made all arrangements for her passage with "Cook's."

She, poor girl, would probably be leaving her family for good, never to see them again.

Life is very sad sometimes. Often, now, I saw her silently crying, and I couldn't do anything to help her. We must all part with our loved ones some day, and it is the thought of this which makes death so bitter.

On the voyage home I again gave up using drugs.

Arrived in England, I first had a good holiday, and then got employment as a draughtsman with a well known steelworks on the Teeside.

Meanwhile Mulki arrived in London, and I went through to meet her, and bring her home.

For about a year I worked on the Teeside with the firm mentioned, but was on the look-out all the time for a chance to get to China.

One day I had a letter from a firm with whom I had previously been employed, asking me whether I would care to go out to the west coast of Africa.

It was a job as engineer at a gold mine on the Gold Coast. The pay was very good, and moreover the term was only for twelve months, of which only eight months' actual service was required, the other four months being leave on full pay.

This was, no doubt, on account of the very unhealthy climate.

I decided to accept, chiefly because I wanted to see the African jungle; I wanted to see whether I could find any plant similar to the Sumatran one from which I had made the wonderful drug I had brought home; besides, I was confident that the climate would not affect me. Eight months was nothing, I felt that I could thrive in any jungle in the world.

There was something about jungle life which was very attractive to me.

Before sailing, I thought I would have a week's holiday in London, and I took Mulki with me, as I was leaving her in England this time.

For some time I had been using drugs again, moderately, with the exception of occasional week-end experiments, so now I thought it was a good opportunity to indulge freely. Of course I knew that in this country one had to be more careful than was necessary when out in the wild, but anyway I decided that I had my wonderful drug No. 2, which would almost immediately bring me back to normal, no matter what drugs I was under the influence of. Even the grotesque drunkenness and distortion of all the senses produced by hashish I could banish at once and become cold sober.

I decided to have a good holiday, and one day Mulki and I arrived in London and put up at a private hotel near King's Cross.

Usually, when taking very heavy doses, I stayed at home, but one night I went out for a stroll. I was pretty well lit up by frequent doses of cocaine, morphia, and "cannabis indica."

As I walked down the road I felt that it was glorious just to be alive. Everything, even the least thing around me, was a happiness.

I could hear a faint, far off kind of music, and I could feel the vibrations of the earth beneath my feet, as though a huge pulse was beating in its interior.

I was in no sense intoxicated, as drugs do not affect one that way. I could walk and move about with the same ease and certainty as when in a normal state, only the senses were affected in quite a different way.

The people around me seemed to be abnormal in every conceivable way. Some would appear to be about ten feet high, while others would appear to be microscopic in proportions.

At the first glance the person would appear to be quite normal in every way, and only when I looked longer than a few seconds did the change take place, and then, quite suddenly, but somehow imperceptibly.

There was a dog coming towards me, and as I looked it changed to a crocodile, then, as it passed me, it was once more a dog.

The strange part of it was, that every object did not appear out of the ordinary, for many, both people and objects, seemed quite natural.

My sense of hearing seemed to be playing tricks also, for simple ordinary sounds, like people speaking or walking, or the traffic around me, became sometimes quite fantastic in effect.

All the time there were spirit-like shapes floating around me, constantly coming and going, and being replaced by fresh ones.

I heard a clock chiming the hour, and the first two or three notes seemed natural in tone, but the next few seemed as loud as though I was in the clock tower, while the remainder died away until I could hardly hear them.

I strolled along seemingly in fairyland. I was in an intense condition of happiness, without a single care in the world; I seemed to be walking on air.

I thought that I would see Piccadilly, and I went down into the Underground, and approached a ticket window. Standing at the window there was a Hindu, so I just waited behind until I heard the clerk say, "Where to?"

Naturally I thought that he was speaking to the Hindu.

No reply came.

Thinking that perhaps he could not speak English, I spoke to him in Hindustani, asking him where he wished to go, but again no reply.

I next turned to the booking clerk, and said, "This gentleman, I think, wants a ticket somewhere."

"Which gentleman?" said the clerk.

"This gentleman," I said, pointing to the Hindu, who had not moved.

At once I noticed a strange, scared look appear on the clerk's face, and I put out my hand and felt only air.

"I want a ticket to Piccadilly," I said hurriedly, putting down the money.

Looking back I saw the booking clerk craning his neck round the window, when just then some more passengers came along and he had to attend to them.

I never knew whether he thought I was drunk or was just having a joke.

I walked down Piccadilly. It was a blaze of light from the illuminated signs, and brilliantly-lighted shop fronts, and the pavements were crowded with well-dressed people bent on enjoying themselves; each one a little world in themselves, with their hopes and fears and desires.

No two are absolutely alike; never, probably, from the beginning of the human race, has there ever been two persons who were absolutely exact duplicates of each other.

Dozens of good-looking girls passed me, some with a smile, while some murmured "Dear."

Why do girls call a perfect stranger "Dear"?

I have had this experience many times, not only in England, but in other parts of the world.

I wonder whether, if I had a nose like "Cyrano," I would still be "Dear."

A young girl approached, and when about to pass me, she slightly smiled, and half stopped.

I saw her face and noticed her eyes, and I knew that she was a cocaine addict.

I felt a great pity for her; she was little more than a child. I say child, although she might have been eighteen, because I felt old in experience. I had seen life in many aspects, yet I was only thirty-two years of age.

The girl was small and dark, and refined looking, with nice eyes; but the pupils were dilated until they nearly filled the whole iris. Of course this effect could be produced by a drop or two of belladonna, but there were other signs besides the dilated pupils which told me that it was not belladonna, but cocaine.

I glanced at her nose.

No, I decided, she did not snuff the cocaine, like the great majority of cocaine addicts. Nothing so crude; she must inject it.

I stopped and spoke. I felt myself interested in her, or was it the medical aspect that interested me?

I suggested some supper, and she agreed, but in turn suggested that I should go with her to her flat and she would cook some steak and chips and make some coffee.

I looked at her face, it had such a pathetic little droop, like that of a tired child, and her eyes had a hopeless expression although she had had cocaine, and I knew that the drug was beginning to lose its effects; that she was caught like a rat in a trap, and was scared.

I decided to treat her as one would a sick child, and help her all I could without any other thought.

Arrived at her flat, which was a single bed-sitting-room of fair size, with a gas stove in one corner, and a fire ready laid for lighting in the grate, she became more cheerful, and started to cook the supper.

I looked round the room, and noticed that it was well kept and comfortably furnished. It was on the first floor in a building up one of the streets behind Shaftesbury Avenue. The lower portion of the building appeared to be shops, and the passage and stairs were dark and without carpets, although the room itself was cosy.

I was hungry and made a good meal, but I noticed that she ate hardly anything. She had been out of the room for a few minutes and came back with an increased brightness of her eyes, and appeared to be full of life, and bubbling over with good spirits.

"How long have you been taking cocaine?" I said.

A startled look appeared on her face for a moment. "What makes you think that I take cocaine?"

"Well," I said, "I know a good deal about cocaine, and to me the signs are easily recognised."

"Are you a doctor?" she asked.

"No, I am not a doctor, but I have used cocaine, and other drugs, for over ten years."

"For ten years? Why you don't look as though you have taken drugs for long, you look so healthy," she said. "How do you do it? Perhaps you only take very small doses, occasionally."

I told her something about my system, and I saw a new light come into her eyes.

"Oh! if only I could give it up," she said. "I have tried so hard, many times, and I have lost hope."

I studied her appearance, and weighed up her natural temperament in my mind, and then I promised to help her to get rid of the habit.

I asked her how long she had taken cocaine, and also her usual dose, and the quantity she took in a day, and although I felt certain of her answer, I asked if she used any other drugs besides cocaine.

I found that she was a comparative beginner, and that she used only cocaine; that she could not sleep, and had hardly any appetite, both of which failings quickly tend to undermine the health.

Obviously the first thing to be done was to restore her appetite, and to produce sound sleep, both of which can be done at once by substituting for the cocaine other drugs or combinations at meal times, and opium smoked at bed time, failing which, as this is not very convenient in England for an inexperienced person, morphia injected.

"Let me see your syringe," I said to the girl.

She produced her syringe, one of those with a leather plunger, and with leather washers in the screw caps. Traps for germs and septic accumulations.

"Do you ever take it apart and thoroughly clean it with carbolic or sublimate? "I asked.

She did not.

Her system was becoming poisoned by septic matter, while her vitality was quickly being sapped by loss of sleep, and lack of adequate nourishment.

The continual state of exhilaration produced by the cocaine quickly used up the body's store of energy without it being made good.

When I left her she had regained hope.

Next day I prepared a careful schedule of instructions for her to follow, which would enable her to give up the drug.

It was best so, because drug taking is not for the inexperienced.

As I said before, the indulgence in drugs can produce a life of happiness such as is rarely experienced on this earth, but only for those who are prepared to spend as much time on studying and experimenting with them on themselves as one would give to one of the learned professions.

I never saw the girl again after my second visit, but I was confident that she would have little difficulty in giving up the cocaine habit if she followed my instructions, which were carefully considered, and based on many factors connected with her condition, temperament and drugging method.

It is true that the drug I discovered in Sumatra would have made the result quite sure, but I had none of this to spare; my supply was limited, I wished to save it.

CHAPTER 31

The Gold Coast

I sailed from Liverpool on an Elder Dempster liner and presently arrived at Sekondi, on the Gold Coast, calling at Lagos, commonly known as the White Man's Grave. A beautiful place as regards scenery but not otherwise.

Sekondi, I found, was a small native town, with a few European buildings and good roads, but a bad beach, with great rolling combers coming in all the time, making the landing in the native surf boats fairly exciting, as there was always a good chance of being spilled.

The first night I stayed in Sekondi, being taken to a small hotel by the agent of the company, who presented me with a sovereign for expenses. I was surprised.

In the next room to mine there were three fellows who were going to the same gold mine as myself.

They evidently were enjoying themselves, for they gradually became roaring and singing drunk, and about midnight they came into my room, sat on the bed and started singing a chorus at the top of their voices. As I wanted to get rid of them, I proposed that we should go downstairs into the parlour and have some drinks.

I ordered a couple of bottles of brandy and insisted that they should drink level with me.

Spirit, or in fact any kind of liquor, had not much effect on me, consequently they were all soon asleep and snoring on the floor or elsewhere.

Next morning we proceeded by train through the jungle, and across country to the gold mine, which was a regular camp in the heart of the jungle.

There were many Europeans working there, men of all nations, but chiefly Swedes, Germans, Italians, and English, and they were a pretty rough crowd.

A fight there meant kicking and gouging, and jumping on a man's face with a heavy pair of boots, or even a knife thrust, and fights were not infrequent.

Each man had a room in a kind of wooden barracks, and they all sat down to meals together in a big mess room.

There were about fifty of us, and we each contributed our share towards the cost of the food, of which great quantities of everything of the best was provided by the one who ran the mess. The nigger cooks were first-class.

At mess, the noise and language were terrific, also the table manners, but I felt at home in the crowd.

133

Although I was a quiet man, I always got on well in a rough crowd, especially among foreigners. A Dutchman told me that I was the only Englishman whom he could ever get on with. I was very popular with all in the mess in spite of the fact that I spoke very little; I never made conversation for the sake of making it.

After being there a few weeks I was sent to a new mine which was being opened up further inland, and the only means of getting there was to walk many miles through the jungle, with some black boys carrying my baggage. Here there were only three Europeans, the manager, a clerk, and a foreman miner, while I became the engineer.

The place consisted of a clearance in the jungle on top of a high hill. Here was the shaft of the mine, with a big iron bucket for descending in, and bringing up the ore. A winding engine, alongside of which was a vertical boiler in a rude kind of wooden shelter.

A little further away there was an air compressor and engine-house for compressing the air, which worked the drills underground.

Nearby was a small workshop and steam pump, while further away was a collection of African huts, for housing the native labourers.

Right on top of the hill were one or two bungalows for the Europeans.

Very shortly after my arrival another man arrived to help me, and we took turns on the day and night shifts. Here I was on my first night shift.

I set off, carrying a hurricane lamp. It was dark and raining and stiflingly hot and I wore nothing but a thin cotton suit. The jungle was all around me, dark and silent; a different jungle to what I had been used to. Here was the country of the lion and hyæna.

As I walked along the winding paths skirting the edge of the jungle, I presently came to the mine and buildings, and I entered the boiler house, where I stood in front of the furnace until my clothes were dry.

I next went into the winding-engine-house, and found the nigger who was in charge of the engine asleep on his driving seat. The engine was not winding at the moment, but the bell might ring any time for the bucket to be drawn up, and the driver was forbidden to sleep at his post.

He had his hand on the throttle, but was sound asleep, and required a cuff to wake him.

He woke up and stared at me, and I saw a peculiar-looking type of West Coast nigger, of a dull coal black; even his eyes could hardly be distinguished, as the cornea was nearly the same colour as his skin. His head was coconut shaped, while his features were thoroughly vicious and cruel-looking. A bad type of face, full of superstition and ignorance.

"What for you sleep?" I asked.

"I no lib for sleep, Sah, I stand by at engine boy, Sah. Plenty too much savvy," he replied, with an attempted look of offended dignity.

All the time he was speaking I had a feeling that there was some horrible quality of mind lurking behind his skull, some quality which was abnormal and not to be understood by a human being, producing in me the same sensation as a cobra would.

I cautioned him, and left him muttering to himself in his native dialect.

Next I visited the compressor house and saw that all was working properly there.

I sat down and lighted my pipe, and reflected on what a place I had come to. Everything had an unfriendly aspect here; dark and menacing. Even the natives were different; not like simple negroes, nor the intelligent Malays, nor the happy-natured Chinese coolies; neither were they like the mild Hindus.

There was something cruel, superstitious and ignorant in their countenances.

I could imagine them practising fearful rites and tortures and "Ju Ju."

I had been told tales of the horrors of this place. The blackwater fever, the jigger insect which bores into the sole of the foot and proceeds to lay eggs, multiplying until the whole foot is like a sponge.

The little worm which gets under the skin, and then starts to grow among the veins and sinews, extending inwards several inches, and ultimately having to be extracted surgically.

The vengeful character of the natives, who put powdered glass in one's food and cause death by ulceration.

The centipedes, scorpions and snakes, and a species of poisonous spider which causes a most horrible and painful death by the slow coagulation of all the blood in the body, producing hours of agony before the end.

However, I reflected that eight months would soon pass away. I went outside and stood viewing the scene.

The rain had stopped and the moon had risen, casting a ghostly light on the wooden buildings, and the wood-framed headgear with its spidery bracings.

The jungle around and below me looked very beautiful in its many shadows cast by the moonlight. It was silent, but I knew that it was full of unseen tragedies among its denizens. A thousand cruelties were taking place at that moment. Eat or be eaten was its motto.

I walked over to the shaft and climbed into the bucket, pressing the electric bell as I did so, and as it commenced to descend I saw the black outline of the engineman through the engine-house window.

The bucket started off slowly, and then began to increase in speed. The sides of the shaft, which were pouring with water, rushed upwards past me with a speed that seemed terrific. I felt that there was something wrong, and was becoming apprehensive, when splash went the bucket with me in it, into the sump at the bottom, having passed the proper landing without stopping.

The bucket had disappeared below the water, but the rope had stopped, and I was clinging to it with my head above water.

After a minute or so the rope started to ascend, and I slid down it into the bucket, which ascended a little way until it came to rest at the landing.

I made up my mind that I would have a further interview with the nigger engineman, for I felt certain that he had done it on purpose because I cuffed him.

These natives can only be ruled by fear; they are treacherous and full of hate.

I stepped out of the bucket, and proceeded along the gallery in a crouched position, as the roof was low. Far off in the distance I could hear the pounding of the drills, as I went along towards the face.

Here I had to climb down into a deep hole in the rock, in which there was a pump working.

Ice cold water was coming down from the roof in a perfect torrent, so that if I was not already wet through I would be in less than half a minute. It was so cold and there was so much water coming down that I was gasping for breath, and were it not that I was carrying an electric torch I would be in darkness immediately.

There was something wrong with the pump, and I had to find out what it was, and presently I saw that two bolts in the stuffing box gland were broken; moreover, they were studded into the metal flange of the stuffing box. They were broken off short, so they would have to be drilled out by hand with a ratchet drill, a long and cold job in this icy water.

It would be a couple of hours' work for both of us to-morrow.

I would have to come back after breakfast with the dayshift man, both of us working in half-hour spells, or perhaps less if we couldn't stand that long in the icy torrent.

We would take turns in coming up, and getting thawed out in front of the boiler furnace.

After visiting the workings and examining some joints in a leaky pipe, which would require re-making, I came to the surface for a nigger fitter and some tools, and after booting the winding-engine nigger out and putting a fitter in charge, I returned below and made the joints. By the time I got back to the surface it was about 4 a.m. and still dark.

I was wet through and shivering with cold, but soon dried off before the boiler.

My next job was the one I disliked more than any other. I had to proceed along a narrow path into the jungle, to a small stream, where there was a steam pump working, pumping up water for the boiler and other services.

I took a nigger with me and a hurricane lamp.

The nigger was scared, and I was not feeling any too happy. It was a strange jungle to me, and as I went along I cast glances over my shoulder to right and left, into the thick grass and tangled undergrowth, and bush on either side.

In a strange jungle, even in the day time, one's nerves are in a state of high tension. There is always the feeling that many unseen eyes are watching, some in fear and others with curiosity or savage hate.

A sudden crack of a tree or a branch echoes through the trees with a sound that is startling, and no matter how steady one's nerves may be it will cause a sudden quickening of the heart for a moment.

At night time, especially if the jungle is silent, and you are without means of defence, the effect is much greater – I was afraid.

Although the distance was not great, I did not linger after I saw that the pump was working properly.

The silence was getting on my nerves, because at such a time the greatest danger is likely to be near, in the shape of some great killer, which scares the smaller creatures into silence.

There were no tigers here, I knew, but I did not know yet what other dangers there might be.

I went back, and was glad to get into the friendly light of the engine-house.

Pay day arrived and the cashier of the company came through from headquarters to pay the natives, and he brought my month's pay also, about four hundred two-shilling pieces. Everyone was paid in this coin, for what reason I do not know; there did not seem to be any other coin here except a few sovereigns, which were difficult to get.

Here I was living in a wooden building whose walls I could put my fist through, with nothing but my luggage to keep any money in. The natives were noted as being great thieves, and I had to be out all night, with no lock on the door, although perhaps a lock would not help much.

It seemed like making a gift of a month's salary to some nigger. However, I thought a bit, and then set off through the jungle to the nearest settlement, several miles away. I then went into the Post Office hut, and changed my money into £1 postal orders, which I sent home.

The months passed away slowly, and I was looking forward to getting away from this place and this dog's life.

The jungle had a rotten, decaying smell, and everything was damp, so much so that a pair of boots would be white with fungus if left for a few days without cleaning. Great colonies of black ants crawled up the verandah posts, and I found a long line of them moving across my floor when I woke up in the morning.

It was necessary to stand the legs of my bed and table in tins partly filled with kerosene, otherwise I would be eaten while I slept. Centipedes and great spiders slithered all over the place and disappeared in every crevice; while scorpions were not far away.

In the morning I woke up soaked with perspiration, it was so hot and clammy; there were no electric fans or cooling drinks here.

Everyone except myself took large quantities of quinine regularly. I took my drugs, and I could laugh at all discomforts, and feared no fever.

It is true that many white men drink themselves into D.T.'s in this country.

The West Coast of Africa. Truly the White Man's Grave.

It was pitch dark as I set off for another turn on the night shift and it was stiflingly hot, without a breath of air stirring. Everything was damp and clammy.

I had to take my midnight meal, and a can of tea with me, as, once on duty, I was not supposed to leave the site until 6 a.m.

I looked round my room, and then towards the dark jungle and I felt reluctant to leave. I did not know why; perhaps there is an unknown quality of sense or instinct, which warns us of some pending calamity. Some sixth sense which perhaps was highly developed in prehistoric days, but which now has become almost lost. A survival of bygone ages, when life was savage and full of danger, and nature provided this instinct as a protection.

Anyhow, I felt strangely reluctant to leave my room, and the idea suddenly struck me how easy it would be for any nigger to walk in and help himself.

My thoughts kept turning to the matter throughout the night, and at 6 a.m. I hurried back half expecting something to have happened.

Sure enough, when I arrived, wet and filthy, and pushed open the door of my room, I got a shock.

The room was stripped bare, with the exception of the bedstead, table, and chairs.

My boxes, and suitcases, and all my clothes and books had been taken. Even the bedclothes, mosquito net, towels, and every one of my possessions were gone. There was not even a piece of soap left.

I was stripped clean, and my drugs were gone too, as they were in a suitcase; I only had about a day's supply on me.

Here I was in the heart of the jungle, with only what I stood up in, and no chance of replacing most of my things, especially my drugs, and when I thought of the latter I felt a cold perspiration trickle down under my arms.

It is a terrible thing to be suddenly deprived of drugs even in a civilised country, but here it would be ten times worse.

Now was the time when the new drug would have been a godsend, but unfortunately the little which I had brought out with me was gone too.

I had not even a shirt to change into, nor a towel to wash with.

I went round to my friend's room, and helped myself to a wash and some breakfast, and then set off to walk to "headquarters" to see what I could get there.

I managed to get a few necessary clothes, but no drugs beyond a little raw opium.

I went back to the mine, with a faint hope that some of my things might have been mysteriously found, as I had offered a reward of fifty two-shilling pieces to any of the nigger servants if they could find the small suitcase which contained my drugs and all my papers.

Seemingly a miracle had occurred. The coolies had searched (so they said) all round the jungle and found the suitcase. The drugs and papers were intact. A tin trunk of tools, and drawing instruments and one or two odds and ends which would be of no value to a nigger, were also found.

Among my papers there was about £40 in postal orders, while among the tools, secreted in the hollow of a piece of copper pipe, was over £30 in sovereigns, which I had brought out with me.

Do you know what it is like to come in for a great fortune?

If you do, you will know my feeling then. I would not have exchanged those things, then lying on the floor of my room, for any sum of money. When I turned into bed I fairly made it creak, I felt so happy.

The thieves, who may have been some of the servants or their relations, probably first carried all the things out of the room into the surrounding jungle, and then started breaking the boxes open, and scattering out all the things which were of no use to them, to save themselves the trouble of carrying extra weight.

The tools and papers were of no use to them, of course, and as for the drugs, they would not know what they were, as they were in bottles, labelled in English medical terms.

After this experience, I carried my drugs with me always, fitted into the top of my helmet. The postal orders I sent off home at once, and the sovereigns I left hidden in the piece of copper pipe among the tools.

I lost all my clothes and other possessions, however.

The native camp here was very different from any that I had been used to before, as most of the niggers lived in a hut of their own with their wives and families, and not in big bongsals. As far as I could find out, there were hardly any drugs used among them, though many of them maddened themselves with trade gin.

The young women were fine looking and well built. They were naturally proficient in the art of attracting the opposite sex, by the way they looked at him, and the way they lounged and displayed their figures, and moved about with a panther-like glide and a grin of gleaming white teeth and glittering eyes.

I was very much disappointed in the West Coast of Africa, and I was leaving without the slightest regret, or the desire to ever see it again.

Where is all the romance one reads of in the many novels dealing with this part of the world? I think it must be chiefly in the author's imagination!

I never saw a lion, or the slightest trace of one, nor a witch doctor, neither did I ever come across any "Ju Ju."

CHAPTER 32

Rio-de-Janeiro

I arrived back in Liverpool and found Mulki waiting for me on the landing stage.

She was rather excited about an adventure she had just had in Liverpool, the day before I arrived. She had by this time learned to speak fairly decent English, and could travel by herself, but she was very simple in some ways.

It seemed that she had been walking about the town looking at the shops, and I expect going into many and examining most of their stock, as was her habit, when two young ladies got into conversation with her.

Of course Mulki told them all about herself and her friends, and also mentioned one who had come to live in Liverpool. "Did either of the young ladies know where this friend lived?"

Both of the girls knew the person quite well, and Mulki, in her simplicity, believed them when they offered to take her and show her the house.

They took her through miles of streets, until they arrived at a slum district. By this time Mulki was beginning to be suspicious, and when the girls stopped before a house and invited her in, telling her that they would bring the lady in question, she turned and ran as hard as she could, no doubt to the amazement of passers by.

She had an idea that they intended to rob her, but I had an idea that their object was something quite different; an idea which I did not mention to Mulki.

We decided to have a good holiday, and as I wanted to see many places of historical interest in England, we visited most of the cathedral towns and other old places.

I soon saw that Mulki was getting bored, so I took her to Blackpool, a place which she was never tired of talking about for ever afterwards.

Then I took a position as draughtsman in Rio-de-Janeiro; going out alone, and intending to send for Mulki when I got settled, if I found the place suitable for her. Each time I left her I missed her more than ever.

Rio, I found to be a place with beautiful suburbs of picturesque Portuguese villas, nestling all round the shores of the wide bay, which at night looked lovely with the lights of the shipping strung out for miles around.

Unfortunately it was a very unhealthy place, for Yellow Fever was raging in the city, and hundreds of deaths per day were taking place from this, the worst of all fevers. Ships were lying in the bay without crews, and people slunk about the streets with faces on which could be read the stamp of fear, avoiding contact with each other as much as possible.

Extensive improvements to the harbour were being made, and the work was disturbing the sewage at the bottom of the bay, sewage which had been running into it for many years, and this was supposed to be one of the chief causes of the outbreak.

Engineers on the harbour works were dying off quickly, and fresh men were arriving nearly every week from England to replace them.

Any person suffering from any kind of illness which was not clearly defined was liable to be carted off to the Pest Hospital to be kept under observation, where, if the case was not Yellow Fever, it very soon would be so.

I came intimately in contact with Yellow Fever, and know what a terrible disease it is, worse even than the plague, of which I saw many deaths in India; in fact I saw my own servant lying dead in the garden, when I came home at midday for tiffin, once in Calcutta.

Death from Yellow Fever takes place very suddenly.

One young fellow was sitting at the same table as myself one evening at dinner, when he suddenly started to vomit black-coloured bile, which is one of the first symptoms of the pest, and is called "The Black Vomit."

In a few hours' time he was dead, although when he sat down to dinner he seemed as well and jolly as any one in the company.

Rio-de-Janeiro is a beautiful place to look at, but not to live in.

Neither in Brazil or West Africa had I any opportunity of testing any new species of plants, as I had not my apparatus with me nor had I sufficient privacy for doing so. I confined myself to searching for specimens as near as possible in appearance to the plants which I found in Sumatra.

These I dried and powdered up and put in bottles for future testing.

I was glad to leave Rio, as it was no place to bring Mulki out to, and I did not want to be separated from her. Back in England once more, I got employment as a constructional steel draughtsman in Middlesbrough with one of the greatest firms of steel makers in England.

All the time I was on the lookout for a position in China, and after about seven or eight months with the steel firm, I succeeded.

An advertisement appeared in the *Engineer* for a chief draughtsman, with constructional steel and railway experience, for China, and I applied.

Some months passed away, when one day I got a letter from London from one of the most famous consulting engineers in England, asking me to call on them.

On going up to see them, I was lucky enough to be engaged as chief draughtsman for a railway in China.

This position I held for seven years, serving out two terms of contract. But I am anticipating my story.

Travelling by rail to Marseilles and from there on one of the largest P. & O. mail boats, we stopped at all the usual ports of call, which I had seen many times, but in addition, Hong Kong, which I had never seen before, and finally arrived at the wonderful city of Shanghai.

It was summer time (June, 1906) and very hot, but hot or cold was all one to me, I could make myself comfortable and accommodate myself to any weather.

I had arrived in China, the land of my dreams.

CHAPTER 33

The Shanghai Underworld

When I stepped off the jetty on to the Shanghai Bund, I was at once fascinated with the busy scene; the strange mixture between the East and the West. The fine, broad road bordered by a wide green promenade along the river side; the well-built banks and hotels, and the crowds of well-dressed English people, showed by contrast the other half; the picturesque and gaudily-decorated Chinese buildings, the crowds of rickshaw coolies, wheelbarrow men, and the porters carrying heavy loads balanced from the two ends of a pole, as they moved swiftly along at a half run, chanting their everlasting song "Ho. Ho. Ho."

Well-to-do Chinamen in flowered silk coats, with wide sleeves, in which there were pockets for carrying small stoves, in winter; tall Sikh police in turbans; Chinese women in silk trousers hobbling along on tiny crippled feet; business people going to work carrying their teapots, and the junks and gunboats floating in the river; all added something to the novelty of the scene.

I got into a rickshaw, and, leaving my heavy luggage at the Customs jetty, I proceeded to the Palace Hotel, which we reached after about ten minutes' hard going. After tipping the blandly smiling coolie, I found that the jetty where I had landed was right opposite. No wonder he smiled.

That night at dinner I did myself well. In no other part of the world that I have visited have I found the hotels provide such a variety of food.

Not the meagre half dozen dishes one meets with at the average English hotel dinner, but the courses were there by the dozen. Every kind of meat, fish and fowl, cooked in many different ways, came on one after the other.

There were many different dishes provided to suit the many nationals to be found in Shanghai.

With so much to choose from, one hardly knew what to leave out, and even with my appetite I could not sample half the things provided.

In the cool of the evening I strolled out on to the Bund, and the banks of the river, then into the gardens where a band was playing.

Crowds of people of all nations in white or Chinese silk costumes were strolling round or sitting listening to the music. Slender Chinese girls, and tiny Japanese girls with elaborately coiled hair, white socks and wooden sandals, mingled with the crowd.

I moved out of the garden and walked along the river bank, and presently sat down on a seat facing the river.

Chinese junks and sampans, and craft of every description, lay in the stream, making the scene one of great interest.

A pretty little Japanese girl came along, and sat down on the seat, and producing a cigarette put it in her mouth. After waiting a minute without moving, she turned to me and said:

"You have got match?"

I produced a box of matches and gave her a light, thinking that perhaps it was the custom to offer a match to a lady without being asked.

Soon she was talking to me quite freely; telling me all about herself and her family and asking me many questions, so that soon I felt as though I had known her a long time. Japanese girls, I think, are freer and broader-minded than almost any other race of women, and are therefore charming.

We talked quite a time, then presently she got up, bowed, and toddled away.

I wandered down a street leading off the Bund and running parallel to Nanking Road. Its name I forget. It was brilliantly lighted. Chinese shops with wonderfully ornamented fronts, and scores of Chinese lanterns, added to the gayness of the picture.

Chinese theatres and tea houses with open fronts met my eye on either side of the street, while festive groups of Chinese were sitting on the overhanging balconies above.

As I walked along I saw at the entrance of numerous courts leading into the streets, groups of young Chinese girls, with highly-painted faces, and costumes splendid, standing chatting among themselves, meanwhile eyeing the passers-by out of the corners of their eyes.

Most of them appeared to be girls of from twelve to eighteen years of age, the latter age being considered quite matronly for girls of this profession.

When a likely customer approached, they stood with a demure expression and downcast eyes.

Most of these girls, to all intents and purposes, were little better than slaves.

At the age of ten to twelve they would be bound by contract, that is sold for a fixed sum of money paid to their parents, to remain an inmate of the house until they reach the age of twenty.

The house would generally be run by an old Chinese woman who probably, in her young days, started in the same way as the girls.

In this quarter of the town these houses catered chiefly for the better class of Chinese.

There were quarters in Shanghai where almost every house in the street was in this profession, and each was a class apart.

For instance, down by the creek and leading off Seward Road, nearly every house facing the creek was licensed and patronised chiefly by sailors and naval ratings.

Many sanguinary battles had taken place down here when a party of Japanese and American navy men happened to meet, and on one occasion an American sailor was found with his throat cut after one of these fights. The Americans generally used bottles or clubs.

In Shanghai, the different Nationals lived in their own quarter chiefly; there was French town, where one might almost fancy himself in France; also the Japanese quarter and the Chinese city.

Shanghai, on the surface, appeared to be a highly respectable city, but to anyone who could look below the surface, it would be revealed as a city in which vice flourished to a greater degree than in any other part of the world.

To some extent this was accounted for by the fact that it had a large floating population of all nations. It was one of the show places, visited by large numbers of very wealthy people who were prepared to spend freely.

Also the Chinaman is by nature so clever, secretive and cunning, that where money is to be made, he can carry on illegal practices right under the eyes of the authorities without being suspected.

Whatever country I have resided in, I have always made it a practice to become friendly with the natives, and by this means I have seen more of the hidden side than I would have done otherwise.

Shanghai is a city where enormous quantities of cocaine, morphia and opium were used (I am speaking of the year 1906–7), specially cocaine, which could be bought from the Chinese chemists by the sixteen ounce bottle.

I soon became friendly with one or two well-to-do Chinese who used drugs, and who knew the underworld of the city thoroughly, so that soon I had the entry of places of which very few Europeans had any idea of the existence.

There was a gambling house situated not far from Nanking Road. It was a highly respectable-looking building, but even so, it had come under suspicion, and had been raided, I believe, more than once, but never had anything suspicious been found.

On each occasion several people, mostly Chinese, and all apparently friends, had been found sitting round a table drinking tea; whereas one minute before a game of "Fan Tan" had been in full operation for high stakes.

How was this done?

The place was fitted up mechanically for a quick change.

The table on which the gambling was being done was suspended from the ceiling by four wires, running through the ceiling into the room above; apparently a private apartment. The table had no legs, and the underside of it exactly matched the ceiling, fitting into a recess, so that when drawn up quickly by mechanical means with all evidence of the game, it couldn't be distinguished from the surrounding ceiling.

Even the pattern of the underside of the table matched the ceiling, and looked like an ornamental centre-piece.

The tea table was always in the room, ready set out with tea pots and cups, etc., and at each corner of the table stood an ornament on which the gambling table rested when it came down from the ceiling. The winding apparatus was set in motion by simply pressing a button.

Outside of the settlement, in Chinese territory, practically any kind of vice can be carried on, as the British, or rather the European powers, had no authority.

There were many places in Shanghai where gambling was carried on, especially on the rivers and creeks, about which I will have something to say later.

Among my Chinese acquaintances was one whom I will call "Wong." He was a merchant in a large way of business; well educated and speaking English perfectly, having been at one of the Universities in England.

He was a confirmed opium smoker and cocaine sniffer, and he knew the underworld of Shanghai and many of the treaty ports thoroughly.

I wished to see and learn everything that was new and strange, therefore I went about with him a good deal on secret excursions.

One night Mr. Wong said to me: "Let us go to the pictures."

I was not particularly interested, but as he seemed to want to go, I agreed, so we called a couple of rickshaws, and started to ride along Nanking Road. After proceeding some distance, I called him and said, "Here, there are no cinemas along this way as far as I know. Where are we going?"

'There is a new place out "Bubbling Well" way,' he said.

I thought it strange, because it is a district of fine houses chiefly, many of them mansions. Still I did not say anything more; he appeared to know all about it.

After driving more than a mile out, we turned into the grounds of a large private house, or what seemed so.

"What place is this?" I said. "It does not look much like a cinema."

"Wait a bit," replied Mr. Wong.

The entrance hall was like the hall of a large private house and was sumptuously furnished. A well-dressed man, who appeared to be either a Greek or Turk or some similar nationality, came out and shook hands with Mr. Wong, who introduced me, and I noticed that Mr. Wong handed the other two ten dollar notes.

We were led into a small room, in which there were several people, mostly Chinese, although there were one or two foreigners of both sexes there. Here, drinks and drugs of all kinds were being served by an attendant at stiff prices. Presently we were conducted to a large room which was fitted up as a Cinema Hall.

It was almost in darkness, but I could see about twenty or thirty people sitting on comfortably upholstered seats.

There was a picture being shown at the moment, and when I looked at the screen I got a shock.

The picture was horribly lewd, not just ordinarily suggestive, but absolutely as lewd as it is possible to make, and it had evidently been prepared by a past master in this kind of thing.

After the film was finished, the lights were put on, and Mr. Wong left me and went over to some friends.

I could see that there were a good few ladies among the audience, and one of them, a young woman of some continental nationality who spoke English with an accent, came and sat down beside me, first asking for my permission with a wide smile, which exposed three or four gold teeth. She evidently took this as an introduction, for she continued the conversation.

Another picture, even worse than the last one, was put on the screen, after which the young lady moved away to another seat, probably thinking that I was no sport.

Upstairs there was dancing, and other things going on, and there was one room in which several people were smoking opium.

The house itself stood in large grounds of its own, with a wide carriage drive up to the door.

I noticed, however, that the big iron gates at the entrance were kept locked, and had to be opened by a porter in a small lodge, and it was a fair distance from the gates to the front door. No doubt there would be electric signals from the lodge to the house.

CHAPTER 34

The Chinese City

It was a beautiful evening towards the end of September; the time when the evenings are beginning to become comfortably cool, and when the European population of Shanghai are beginning to brace up after the long and stifling hot summer.

I had just had a good dinner in French town, where I often used to go when I wanted a perfectly cooked and served meal with many tasty little side dishes.

I had had a comfortable dose of mixed drugs, and was in a mood in which strange sights and scenes can best be enjoyed.

I wandered down in the vicinity of the creeks and the river. Great junks of strange shape were moored along the banks; their shape, and their large sails made of bamboo matting, were exactly the same as has been in use for over a thousand years. They had an eye painted on each side of the bow, as no Chinese pilot would feel safe without these, the boat would most certainly come to grief – it would be blind.

There were smaller junks, which were sailed almost entirely by a family – father, mother, children and near relations.

Sometimes three generations might be seen on board, including a wrinkled and toothless old grandmother, who seemed to have more authority than anyone, and to whom all bowed, listening to her abuse with the greatest meekness.

Along the creeks were moored many hundreds of sampans each with painted eyes, and a grass-covered shelter in the stern of which an entire family lived, hardly ever putting a foot ashore. They were born in the sampan, and would die there. Smaller sampans handsomely decorated, and with silk curtains, lay quietly moored all day, with the curtains drawn close, but at night time these sampans might be seen gliding slowly along the creeks and canals, while peeping out of the curtains would be a young Chinese girl plying her profession.

In some parts of the waterways there were whole streets of moored boats all plying this most ancient profession in the world.

China is a place of canals, and the whole country is a network of waterways, so that it is possible, I believe, to travel by water to any part of the country, for thousands of miles. The scene during the daytime on the canals and creeks was a wonderful one. Thousands of traders of every description were moving about, plying their trade.

There was the barber's boat coming along in which Chinamen were being shaved, and the restaurant boats, in which he could get a meal. There were even beggars and lepers in rags soliciting alms.

In some parts of the creeks and backwaters the boats were packed so close together that it was possible to travel by simply stepping from one boat on to the next.

I passed a large mill which was just knocking off work. A long line of wheelbarrow coolies were waiting outside. The barrows have a large wooden wheel, with a platform on each side of it.

Presently hundreds of Chinese women came out of the mill and took their seats on the wheelbarrows, six on a barrow – three on each side, sitting back to back – and then the long line set off. Most of the women had small feet, and were unable to walk much. Their toes had been doubled under the foot, when they were little children, and the foot bound in that position, until the toes had grown into the sole of the foot.

When one sees a pretty Chinese girl, one tries not to remember her feet. Not all are like this, however. There are some who have good shaped feet, and they are ashamed of them. Their parents have neglected them as children.

The months rolled on, and summer passed and winter came. It was cold; a biting cold such as is rarely experienced in England. We Europeans went about in heavy, fur-lined coats and gloves, but I noticed the poor rickshaw coolies still wearing the same clothes they had worn all the broiling hot summer. One sees them pulling their rickshaw through the snow blizzard, dressed in a thin cotton pair of knee length pants, and thin cotton coat, with nothing underneath.

Their feet and legs are bare, although the snow may be a foot deep. Inside the rickshaw may probably be seen a European wrapped and muffled up in furs, but still with a blue nose and face.

How do these coolies do it, especially as their food is chiefly rice, and perhaps only two meals a day? Is it that they are a hardier race than we are?

I have observed them closely in the bitterest weather, and I did not notice any signs of shivering, or that their bare hands which gripped the rickshaw shaft were cold.

Often their coats had no buttons on, and were wide open, exposing their bare chests and stomachs to the cold wind and snow; a snow which was dry and fine like dust, and cut like glass. The cold was so intense that, although I had a big fire in my bedroom, the water in the jug on the washstand at the other side of the room generally had a cake of ice on top of it.

One day Mr. Wong took me to see the Chinese city. This is quite distinct and some distance from Shanghai proper.

It is an old walled Chinese city; a place of smells and narrow courts, where horrible punishments are inflicted and carried out in public, at the will of the Chinese Mandarin governing it.

At the time of which I am writing, there were places in it where a European would not be alive five minutes unless he was accompanied by a Chinaman who was known.

Here the fumes of opium smoking met one at every turn. They issued from the open doors of houses and shops, and the very air seemed to be flavoured with a faint smell of burning opium.

The narrow streets and passages, so narrow that there was just room for two people to pass each other, were full of beggars with hideous mutilations, and distorted limbs, and lepers, who were hardly recognisable as human beings, might frequently be seen.

Mr. Wong led the way up one of these narrow passages, the middle of which was an open drain or channel, littered with garbage and refuse, so that we had to crowd close to one side to prevent ourselves falling in.

About half way along the passage we turned in at an open doorway, and into a dimly-lighted room or cellar, containing a great variety of strange looking stuff, most of which smelt powerfully.

Passing through this place, we came to another room behind, in which there was sitting an old Chinaman.

After a little talk in Chinese from Mr. Wong, the old man led the way up some stairs, which were somewhat like a wide ladder, into a room above.

When my eyes became accustomed to the dim light of the place, I saw that we were in a large room entirely bare of furniture. On the boards of the floor were stretched, alongside of each other, about a dozen grass mats, and on most of them there was a Chinese coolie.

Some of them were already lying insensible like dead bodies, while others were still smoking opium.

Some were filthy and in rags, and I noticed that some were quite young boys, although there were old men too.

"This is how the poor coolie smokes his opium," said Mr. Wong. "Each man, for the sum of ten cents, is given a mat to lie on, and the use of a pipe, lamp, and skewer, and a little opium smeared thinly on a kind of thick green leaf. The opium is not pure opium, it is called 'Tye'."

It is a mixture of opium and the leavings or residue of opium which has already been smoked by more fortunate or more wealthy individuals.

'The very poor among the customers, who are unable even to afford the ten cents, may purchase for a few cash (a fraction of a cent) a pellet of "Tye" which they swallow.'

Discussing the matter with Mr. Wong, we came to the conclusion that one in every four of the male population of China used opium in some form or other.

This was before the Chinese Government issued the order for the discontinuation of opium smoking, with the death penalty for disobedience.

There are some terrible punishments in China for the Chinese, and I think "Ling Hi" is the worst. It means, "The death of a thousand cuts," and the penalty is carried out in public.

The victim is fastened by the feet on to a pedestal, and the executioner, who is an expert at his business, can snip off an eyelid or a lip with one stroke of the sword, or knife. The object is to get in the whole thousand cuts before the condemned dies, and the executioner first proceeds to put in about two hundred cuts on the chest, back and arms; just cutting through the skin in a herring bone pattern.

After the ears, nose, lips, and eyes have been cut out, near the end of the execution, the final cut is given, and the head falls.

It is possible, however, for the executioner to make a slip with his sword and finish the execution much earlier, if he receives a substantial bribe from the friends of the condemned.

Mr. Wong led the way along another passage or street of rather a better class, and stopped before a shop which seemed to deal in food stuff chiefly, but which later I found dealt in other things.

We entered the shop, and Mr. Wong said a few words to the proprietor, who invited us to be seated and offered us tea. Leaving us for a while, we waited patiently for about ten minutes when we were conducted upstairs into a room.

Sitting on a long form of peculiar pattern there were several little Chinese girls, whose ages seemed to vary from about twelve to sixteen or seventeen years.

They were painted, and dressed in gorgeous costumes, and their feet displayed in front of them, as this was an important point.

"If you are requiring a female servant or housekeeper," said Mr. Wong, "you can buy any of these, from about a hundred dollars upwards. She will then become your property until she is twenty, after which the contract will be finished."

I was not thinking of buying any one of them, and there were some beauties amongst them, but I wanted to learn all I could about the matter.

"Suppose that I bought one of them, and then she ran away," I said, "I suppose I would lose my money?"

"There is no fear of that," said Mr. Wong; "besides where could she run to? Moreover, the proprietor would guarantee to get her back or refund a proportion of the money paid. It would not be wise to run away, and the girl knows that," said Mr. Wong, and I thought that I understood his meaning.

I learnt that many Chinamen, and even others, make these purchases.

Female children have little or no value in China; in fact, many thousands are dipped in the canals and creeks and drowned at birth, and then buried in the countryside. A girl is only a source of expense, and without earning capacity in the country districts, and only a few who are good looking can be sold when they reach the age of ten years or so.

To have a son is to make provision for one's old age, because a Chinaman will work his fingers to the bone to provide for his parents, whom he venerates.

The girls sat in a row, with a shy expression and downcast eyes, all except one, a little girl of about twelve or thirteen, with rather a cheeky countenance.

Every time I looked, I met her eyes staring at me, and for this reason perhaps I looked a few times, as I felt her eyes on my face all the time.

"You likee me?" she said. "Me velly good girl. Talkee Englis allesame white girl. Makee sing song too much good. You buy?"

"How old you belong?" I asked.

"Me no savee. Plenty small feet," she said, sticking her foot out.

Although she was a pretty little thing, when I saw her foot, a cold feeling went down my back. "You no likee stop this side?" I asked.

"Likee this side allitee, me fear too much bad Chinamans makee buy me."

"You no fear me buy?" I said.

"No fear. Me likee you. You velly good."

I felt extremely sorry for this poor little girl, and for a long time after I felt sad.

What would be her ultimate destination?

What do these girls do when they reach the age of twenty and afterwards? There are no pensions, doles, institutions, or charities here. Most of them have no families or relations that they remember or know of. Many don't even know what part of China they were born in.

We made our excuses and left, and I was glad to get back into French town, which is not far from the Chinese city. We had a good dinner at the house of a friend of Mr. Wong.

There we talked and smoked opium till late. The conversation of really well educated Chinamen is very interesting. Most of them know the whole history of their country for 3,000 years back, and many legends extending for many thousands of years earlier than this. Legends which may even be true.

Mr. Wong informed me that there are records to prove that once, many thousands of years ago, Japan and China were all one country, with Japan as the sea coast. As the great mountains and volcanoes now in Japan rose, the land on the other side sank and became the strip of sea in between the two countries.

CHAPTER 35

A Trip to Japan

All this time I had been living at an hotel, but now Mulki had arrived, and we had a small house near the end of the Broadway. It was only a small place of four rooms and a kitchen, but there was a verandah both upstairs and downstairs, and a little coachhouse at the back, in which I used to keep my three-wheeled Rexette motor car. Besides this, there were a couple of small rooms above the coachhouse, which did for my Chinese servant and the amah.

The cool season was just commencing again when I decided to have my holiday in Japan, so one evening, with a young fellow who had arranged to go with me, we went on board one of the Nippon boats.

Nagasaki, our destination, was only about thirty-six hours' journey, so we arrived there on the second morning, to find we were quarantined.

A Japanese official arrived on board and presented the steward with a small tin and a bottle for every passenger, and we were not allowed ashore until the tins and bottles had been filled and taken ashore and tested. Even the ladies had to submit to this embarrassing formula.

Late next night the two of us went ashore, and put up at one of the best hotels, The Belle Vue.

It was late and of course dinner was over long ago, and instead of ordering anything in the hotel, we decided to see if we could get something to eat outside, even if it was midnight when we set off.

Just outside the hotel we met a rickshaw coolie, whom we engaged and sent off for another rickshaw.

One of the coolies spoke English, so we told him we wanted to go somewhere and have supper.

Although it was now nearly half-past twelve, this seemed to be a quite ordinary request, as the coolies started off at once. Presently they stopped before a house which was in darkness, and commenced to hammer on the door.

Soon lights appeared and the door was opened. Entering, we found a large room furnished with tables and chairs and a bar at one end.

After ordering steak and chips and coffee, we sat down and had some whisky from the bar.

The Japanese proprietor now left us, and presently three pretty Japanese girls came in and entertained us with chatter in pidgin English, and joined us in another drink, which was "saki."

We made a good supper, and it was after 2 o'clock when we finally left. Altogether a pleasant evening.

"Well," I said, "shall we get back to the hotel?"

"No," said my friend, "I don't feel much like sleep, let's make a night of it."

Considering that it was after 2 a.m. I thought that we had done very well the first night; however, I told the rickshaw coolies to take us somewhere else.

"Let us have another drink," said my friend, who had already had a good few and was inclined to be festive. I had had the same number of drinks, but did not show any signs.

"Master like look see Geisha?" said the rickshaw coolie.

My friend evidently thought that the Geishas were something quite different from what they really are, and he got quite excited, and would insist on first having another drink, so we knocked somebody else up. Strange to say they supplied us with drinks with great politeness, and without the slightest sign of annoyance at being knocked up at that time in the morning.

We told the rickshaw coolies to take us round to the Geishas.

Arrived at the house, we found it in darkness as I expected, but I was determined to see whether there was any limit to Japanese politeness, so we knocked them up.

Soon lights appeared in the house, and we were invited inside, first being provided with grass slippers which we put on at the door, leaving our boots just inside.

The floors and walls were made of beautifully woven grass, almost as fine as a Panama hat, and spotlessly clean.

We were received with bows and smiles, and conducted upstairs into a room with a similar floor, on which we sat, finding it soft and springy.

Presently the Geishas came in, six of them, beautifully dressed and with elaborately coiled hair decorated with gold ornaments.

Four of them were dancers and the other two played the music. They were very pretty girls, but I can't say that I was particularly struck with the dancing and music.

After the first dance, my friend asked for something to drink, and wine was brought in.

The Geishas, on being invited to join us in the refreshment, squatted down alongside of us, and became quite merry, until my companion, mistaking their attitude, put his hand under the chin of one of them. She appeared startled, and I noticed that the smiles and friendly expressions disappeared, and they started talking in Japanese to each other.

The Geishas are as a rule good class girls, and naturally they were offended.

A few words of apology, and compliments to their dancing, quickly put matters right, and they were friendly again, giving us another dance and song, after which we left, amidst many expressions of good will, and invitations to come and see them again.

While we were being shown out by the proprietor, or whatever he was, I asked him if he could tell me where I could buy some cocaine.

"Yes," he said, "cocaine have got," and going away, he returned with an ounce bottle, for which I paid two yen.

"Come on, let us go home," I said, and in half-an-hour I was in bed, dropping off into a beautiful sleep, preceded by a feeling of intense comfort, with sleep gradually stealing over me, the result of two grains of morphia injected.

A few minutes before, sleep was the least thing I felt like.

Next day we went sight-seeing, engaging the same rickshaw coolies who were waiting outside the hotel.

We told them we wanted to see all places of interest in Nagasaki. After taking us round to several temples and tea houses, we said we didn't want any more tea, neither did we require to see any more temples.

My friend suggested a drink, and I noticed the coolies' faces brighten up. Perhaps they get a bonus. I don't know, but I became suspicious, remembering the Port Said and Calcutta experiences.

We drove along, and presently stopped before a large building. It was about the size of a big hotel, but somehow it did not look like one.

"Do they keep drinks here?" I asked the coolie.

"Yes. Can do," he replied. "Master go inside."

We went up a wide flight of stone steps, and entered, to find ourselves in a large hall room, comfortably furnished in half European and half Japanese style.

There seemed to be nobody in, but just then the coolie ran up the steps and rung the bell, and a middle-aged Japanese lady came out of a side room and greeted us with the usual Japanese politeness.

We explained that we wanted something to drink – beer or whisky.

In a few minutes a young Japanese girl came in with two bottles of beer, and lingered chatting in pidgin English. My suspicions were beginning to be lulled, as everything appeared all right except that the price of the beer was uncommonly high.

I noticed that there were many doors leading into the room we were sitting in; in fact there were doors all round, and it struck me that the rooms behind must be very small.

Glancing round, I saw another girl's face peeping out of one of the doors, then another and another.

In a few minutes the room was full of girls, dozens of them there seemed to be. They were standing all round us, some squatting on the floor at our feet, and the room was full of chatter, mostly among themselves.

I knew that we were the subject of the talk by the way they looked at us, and I felt very much embarrassed.

A few of them spoke a little English and talked to us. Most of these girls were very refined-looking and dainty in appearance, and there were no children of ten and twelve, such as I had seen in this profession, in some parts of the world. Very few of them appeared to be over twenty years of age, as they quickly marry, and become good wives; in fact many girls enter these houses with a view to marriage.

I noticed no coarseness or signs of dissipation amongst any of them, although I could see that a few of them used cocaine.

Well, we had been taken by surprise, and we thought the best thing we could do would be to invite them to have some refreshment, and soon they were all drinking a sweet kind of Japanese red wine, and became quite a merry party, but I noticed no sign of any immodesty.

By and by we made our excuses and departed amidst much bowing, and promised to come and see them again.

Altogether, it seemed just as though we had been on a visit to a friend's house.

An Englishman in Japan was received everywhere with the utmost friendliness and good will. Everyone we met, or came in contact with, seemed eager to show their friendliness. We were their friends and Allies.

I was sitting in my room, and I had just had an excellent dinner followed by a combination of drugs of just the right kind and quantity to produce a perfect state of peace and happiness.

It was a beautiful night and I was sitting with the window open on to the balcony.

My room was in the annexe, and looked down on to a lane at one side of the hotel.

I heard whistling under my window, and looking down from the balcony I saw a pretty little Japanese girl, and recognised her as one of the girls we met when we went to have supper at midnight on the day we arrived.

Of course I must go down and speak to her, and I wondered how she knew where I was staying, and even the room I occupied. I came to the conclusion that the rickshaw coolie was the culprit.

Routing out my friend, we both went down to speak to the young lady.

"You no belong angry, me come whistle?"

"No," I said, "I am very pleased to see you."

She informed us that she was going to the Japanese Picture House with another girl, and would we like to come with them. She would explain all the pictures to us she said.

I can't say that I was much struck with the picture, which chiefly featured a kind of bare-legged and grotesquely costumed bandit, with a long sword, who kept popping out of all kinds of places and killing people. Several times he was chopped and left for dead, but always reappeared apparently no worse for being run through many times.

The young ladies were greatly excited, and kept up a running fire of explanations.

Presently they were assisted by others sitting behind us, but, even so, I had no idea what it was all about. After the performance we went with them to the house and had supper the same as before.

After a few more days in Nagasaki, we decided to move on to Kole, then Tokio and Yokohama.

We spent a pleasant fortnight in Japan. It is a lovely country and the people are fine. The women have perfect freedom, and can associate with the opposite sex as freely as they would with a girl friend without causing any scandal.

I returned to Shanghai with my friend, and as I had still another fortnight's holiday, I took Mulki for a trip. I hired a small motor boat with a cabin, and taking one Chinaman to look after the boat, and my Chinese cook with us, we set off along the canals and waterways to see something of the interior.

The countryside had a very dismal appearance, as there were no hedges or fields as we know them in England.

We passed through flat country extending as far as the eye could see on either side, mostly sodden rice fields, the only roads being narrow mounds or tracks just wide enough for two people to pass each other.

The whole country was dotted over with mounds. Wherever I looked, I could see these graves which may have been there for hundreds of years. They stood as high as one's waist above the ground, and in some spots they existed in clusters, the coffin being laid on the ground, and a mound built over it.

As we got further into the interior, it was like travelling back through time to the middle ages.

The people's mode of life, the appliances they used in their work, the hand labour, their costumes, and in fact practically everything was the same as it was hundreds of years ago.

We stayed all night in an old walled city.

Instead of sleeping on board the boat we decided to sleep inside the walls, and secured a room in an inn or rest house.

To reach our room we climbed a ladder, and entered it through a hole in the floor, covered by a trap door.

There was nothing in the room except a bed, which was a heavy structure made of wood, the bottom, or sleeping place, being made of a kind of plaited grass matting stretched on the framework.

We had brought with us two pillows and some blankets, so we were fairly comfortable.

Beneath us was the common room, which was full of Chinese all talking loudly in the usual sing song tone, and even with the trap door closed, the noise was awful.

We were just dropping off to sleep when up went the trap door, and the old Chinawoman, who appeared to be the boss, came in, followed by three or four men and women.

They stood staring at us for some time and then bowed and shook hands with themselves, the right hand grasping the left hand, and then went down the ladder one after the other.

We talked for some time, trying to fathom the meaning of this strange behaviour, and then settled ourselves down to sleep again.

"Listen," I said to Mulki, "I believe there is somebody coming up again."

Sure enough, the trap door lifted once more, and the old lady came up with another crowd, who went through the same actions as the first lot.

As we hadn't our servant with us we couldn't understand anything they said, although I had a faint idea of the position.

For a long time afterwards we did not venture to sleep, expecting another visit, but they did not come up again.

Next morning, when the boy came up with some tea and fruit, I enquired the meaning of this strange happening.

"Chinawoman, she chargee five cents look see Master, Missie," he replied in a matter of fact voice, as though the happening was quite in order.

As we walked through the streets, or entered shops, we had an interested audience with us all the time.

People came to doors, or craned their necks out of windows to see us, while a crowd of beggars and horribly-distorted cripples followed, holding out their hands, and we found that to give them anything only increased their eagerness, and attracted others.

Eventually we had to take refuge in a shop of the better class, the proprietor of which went out with a stick and laid about with it.

Which direction our boat lay in we had no idea, and if it had not been for our boy, who seemed to know the way, we would have been lost.

In another walled town where we passed the night, we woke up about 4 a.m. probably owing to a most horrible and ghastly smell, which was coming in at our open window.

When I got up and looked out, I found a garbage boat moored right under the window in the narrow creek or canal below.

Quickly we packed up our things and called "Ling," the boy, who was sleeping below.

We decided to get back to our boat, and proceeded towards the main gate of the city, which was locked when we got there.

After about ten minutes' hammering on the keeper's door he came out, and we explained that we wanted to leave. A slanging match now took place between him and Ling, the latter appearing to be the winner, and the keeper, an ancient and withered individual, went in for the key. A long time we waited, for it appeared that the key could not be found.

By this time, I was beginning to be annoyed, but fortunately the little son of the keeper came running out with the key, which he had found.

It was a great rusty thing, and looked as though it had been buried for half a century.

Finally, after a lot of hard work by the keeper and some coolies who had come to his help, the gate, with much resistance and creaking, was pushed open and we passed out.

It was now beginning to get light, and I could see my surroundings.

Outside the gate there was a crowd of coolies, interested spectators of the ceremony, and I knew that they had not come through the gate, so how had they got outside?

The explanation was simple, I could see clearly by now, as it was almost daylight.

The gate stood practically by itself, with a little bit of broken wall attached to it on either side, and then there was a gap of thirty or forty feet in the wall, through which I could easily have walked.

CHAPTER 36

How the Poor Live

The years were passing away and I was getting older, not only in years, but in experience. I knew Shanghai and district as few Europeans ever know it, and some of the things that I saw saddened me.

I had just finished making a plan of part of the city through which it was intended to extend the railway, and for this purpose, I had to do a good deal of measuring up on the site.

I entered a narrow court in which there were a maze of ramshackle rooms like rabbit warrens.

Opening the door of a room I entered. It was daytime, yet the gloom inside of the place was such that at first I could hardly make out the inmates. There was a horrible smell of unwashed bodies, and inhaled breath, mixed with the smoke from small, naked oil lamps, which cast out a faint light for a few feet all round.

My eyes, becoming more accustomed to the murk of the room, were able to make out several Chinamen stitching and performing other jobs on different garments; working feverishly as though they were competing against time.

Their faces had a strained expression, and most of them were pallid and wrinkled, while others had faces like corpses.

The light was so bad that it was necessary to stoop low over their work.

I learned that they worked from six in the morning until 10 o'clock at night, and sometimes later, and that they all lived in this room, working all day long, with only an occasional break for a basin of rice and salt fish or a few pieces of horribly-looking Chinese pork, from pigs which generally run loose about the country villages and towns, feeding on garbage.

At night time, when they stop work, they lie down on the floor alongside of their work place.

There was a clinging odour of stale opium fumes, so probably at night the room would be full of opium smoke, in addition to the smoke of the lamp, the smell of oil, unwashed bodies, air which had been breathed by many people, and the smell from the open drain outside.

They had nothing else to look forward to for the rest of their lives, and, when their earning powers failed, gradual starvation and disease.

The boat dwellers and the peasant in the country had a place of their own to bring up a family in, so that their sons would look after them in their old age, but how could these slum dwellers have families? Space was scarce in the city, and thousands of coolies only had sufficient floor space to stretch out on in such a place as this.

Coming out of this place and getting back to the main road, I saw a Chinese wedding procession, probably of the trader or shopkeeper class.

The bride and bridegroom sat in rickshaws and paraded round the streets, followed by many coolies, carrying, slung on poles, all their household goods, a roast sucking pig and other eatables, displayed for the edification of the community.

Sometimes, outside of the settlement, one may see a poor man's funeral. First will come the enormous coffin, slung on poles, and carried by coolies moving at a half trot, to the accompaniment of a chant "Ho, Ho, Ho"; then come the mourners letting off innumerable crackers, to scare away any evil spirits that may be lurking about.

Inside the coffin there would be a little fortune in ingots of silver for the use of the dead man in the next world. Only they will be made of silver paper and will be hollow. Anyway, the dead man will not know the difference, reasons the Chinese mind.

Great precautions are taken to prevent the soul from being contaminated by evil spirits; in fact, this idea seems to prevail right through life. Confucius teaches that man is born good, and evil can only enter the soul through contact with outside influence. That if a man could live an entirely isolated life, without contact or communication with his fellows, his soul would be pure at death.

This is why the Chinese character is reserved and secretive; why he builds high walls round his house and his cities; his poker or expressionless face, so that he may hide his thoughts from others. He fears outside influence.

Outside of the International Settlement, the country was seething with excitement, as the Chinese revolution was in progress. Sun-yat-Sen, against the Government, and at the moment there was a duel of big guns taking place between Woosung Forts and Kiang-an Arsenal; the shells passing on their many miles' flight over the city. Almost over my house it seemed to me, as I was awakened in the early morning by the roar of a shell passing over.

A little distance, just outside of the settlement, hundreds of young bodies were being torn and mutilated. As each shell passed with a roar, I thought of the agony and death that some poor human creatures would suffer within a few minutes. I saw some terrible sights on the battle-fields in the surrounding country. Order was maintained in the Chinese cities very effectively by the authorities.

An executioner with a two-handed sword paraded the streets. He was accompanied by an officer and a squad of soldiers, and woe betide any Chinaman who causes trouble or commits a crime, for he would be seized and forced down on his knees, and in a couple of minutes his head would be rolling in the dust.

Cases were tried on the spot, and witnesses listened to, and a man might be tried and executed in less than half an hour.

I have heard that it is a convenient method of getting rid of an enemy sometimes.

You simply hire a few witnesses and make a complaint when the execution squad comes along, and the thing is done.

Crime was very rife in Shanghai, too, and a great many burglaries had occurred, and often if the householder woke up and disturbed the robbers they took out his eyes, so that he could not identify them.

Since the revolution started, I noticed a change in Shanghai. The Chinese did not appear to be so friendly as before, while the lower class Chinese seemed to be more inclined to assent their equality. There was not the same deference to a European as formerly; moreover, the city seemed to be full of strange Europeans, many of them Russians, swells in expensive furs and top boots.

Some of them did not wash much in the winter time, and when they came into a room one got two different smells; one was a horrid smell, while the other was some odour which appeared to be struggling to blot out the former. Someone told me that they poured scent into their boots instead of washing their feet.

Mulki and I had been home to England for six months and returned. I was very sad at leaving my family once more, and going so far away. They were all getting older, and some I might never see again.

This had already happened once while I was in India; my sister came to London with me then to see me off, and I never saw her again.

Now my mother came through to London with Mulki and I, and I saw her in my mind again.

A frail old lady well over seventy, standing on the platform at Victoria as our train steamed slowly away.

She was making a brave effort to restrain her tears; perhaps she knew that she would never see me again.

Shortly after we reached Shanghai, I was sleeping one night, when I heard a voice whispering my name. It was my mother's voice, and I immediately woke up and saw her bending over me.

The vision was clear and distinct, but lasted only a moment, and then it was gone.

All next day I was in fear. I waited, and as each hour passed and the afternoon wore on I felt a little easier, but, sure enough, I saw the telegraph messenger coming up the garden. I took the telegram and opened it, although I knew what it would tell me. My mother was dead.

CHAPTER 37

Visions

I sat in my bedroom one evening as the sun was going down; I was testing a new combination of drugs.

The room was on the first floor, and the large French windows which opened on to the veranda were open. The house was set back from the roadway, and between it and the house were some large trees with many branches and thick foliage.

From time to time I would glance at these trees, because the first indication of the vision stage approaching would be that faces and figures would appear to be among the branches.

Always would visions appear at some distance away at the commencement and then gradually become nearer as time went on, and as I continued taking more drugs.

I had found, by means of several tests, that the visions would always disappear, no matter what kind they were, nor by what drugs produced, when I took sufficient of the No. 2 drug. Then I would be normal in every way. Otherwise the vision stage advanced gradually, starting with a wonderfully fertile imagination, a sensation of being within touch of everything in the world, or even in the universe; the power of seeming to know almost anything I wished to know.

It is true that afterwards many of my thoughts appeared strange, grotesque, or absurd, but this did not make them any less real and interesting at the time experienced.

Strange new thoughts came into my mind, and problems which before seemed impossible to solve now seemed easy.

The advance of civilisation. Why does civilisation advance or increase, and not decrease?

I saw that it does so in accordance with the Law of Evolution. Knowledge accumulates and concentrates, just as units or atoms come together and concentrate.

There is a definite connection between the earth's gravitation and the advance of civilisation.

The intensity of the gravitation depends on the earth's mass. It has been shown that millions of tons of meteorites, star dust, and nebulous matter fall on to the earth every year; also the sun is transferring some of its mass

163

to the earth in the form of heat, therefore the earth's mass, and consequently its gravitation, is increasing.

To resist this increased gravitation, every part of our bodies must gradually be getting stronger. The heart, the lungs and every organ in our bodies, including our brains, meet with greater resistance to their action, so the strength and quality of each must increase, and the only way this can occur is by the cells or atoms of the body increasing in number and coming closer together.

Every single piece of knowledge we possess may be likened to a unit or atom, and when these atoms of knowledge accumulate and concentrate in accordance with the Evolutionary Law, civilisation advances.

Prehistoric man had no consideration for any other person but himself, he was an isolated unit. But as evolution went on, mankind gradually became more and more connected and bound up with each other so that in time the human race will become perfect, and the welfare of all will be considered by each, knowing that the welfare of every other person will mean the welfare of himself.

Science, religion, sport, trade, etc., are not so distinctly separated as formerly, each are making more and more use of the other, and in many branches there is already a connection – sport to trade, trade to science, and science to religion.

Velocities of travel are increasing, which means that distances are decreasing, and every part of the earth is coming closer together, if we measure distance by a time factor, which is the correct way. Fifty years ago a journey to Australia took months to perform, whereas now it can be made in a few days.

I continued taking more drugs, and as time went on the room became full of ghost-like shapes, which gradually grew clearer and more distinct; then for the first time during all the years of my drug-taking experiences the visions were animated. No longer did they simply float past me as before, their movements were perfectly natural and life-like. Although the figures appeared luminous or slightly transparent, so that I could see the background of the room through them, I was not conscious of this, unless I specially looked for it.

The walls of the room began to recede, until they finally disappeared, and I lost all sense of personality, until I was just an intelligence with the power to observe and think. Time and space had no confining limits for me; I could live many lives, in many different places and periods. My condition was like a perfect and unique form of self-hypnosis.

I could experience anything that I wished. I willed it to thunder, and I heard the crash distinctly. For lightning, and I saw the flash. I could sit in the "circus," and see the games, and gladiatorial contests as they took place in the time of Nero.

I could see a close-up view of the sun; the waves of molten white hot matter rolling and leaping to a height of a hundred miles between crest and hollow, sending off tongues of flame of blue heat, leaping up to a height of two hundred thousand miles in a few minutes of time. Flames, each one of which could entirely envelop a hundred globes like our earth.

There was a point beyond which I could not go; a point which, when reached, the visions would be at a maximum state of clearness, and any further drugs would cause them to become blurred and dim. When this point was reached I slept.

CHAPTER 38

An Adventure

Hire a Chinaman to do a piece of work and he will most likely hire someone else to do it a little cheaper, pocketing the difference himself.

Buy anything at one of the stores or elsewhere, and later your servant will call on them and collect "Kumshaw," or interest. Even the big stores will often pay, for suppose that it was a suit of clothes that you had bought, and the seller refused to follow this custom, then most likely the suit would fray out, or wear into little holes, or become discoloured in places, and you would not go back to the same place again.

A Chinese dollar is nominally a hundred cents, yet any money changer will pay a rate which fluctuates every day – one day it may be one hundred and forty cents in small change, and next day it may be more, so that when making a purchase small change will only be accepted if the price is under a dollar.

Chinamen managing businesses will therefore pay over their takings to their employers, in sums containing as much small change as they can, explaining that a good proportion of the purchases have been made in small sums of under a dollar.

Mr. Wong had several branches of his business in the interior, and he was complaining that he was being robbed.

Sometimes the takings of some particular business would arrive in a sealed bag, with a statement of the amount contained, but when the bag was opened and the money counted by his cashier, the latter would say that the amount was considerably less than it was supposed to be. The sender would swear that he had sent the correct sum, and the other would maintain that he had not received it.

It was for the purpose of investigating a similar occurrence that Mr. Wong intended making a trip into the interior, and he suggested that I should go with him, as I was on holiday at the time.

We travelled on the upper deck of one of the river steamers, plying on the Yangtse. For about a thousand miles we travelled, taking on a fresh pilot most days, as the deep channel in the river is constantly shifting.

When we reached Hangkow, we disembarked, and struck inland.

The country round about was in a very unsettled state; bands of soldiers or brigands, under leaders who called themselves generals, scoured the country, robbing and pillaging. Sometimes two hostile bands would meet, and then it became almost like a game of chess.

The two armies would camp at some distance from each other, and wait to see what would happen. Then some morning one of the generals would wake up to find nearly all his army gone over to the other side, and would have to flee if he wished to save his head. There was a regular rate of payment in force for desertion, so much for a private, more for a sergeant, and if a colonel went over with a whole regiment he would make a nice little sum.

We travelled inland by houseboat on the waterways, the banks of which were considerably higher than the surrounding country, and I enquired of Mr. Wong why this was so.

It seemed that originally these waterways had been made in the usual manner, plain channels, excavated to give the required depth of water, but as time went on they had become shallower and shallower owing to silt, until finally the level of the water had risen until it overflowed the banks. The obvious remedy would seem to have been the dredging and deepening of the channel. Instead of doing this, the banks were raised higher, and the same method had been adopted for hundreds of years, until the canals now appeared to be up in the air. The original work had been done by people who were sent in chains from overcrowded districts, to colonise this part and to do the work.

Of course this story may be true or it may not. I cannot vouch for it.

I saw some horrible instances of foot distortion. Young girls who could only hobble along with the aid of sticks, and even, in some cases, had to be carried, if they were of the well-to-do class, and could afford it.

There were various methods of producing the small foot so much admired by the Chinaman. One of them was to bind the foot tightly and encase it in a boot, which was worn continuously night and day, in spite of the pain until the girl was well grown.

In other cases, the toes were doubled underneath the foot, and bound there, until they had grown on to the sole. The worst cases, however, were those in which the girl had been allowed to grow too much before her feet were operated on. Perhaps the parents had been of the coolie class, or they may have been neglectful, and then have suddenly become aware of their obligations; in which case the toes were entirely cut off.

We Europeans, as a rule, have nothing to be proud of in our feet. Witness the unnatural-shaped boots with pointed toes, which cramp and cause the toes to grow all in a bunch, producing corns and bunions. The women who wear shoes with ridiculously high heels set back almost under the instep, causing an unsightly and exaggerated arch; a distortion.

To see it gives one a cold feeling; one imagines what the foot must really be like.

By contrast, compare the beautifully-shaped feet of the Hindu women.

There is a slight but natural arch. There is a little space between each toe, which are flat and straight, like fingers. The feet are turned slightly inwards when walking, because to turn them outwards is unnatural; it throws all the weight on to the big toes when the foot bends, leaving the little toe off the ground, causing it in time to become useless.

Why do people not use their own judgment, instead of following idiotic fashions? Realise that anything which is unnatural, is ugly. The human foot in its natural shape is a thing of beauty, designed in a wonderful manner, with perfect symmetry, to resist the many contrary stresses and strains to which it is subjected.

Fishing boats of strange shapes and many kinds, some with sails like kites, fishing in many different ways, were strung along the waterway.

Many were using cormorants, a method of fishing so often described that most people know it. The birds sat on the side of the boat gazing into the water with a fixed stare until they saw a fish, only to be robbed of it by their owners time after time.

Another method adopted was by line, but in place of a hook, was used a thin sliver of bamboo, sharpened to a point at each end and then bent double, the two points practically touching, and fixed in that position by means of a lump of rice boiled to the consistency of glue almost. When the fish swallowed the rice, the bamboo opened out and formed a kind of hook.

Some were fishing with a piece of white painted board, lowered just below the surface of the water, and fish coming along jumped over the board, right into the boat.

Further along the canal, Mr. Wong pointed out a temple. "That is a temple of the Taoist priests, where for 4,000 cash the relatives of a dead person can purchase a letter to Fengtu, the Chinese Hades, otherwise Hell.

"The priest writes the letter and then burns it. By this means it will go direct to headquarters, and if by any chance the spirit of the dead man goes there, the letter will be of great service. They will even write you a letter in English for the same price, although you are not yet dead. There are only two Emperors," continued Mr. Wong, "the Emperor of the living, and the Emperor of the dead and the Taoist priests are in communication with the latter."

"Very curious," I remarked.

"Not more curious than some of the religious customs of your own country," he said. "Can you not buy in some Christian countries forgiveness for some sin committed, or even forgiveness for a sin you are about to commit? Most of the customs of my country have been in vogue for thousands of years, and we venerate anything that is ancient, and therefore are reluctant to change.

"You see that kite up there," he continued, pointing to a large kite high up in the air. "Well, on that kite are written supplications to Heaven; kite flying is a very popular pastime throughout the whole of China, but most of them are flown for a purpose. When a person dies, messages will be sent to both Heaven and Hell. Imitation paper money, paper models of household goods, horses, servants, concubines and other things which the dead man is likely to require in the next world are burnt, so that they may reach him. Originally thousands of years ago, real silver and gold and real people and animals were sacrificed, but the practice gradually died out, and imitation ones were substituted."

As we proceeded slowly along a canal, we passed a large receptacle, something after the shape of an ashpit, built of loose stones. It had a sign in Chinese characters on it, and Mr. Wong informed me that it was a dump into which the bodies of girl babies that were unwanted could be dumped. Some of the new-born infants were just dumped in even while alive.

Up some of the narrow creeks we occasionally came to an old junk moored across and blocking up the waterway. It would be serving as a toll bridge for foot passengers who wanted to cross the stream. They would pay a few cash for the privilege of being allowed to walk along the deck and step off on the opposite bank. As soon as a boat came along, the whole family – father, mother, children and grandparents – would bustle round and turn the junk out of the way. These junks would sometimes be moored in the same place, carrying on the same business for generations.

On the wider waterways there were "Flower boats"; large craft, well furnished and decorated. On board of these would be a dozen or so young Chinese girls, plying their profession of entertaining the opposite sex.

There were also other junks which did not advertise the nature of their business so openly. On these, things which cannot be described were carried on.

The more I saw of China, the more I marvelled; it is truly a wonderful country. Everything used, in every walk of life, is the simplest in design, yet being very efficient in a primitive way. Even the Chinese wheelbarrow is so designed that ten persons can sit on it and all be perfectly balanced, so that the coolie can walk away with the load quite easily.

It is true that there are some callings in which unnecessary labour has to be expended. A Chinese typesetter has to deal with and be able to pick out at once any one of thirty thousand different characters. To do this he must constantly be walking about a long room, picking out the type. The next character he requires may be twenty feet away. Imagine what a memory he must have.

Back again in Shanghai, I found Mulki exceedingly worried, and angry. For the third time some horrible scoundrel had stolen the cat. On each of the previous occasions when it had disappeared she had offered a reward of five dollars for its recovery, and each time it had been brought back by some Chinaman, who had claimed the reward.

I was beginning to suspect that the cat was becoming known in the district to certain enterprising Chinamen, who saw in it an easy source of income. Cats are difficult to keep in Shanghai because they are prized as food by the Chinese, and the eyes especially are great delicacies.

Only well-to-do people can afford to indulge in a dish of cats' eyes. They are arranged tastefully on a dish, and picked out delicately with the aid of a pair of chop sticks, viewed for a moment by connoisseurs, and then dipped in sauce, and swallowed like oysters.

It was difficult to know what to do, because I felt sure that the cat would be stolen time after time, as long as there was a five-dollar reward for its return. We reduced the reward to slightly above the market price of cats, and after a while it was returned by a coolie, who probably considered himself cheated.

The years passed away, years the story of which I intend to tell in another book, as I have not room in this one to do so.

I will tell of my remaining years in China. My adventures while slowly making our way home to England in 1913, in Japan, San Francisco and New York, and also my strange experiences during the war years up to the time when the Dangerous Drug Act came into force, and I gave up drugs for good.

I was able to give them up easily with the aid of the drug I called the "Elixir of Life."

I will tell of the death of Mulki in London and her burial in Stratford Cemetery. She had been all over the world with me between the years of 1895 and 1915.

For many years I have intended writing this story, but always have I hesitated to do so. I feared the publicity, but now I have given up my profession, and most of my friends are dead and gone, so I have no longer any reasons for delay.

Years ago I destroyed all my syringes, apparatus and drugs, but somewhere in the island of Sumatra there exists the plant from which I made the drug I called the "Elixir of Life."